THE RISE OF THE ENGLISH POLTERGEIST

The haunting by demons of the Mompessons' home, 1662–63. Detail from William Fairthorne's frontispiece for the second part of Joseph Glanvill's posthumous *Saducismus Triumphatus* (1681), containing his collection of Relations. (Hand-tinted by author)

The Rise of the English Poltergeist

ANDREW PICKERING

THE HOBNOB PRESS

First published in the United Kingdom in 2025
by The Hobnob Press,
8 Lock Warehouse, Severn Road, Gloucester GL1 2GA
www.hobnobpress.co.uk

© Andrew Pickering 2025

The Author hereby asserts his moral rights to be identified as the Author of the Work.

All rights reserved. No part of this publication may be reproduced, stored in a retrieval system, or transmitted in any form or by any means, electronic, mechanical, photocopying, recording or otherwise, without the prior permission of the publisher and copyright holder.

British Library Cataloguing in Publication Data
A catalogue record for this book is available from the British Library

ISBN 978-1-914407-93-2 paperback
ISBN 978-1-914407-94-9 hardback

Typeset in Adobe Garamond Pro, 11/14 pt and Caslon Antique
Typesetting and origination by John Chandler

Cover design by Rachael Hunt

CONTENTS

Acknowledgements	*vii*
Foreword	*viii*
Introduction	1
1. The Rise of the English Poltergeist	13
2. Haunted Houses and the 'Great Rebuilding'	29
3. Paranormal Activity? Experiences and Interpretations	47
4. 'Whistle if thou canst': Living with Demons	59
RELATIONS	73
1 Strange and Wonderfull Accidents: North Aston, Oxfordshire, 1591-92	74
2 Peter Pain's Poltergeist: Bristol, 1630s	84
3 Extraordinary Rumblings in a Godly Home: Edinburgh, Scotland, *c.*1635.	87
4 Mad Frolics of Witches and Demons: Plaistow, London, 1645	88
5 The Just Devil of Woodstock: Oxfordshire, 1649	94
6 A Violent Ghost and a Wily Wench: Greenwich, 1650	107
7 'Satan is my Father': Glenluce, Scotland, 1654	110
8 Strange Vomiting and a Haunted House: Welton, Northamptonshire, 1658	117
9 Mr Lloyd's Story: Bleddfa, Powys, *c.*1659.	120
10 Andrew Paschall's Troublesome Spirit: Soper Lane, London, 1661	122
11 Mr Mompesson's Goblin: Tidworth, Wiltshire, 1662-63	126

12	The Demon of Burton: Weobley, Herefordshire, 1670	146
13	The Riddle of a House Disturbed: London Wall, 1674	151
14	'What are you?': Puddle Dock, London, 1675	153
15	Old Gast's Ghost: Little Burton, Dorset, 1677	157
16	The Story of the Stirs, Leasingham, Lincolnshire, 1679-80	160
17	A House Infected with Demons: Newburyport, New England, 1679	163
18	The Foul-Fiend of Ormiston: East Lothian, Scotland, 1680	168
19	Strange and Wonderful News: Ewell, Surrey, 1681	170
20	The Stone-Throwing Devil: New Hampshire, 1682	172
21	The She-Demon of Spreyton: Devon, 1682	185
22	A Thief Discovered by a Demon: Brightling, Sussex, *c*.1690	188
23	The Violent Infestation of a House in Rerrick: Dumfries and Galloway, Scotland, 1695	191
24	The Devil of Deptford: Deptford, 1699	201
25	A House Infected with Demons: Butleigh, Somerset, *c*.1704	204
26	'Old Jeffries' and the Wesleys: Epworth Rectory, Lincolnshire, 1716-17	206
27	'All nipped to pieces': Kinross, Scotland, 1718	221

Afterword 225

Appendix 228
Bibliography 230
Index 237

ACKNOWLEDGEMENTS

The Rise of the English Poltergeist is a companion piece to my previous publication, *The Witches of Selwood: Witchcraft Belief and Accusation in Seventeenth-Century Somerset* (2021). While it is not another regional study, this history also focuses on the significant role played by the West Country's seventeenth-century demonologists and their associates in shaping it. In particular, it builds on the extraordinary set of relations in the *Saducismus Triumphatus* (1681) collected by Joseph Glanvill, the Somerset vicar and Fellow of the Royal Society who encountered a poltergeist at Tidworth in Wiltshire.

Once again, I am indebted to my friends at the Hobnob Press, Dr John Chandler and Dr Louise Ryland-Epton, for their support, editorial advice and commitment to local and cultural history. Also to Rachael Hunt and Loren Ryland-Epton for graphics and publicity. I am very grateful to the four anonymous expert referees involved in bringing to light my recent paper on the subject in *Folklore*, the journal of The Folklore Society.[1] The critical advice and guidance of its editor, Dr Jessica Hemming, has been of immense value in both the broadening of my horizons and the refining of my arguments. This book is dedicated to my wife, Lisa, who shares my enthusiasm for exploring historic and haunting – if not haunted – houses, and the stories of those that have survived and those that have long since disappeared.

---

1   Andrew Pickering, 'The Rise of the English Poltergeist c.1590–c.1720', *Folklore* 136, no. 2 (2025), pp. 314–55.

FOREWORD

'My mother tells me a very strange story of disturbances in your house [...] and I cannot think at all of any interpretation. Wit, I fancy, might find many, but wisdom none.'

Samuel Wesley to his father, 1717.[2]

I AM HAPPY to declare that, although I live in a house which was probably built (or rebuilt) some five centuries ago, I have not yet been bothered by a poltergeist. This is despite the abundance of tales of English poltergeists and the antiquity of the building which has been a hub of human activity, as a farmhouse, inn, and shop, for so long. The house is even the probable location of a well-documented witchcraft case in which the blood of a supposed nineteenth-century witch was drawn by a near neighbour who considered himself cursed. Houses like this are prone to hauntings. Not a 'grand' house by any means but, rebuilt around the start of the seventeenth century, it is a warren of passageways, staircases, small rooms, and multiple doors. When we first arrived icy Easter winds sent drafts from the open grates in the cellar through the cold damp rooms above, rattling ill-fitting doors and ancient windows. At least one member of the family that preceded us thought it was haunted and, just a few months ago, my grown-up son, on a return visit and alone in the house, was disturbed late one night by the unmistakeable sound of unexplained footsteps in the passage outside his bedroom door. When, almost thirty years before, we first investigated the large, black, filthy attic directly above, we discovered, hidden beneath an ancient beam, the skin of a small lightly furred animal, a rabbit or a mole perhaps, stretched on a flimsy twig frame

2   Joseph Priestly, *Original Letters by the Rev. John Wesley, and His Friends, Illustrative of his Early History, with Other Curious Papers* (Birmingham, 1791), p. 122.

and suspended by horsehair: a mode of house protection against evil spirits. However, I am not haunted by the house I live in, not in a bad way at least. 'Kind and dear is the old house here', as William Morris once said of his beloved Kelmscott Manor. Being haunted, I suspect, is primarily a state of mind. In part this is culturally determined but, as those ghosts in the attic remind us, it is also shaped by the complex relationship between environment and animal instinct. It has been necessary to consider belief and context in equal measure in exploring the development of encounters with poltergeists.

This book imitates the form of several later seventeenth- and early eighteenth-century demonologies in so far as it is divided into two main parts: the first being a broad and theoretical discussion of the subject with multiple allusions to documentary sources and other forms of evidence, while the second is a collection of twenty-seven 'relations' of narratives which in modern parlance would be described as poltergeist stories. These include a case from Wales, a couple collected in New England, and a handful from Scotland spanning the period of its unification with England.[3] They are drawn exclusively and directly from the contemporary sources in which they were recorded. A few are well-known, most, however, are not. Each contains a measure of introductory and editorial comment but, for the most part they are left to speak for themselves. I hope they will prove a useful and interesting resource for readers developing their own enquiries into this most esoteric of subjects.

---

3   Prior to the formal Act of Union in 1707 England and Scotland had a practical union in sharing a single monarch after James VI of Scotland became James I of England in 1603.

INTRODUCTION

'I Know [w]hat I Heard and Saw'
Joseph Glanvill concerning his 'poltergeist' experience at Tidworth in 1663[1]

THE EARLY MODERN period – commonly regarded as that of the late fifteenth to the start of the eighteenth centuries - was the era of the so-called witch craze,[2] the unprecedented persecution of alleged witches across central and Northern Europe and European settlements in North America. This was an age of social, political, and religious turmoil, and one in which all kinds of real and imagined dangers haunted the lives of those who lived through it. Post-medieval existential doubts manifested as fears of witchcraft and reinvigorated concerns regarding other demonic interventions.[3] Jean-Claude Schmitt, in his study of ghost-lore before c.1500, spoke of the Protestant 'diabolization of ghosts'.[4] The rise of the English poltergeist in the seventeenth-century was part of that process. It is probably no coincidence that the witch craze coincided with what appears to be the take-off of what in the English-speaking world, since the introduction of the German term in 1849, are considered cases of poltergeist activity. The record for poltergeist cases in England, as explained in Chapter 1 of this book,

---

1   Joseph Glanvill, *Saducismus Triumphatus* (London, 1681), p. 330.
2   See, for example, Lyndal Roper, *Witch Craze* (Yale University Press, 2004), Anne Barstow, *Witchcraze: A New History of the European Witch Hunts* (Harper Collins, 1994).
3   Ronald C. Finucane, 'Historical introduction: the example of Early Modern and Nineteenth-Century England' in James Houran and Rense Lange (eds), *Hauntings and Poltergeists: Multidisciplinary Perspectives* (McFarland, 2001), pp. 9–10.
4   Jean-Claude Schmitt, *Ghosts in the Middle Ages: The Living and the Dead in Medieval Society* (Chicago University Press, 1998), p. 224.

is slight before the start of the seventeenth century yet comparatively abundant thereafter.

In recent times the once esoteric study of witchcraft belief has become a mainstream subject in British universities and schools. Practitioners have found it an excellent vehicle for enabling students to explore the implications of problematic evidence and culturally nuanced approaches. It prompts the discussion of a wide range of perspectives – feminist, Marxist, psychoanalytical, theological, geopolitical and so forth. Likewise, poltergeist accounts offer another rewarding platform for the wider consideration of what academic history is all about. These odd stories invite the analysis of mentalities, actions and circumstances. Context – cultural, social, and physical environments -, as discussed below, is at the heart of the matter. While multiple causes account for the rise of the English poltergeist, the study of tangible as well as intangible contexts, primarily the houses they haunt, the focus of Chapter 2, is essential in any attempt to make sense of it all.

The histories of the malefic witch and the mischievous poltergeist in England are closely intertwined. However, they do not share the same trajectory. Where the one legend has finally been laid to rest, the other, that of the active poltergeist, flourishes. In his preface to a transcription of the 1670 *Demon of Burton* pamphlet, John Ashton noted 'the trivialities to which this species of Devil [the poltergeist in the case] could descend, apparently, with no object'.[5] The same could be said of much of the *maleficia* [harmful activity] of seventeenth-century witches. Often the most dramatic element in witchcraft episodes is not what they did, but what was done to them: various tortures and executions, some of the cruellest kind. In the popular imagination, witchcraft persecution conjures thoughts of Black Sabbath orgies, the tearing of limbs by the *strapaddo* torture device, and death by burning at the stake, none of which, incidentally, were part of the English tradition. Nevertheless, English witchcraft cases, which identify human perpetrators, have received a great deal more academic attention than those of poltergeists which, by and large, have not. The nature of 'poltergeist' activity, as it is presented in the contemporary accounts, is considered in Chapter 3.

---

5   John Ashton, *The Devil in Britain and America* (Ward and Downey, 1896), p. 60.

INTRODUCTION

'Strictly speaking', Keith Thomas noted is his epic *Religion and the Decline of Magic*, 'the belief in demonianism [demoniacal possession] was distinct from witchcraft'.[6] One of the striking features of the collection of poltergeist accounts in this volume is how rarely they were explicitly and unequivocally associated by their authors with witchcraft. The common assumption that episodes of the paranormal in the period were routinely interpreted as the work of witches and their familiars is not well supported by the materials under scrutiny here; for many it is, at best, an unwritten assumption. This, surely, is the principal reason for the neglect of poltergeist history in the major studies of English witchcraft. Furthermore, possession, which, as Thomas observed, 'came very near to being synonymous' with the epithet 'bewitched' in seventeenth-century England is very rare in early modern English poltergeist cases.[7] Conversely, poltergeist activity, as it appears in these accounts, is rarely a characteristic of the classic witchcraft cases of the period. How it was interpreted in the period by both believers and sceptics is explored in Chapter 4.

~~~

Most of the poltergeist cases in the 'Relations' section of this book have received little academic attention. Historians of witchcraft belief in early modern England have written extensively about the possession of people but not a great deal about the demonic possession of people's homes.[8] Only one poltergeist account, for example, receives much attention (as an appendix item) in Darren Oldridge's otherwise comprehensive *The Devil in Tudor and Stuart England*.[9]

The era of unprecedented investigation and persecution of witches and witchcraft in England was relatively short-lived, starting in the late

---

6   Keith Thomas, *Religion and the Decline of Magic: Studies in Popular Beliefs in Sixteenth- and Seventeenth-Century England* (Weidenfeld & Nicholson, 1971), p. 570.
7   Thomas, *Religion*, p. 570.
8   This includes the most comprehensive single-volume source for the subject, James Sharpe's *Instruments of Darkness: Witchcraft in Early Modern England* (Penn, 1986).
9   Darren Oldridge, *The Devil in Tudor and Stuart England* (The History Press, 2010), 'The Demon of Tedworth', pp. 211-14.

1500s and pretty much over by 1700. Magic and witchcraft continued to play a part in the lives of ordinary folk in the centuries that followed but, over time, old beliefs and superstitions eroded to the point of disappearance. The poltergeist, on the other hand, remains at large - an enduring popular obsession that is as pronounced now as at any time in the past five hundred years. Episodes of poltergeist activity continue to be reported; movies, TV programmes and podcasts investigate and sensationalize them, and at least one professionally written history has placed them in their broader context over time and across place. The search for the historical roots of ghost stories, in the wake of the modern preoccupation with high-tech scientific analysis, seems to be enjoying a revival of interest not seen since the pioneering days of the late Victorian and Edwardian folklorists. The archaeologist, TV presenter, and writer of many informed popular histories, Neil Oliver, recently put out his book on the subject, *Hauntings* (2023), and a new history of paranormal investigation by Alice Vernon should appear at much the same time as this one.[10]

One thing these enquiries reveals is that, while explanations of poltergeist phenomena have varied greatly over time, the phenomena themselves have proved remarkably consistent. In recent years a host of popular monographs has been published regarding intriguing twentieth- and twenty-first-century British poltergeist cases. Unlike other histories, I tend to read these controversial accounts discreetly on my e-reader. Looking through my virtual library I am reminded of Sean O'Connor's masterful exposé of *The Haunting of Borley Rectory* (2022), Kate Summerscale's acclaimed account of *The Haunting of Alma Fielding* (2020) concerning peculiar and suspicious events in 1930s Croydon, Jenny Ashford and Steve Morris's tale of *The Rochdale Poltergeist* (2013) which was active in an otherwise unremarkable bungalow in Rochdale in the mid-1990s, and Mark Chadbourn's *Testimony* (2014) which investigated the haunting of a Welsh farmhouse in 1989 and inspired the hit BBC Radio 4 series *The Witch Farm* (2022). In 2008 Darren W. Ritson published his account of *The South Shields Poltergeist* in the wake of extraordinary events in 2006, while another story, this one set

---

10   Alice Vernon, *Ghosted: A History of Ghost Hunting, and Why We Keep Looking* (Bloomsbury, due date: September 2025).

in Battersea in the 1950s, was told by Shirley Hitchings and James Clark in *The Poltergeist Prince of London* (2013). In 1980, the account of the most famous of modern English cases – that of the Enfield poltergeist in the late 1970s and the inspiration for blockbuster movies – was published by its investigator Guy Lyon Playfair in *This House is Haunted*. Following several movie and TV documentary adaptations, among its latest manifestations is a London stage play starring Catherine Tate and David Threfell.[11]

Collectively these accounts add weight to the evidence that unexplained, 'paranormal', things happen. Those who explore reports of such phenomena are hard-pressed to find simple explanations such as coincidence and fraud in all poltergeist cases. While seventeenth-century commentators might have been quick to find supernatural causes, scientific ones such as string theory, spontaneous psychokinesis tend to steer the discussion in the twenty-first. Few things in human experience are more alluring and, for that matter, disconcerting, than the experience of the seemingly impossible.

Historians have long been the apologists for 'witches' as the maligned scapegoats for natural catastrophes but not, to the best of my knowledge, for the actions of poltergeists. However, for better or worse, any historian with just a hint of uncertainty regarding the impossibility of poltergeist phenomena is bound to consider, privately if not publicly, this noisy elephant in the room when exploring these weird stories. To the dismay, no doubt, of some who bought his ground-breaking book, Schmitt introduced *Ghosts in the Middle Ages* with the opening gambit, 'The dead have no existence other than that which the living imagine for them'.[12] While most would agree with Daniel Walker's view that 'Whatever their personal beliefs, historians should not ask their readers to accept supernatural phenomena',[13] not all academic commentators

---

11   Paul Unwin, *The Enfield Haunting*, Ambassadors Theatre, 01/12/2023-02/03/2024.
12   Schmitt, *Ghosts*, p. 1.
13   D. P. Walker in Carlos M. N. Eire, *They Flew: A History of the Impossible* (Yale University Press, 2023), p. 317; in his 2011 reprint of his account of the Enfield case, Playfair remarked '[what] appears to us today [is] as strange, unbelievable and impossible as, say, the idea of an internet would have appeared to Newton or even Einstein'; Guy Playfair, *This House is Haunted* (White Crow Books, 2011), p. 274.

on historic poltergeist cases entirely rule out the possibility that those involved witnessed actual phenomena because no known natural law explains them. Richard Sugg has found the evidence for poltergeist activity in the past and present hard to ignore, 'Poltergeists', he has written, 'are clearly real. Or, rather: the set of bizarre effects [...] clustered under that name are clearly real'.[14] Whatever their cause the *experience* for observers is a real one and one which might reaffirm or even realign their way of thinking. Shortly before his death in 2006 the controversial parapsychologist, John Beloff (1920–2006), in the tradition of many of those who wrote about such things in early modern England, declared,

> I have never seen an apparition or been present at a poltergeist disturbance [....] However, that is no reason to doubt the testimony of those who have [...] If there are compelling cases of poltergeist activity then it is futile to dismiss, in principle, all reports of such phenomena, although we have an intellectual duty to be as cautious and critical as we can.

With the famous 'demon of Tedworth' haunting in the early 1660s in mind, he further observed, '[In] cases from the past where the investigator was a prominent academic with a reputation to uphold [...] I find it easier to believe than disbelieve, however much believing may complicate my world view'.[15]

Few historians are psychologists, but they do sometimes explore the history of mentalities, of which this book is an example. It is an investigation into things people *thought* had happened and how people interpreted things that *did* happen. It is, in turn, a study of elite and popular culture, of the resilience of established attitudes and, also, their propensity for change.

Narratives of the impossible are products of the cultural milieu from which they emerge. Carlos Eire has suggested the surge in early modern Europe of accounts of levitation and bilocation (being in

---

14   Richard Sugg, *A Century of Supernatural Stories* (Createspace, 2015), p. 12.
15   John Beloff, 'Foreword' in James Houran and Reese Lange, *Hauntings and Poltergeists: Multidisciplinary Perspectives* (McFarland, 2001), p. 2. The opening chapter of Houran's and Lange's book begins with a discussion of the Tidworth case.

two places at once), the focus of his recent study, could have been something of a last gasp of an older, more superstitious world in the face of the rising of a more rational new one.[16] For whatever reason, the period witnessed an outpouring of demonologies and these both related existing narratives and helped inspire more. All this begs the question, 'Why so much interest in such things in the first quarter of the twenty-first century?'. This is a time in which humanity has surpassed itself in its ability to delude itself. Maybe all this poltergeist reportage has at least something to do with an urge to find 'impossible', wonderful things in our own time which are not necessarily CGI or AI deceptions. In like manner, another once 'impossible' feat - landing man on the Moon - undid any number of treasured mythologies but helped spawn new ones (and a wave of UFO sightings) in the last quarter of the twentieth century.

The interpretation of historical events sometimes has as much to do with semantics as it does empirical evidence. Is 'poltergeist', in the way it is understood now, an appropriate term for the supposed entities haunting seventeenth-century houses? 'The poltergeist', the twentieth-century ghost-hunter Harry Price once declared, is 'mischievous, destructive, noisy, cruel, erratic, thievish, demonstrative, purposeless, cunning, unhelpful, audacious, teasing, ill-disposed, spiteful, ruthless, resourceful, and vampiric'. Where a ghost *haunts*, he concluded, 'a Poltergeist *infests*'.[17] While the modern label had yet to be invented, Price's definition is a good fit for much of what was recorded in early modern 'poltergeist' hauntings. Equally, his identification of the poltergeist as something distinct from a ghost also matches the broad impression conveyed by earlier investigators. While Brendan Walsh's conclusion that 'English theologians never fully resolved the question of whether sprits were the remnants of dead people or demons'[18] is valid, those infesting early modern English houses in the way Price envisaged very rarely were declared to be ghosts in the sense of spirits

---

16 Eire, *They Flew*, p. xiv.
17 Harry Price, *Poltergeist Over England* (Country Life, 1945), p. 1.
18 Brendan C. Walsh, '"He Could Raise and Lay Ghosts at His Will": Victorian Folklorists and the Creation of Early Modern Clerical Ghost-Laying', *Folklore* 134, no. 3 (2023), p. 282.

of the deceased.[19] Despite Anglican-Protestant difficulties regarding the Roman Catholic doctrine of Purgatory,[20] popular belief in ghosts remained strong throughout the period but they were rarely invoked, let alone likely to manifest, in poltergeist encounters.

In his consideration of analogous entities in a paper principally concerned with the 'Men in Black' (MIB) associated with modern UFO folklore, Peter M. Rojoewicz wrote, 'the MIB possess a nature very similar to the mythological figure of the Trickster [who] is known to play pranks upon people'. This elusive Trickster 'is both subhuman, superhuman, bestial and divine', a complex 'archetypal shadow figure'.[21] The seventeenth-century poltergeist, it has been argued,[22] sits comfortably within this ancient Trickster tradition.

The distinction between the poltergeist and other *super-* or *preter*natural concepts is fundamental to the purpose of this book which endeavours to build on previous attempts to write about the poltergeist as a unique genre. While there are points of cross-over - and there is no reason, in principle, for why a 'ghost' might not occupy the same space in time and place as a 'poltergeist' - in cultural-historical terms they each have their own natural history. Often subsumed within general accounts of witchcraft belief and persecution, poltergeist phenomena in the early modern period, as now, are comparable but distinct occurrences which warrant their own micro-histories and consideration of their unique collective typologies and paradigms. As any seventeenth-century mechanical philosopher[23] would agree, they demand close observation and classification.

---

19   Timothy Chesters' study of early modern ghost-lore in France confirmed the concept of ghosts in the early modern period as 'apparitions of the dead'; Timothy Chesters, *Ghost Stories in Late Renaissance France: Walking by Night* (Oxford University Press, 2011), p. 3.
20   A condition or place of spiritual cleansing after death.
21   Peter M. Rojoewicz, 'The 'Men in Black' Experience and Tradition: Analogues with the Traditional Devil Hypothesis', *The Journal of American Folklore* 100, no. 396 (1987), p. 154.
22   *cf.* S. D. Tucker, *The Hidden Folk: Are Poltergeists and Fairies Just the Same Thing?* (CFZ Press, 2016) and *Blithe Spirits: An Imaginative History of the Poltergeist* (Amberley, 2020).
23   A form of natural philosophy, 'the claim that everything in nature could be explained in terms of the interaction of matter and motion'; Michael Hunter, *The Decline of Magic: Britain in the Enlightenment* (Yale University Press, 2020), p. 10.

INTRODUCTION

~~~

Over thirty English poltergeist cases are known for the period *c.*1590-*c.*1720. Several are well documented, occasionally by two or more sources. The most famous, and most copiously researched are the case of the Tidworth demon (1662-63) and the haunting of the Wesley family home in Epworth (1716-17). Many more can be found in the pages of mid- and late seventeenth-century demonologies by such writers as Joseph Glanvill, Richard Baxter, John Beaumont, Richard Bovet, and George Sinclair who were all keen collectors of 'providential' accounts of the supernatural. Others appear in often anonymous pamphlets. No doubt some ephemeral publications have not survived or are yet to be found. When Henry More heard of a case in London many years after the supposed events, he noted it was said to have been of 'great fame' at the time, and 'a Book was then said to be printed' though he had failed to find a copy of the earlier work.[24] More's account and that elusive 'book' are the subject of Relation 4 in this volume. It is reasonable to suppose the printed accounts of poltergeist cases in the period represent just a few of many more which were not recorded and have long since been forgotten.

We know a good deal more about the poltergeist's historical bedfellow, the witch, because serious witchcraft allegations were likely to end up in court. This is one reason for why there is a vast amount of literature on the witch craze, and yet the poltergeist cases of the period, have largely eluded the attentions of historians, so much so that Peter Maxwell-Stuart's publishers announced his 2011 publication, *Poltergeists: A History of Violent Ghostly Phenomena,* as 'The first major history of the poltergeist phenomenon ever published'. However, back in 1945, Price, mentioned above, put out *Poltergeist Over England* in which he traced its two-thousand-year-old history to episodes recorded in his own lifetime. When he jumped on the Borley Rectory 'Most Haunted House in England' bandwagon, Price was a blatant sensationalist in turning himself into the twentieth-century's most famous ghost hunter. His critics considered him a liar and, even worse, the instigator of much

---

24 Glanvill, *Saducismus Triumphatus,* p. 431.

of the poltergeist activity he reported.[25] However, his discussion of historical cases in his book is largely objective and rooted in a close scrutiny of primary sources. Respectable history written by a disreputable author. Maxwell-Stuart's own work makes several references to that of Price, even to the point of being his one source for a case in Welton in the late 1650s.[26] Price, in turn, acknowledged his own debt to earlier histories concerned with the subject, notably Hereward Carrington's *Historic Poltergeists* (1935), and Andrew Lang's weighty *Cock Lane and Common Sense* (1894). In 1940 Sacheverell Sitwell, influenced by the emerging discipline of psychology, published *Poltergeists* which included commentaries on the Tidworth/Mompesson and Epworth/Wesley cases. Nevertheless, it is certainly fair to say that, with some notable exceptions, recorded poltergeist episodes *as history* have rarely been addressed. Colin Wilson, whose study of cases predates Maxwell-Stuart's book, concluded that, due to the unspectacular, repetitive, inane, unknowable and unattributable nature of phenomena across so many cases, 'a comprehensive history of the poltergeist would be unreadable'.[27]

Of course, historic poltergeist cases appear in broader histories of supernatural belief and investigation. The 'Demon of Tedworth' turns up frequently. This, together with the Epworth case, and the great precursor of English poltergeist fascination, that of the Devil of Mâcon (1612), have dedicated chapters in Roger Clarke's *A Natural History of Ghosts* (2012). The highly regarded folklorist Christina Hole concluded her influential *Haunted England* (1940) with a chapter on poltergeists. They can be found in Owen Davies's admirable *The Haunted: A Social History of Ghosts* (2007), and in the pages of Susan Owens's equally rewarding *The Ghost: A Cultural History* (2019). S. D. Tucker, a hunter of evidence for a universal 'trickster' fairy over millennia, has commented on several early modern cases in *The Hidden Folk: Are Poltergeists and Fairies Just the Same Thing?* (2016) and *Blithe Spirits: An Imaginative*

---

25   *cf.* Sean O'Connor, *The Haunting of Borley Rectory: The Story of a Ghost Story* (Simon & Schuster, 2022).
26   P. G. Maxwell-Stuart, *Poltergeists: A History of Violent Ghostly Phenomena* (Amberley, 2011), p.134; Price, *Poltergeist,* pp. 65-6.
27   Colin Wilson, *Poltergeist: A Study in Destructive Haunting* (New English Library, 1981), Chapter 3.

History of the Poltergeist (2020). Geoff Holder's *Poltergeist Over Scotland* (2013), makes a valuable contribution in highlighting cases, including several seventeenth- and early eighteenth-century ones, not found in Price's *Poltergeist Over England* or other anglo-centric studies.

~ ~ ~

MOST ACCOUNTS FROM the period surviving as printed and published narratives have at least some overt polemical elements, often in generic statements regarding mortal sin and the reality of the Devil. Some are eye-witness accounts but many are based on hearsay and probably, in some instances, a good deal of invention. Those cases that are built in part or wholly on evidence not written down with publication in mind, particularly those derived from multiple sources, are especially intriguing, persuasive even. In this category the exemplars are the Tidworth (then known as Tedworth) and Epworth cases. It is largely for these reasons they are the best known. However, they are not the most spectacular early modern haunted-house narratives in terms of what actually happens. Wilson rather missed the point when he suggested a book of poltergeist histories would be uneventful, unresolvable, repetitious and boring; the poltergeist is a subtle creature, gradually heightening the tension, usually in mundane ways. The best poltergeist tales are the ones in which the slightest movement of a domestic utensil or a child's toy, the rustle of a dress, the faint whisper of an unknown voice, or the light touch of a hand on a shoulder, are terrifying. The Reverend Samuel Wesley was closer to the mark when he declared the story of the bizarre haunting of his family's home 'would make a glorious penny book for Jack Dunton'.[28]

---

28   Reverend Samuel Wesley to his son, Samuel, 11 February 1717, in Joseph Priestly, *Original Letters by the Rev. John Wesley, and his Friends, Illustrative of his Early History, with other Curious Papers* (Birmingham, 1791), p. 134. John Dunton was a notable bookseller who pioneered the concept of the popular magazine as publisher, from 1691, of *The Athenian Mercury*; he married Samuel Wesley's wife's niece.

1
THE RISE OF THE ENGLISH POLTERGEIST

'He that can be persuaded that these things are true [...] may soone be brought to believe that the moone is made of greene cheese.'
Reginald Scot (1584)[29]

THE FLOWERING OF the poltergeist tradition in the first age of the printing press is not surprising. Very occasionally it, or something similar, is glimpsed in earlier manuscript sources. The haunting by 'unclean spirits' of the Pembrokeshire homes of Stephen Wiriet and William Nott was recorded in 1191 by Gerald of Wales (*c*.1146-*c*.1223). On more than one occasion 'they demonstrated their presence [...] by throwing filth and other things round the place' and 'they seemed', Gerald continued, 'to be playing games rather than doing people harm'. This mischief included tearing and making holes in William's and his guests' garments. The spirit in Stephen's house would converse with its audience and make public scandalous secrets belonging to those who dared abuse it in these paranormal encounters.[30] Meanwhile, in the *Chronicon Anglicanum* (*c*.1200), Ralph of Coggeshall, spoke of an entity haunting the Dagworth home in Suffolk of Sir Osborne of Bradaewelle. It identified itself as 'Malekin', and once manifested in the form of a little boy dressed in a white tunic. In good fairy tradition, the eminent folklorist Katharine Briggs noted, food was left out for him and consumed.[31] In the

---

29 Reginald Scot, *Discoverie of Witchcraft* (London, 1584), p. 329.
30 Lewis Thorpe, (trans.), *Gerald of Wales: The Journey through Wales* and *The Description of Wales* (Penguin Books, 1978), p. 151.
31 Katharine Briggs, *The Fairies in Tradition and Literature* (Routledge and Kegan

contemporary *Otia Imperialia* (Book 1, *c.*1211) 'the homes of simple peasants' were known to sometimes be inhabited by mysterious invisible entities that might 'pelt anyone who comes in with stones, sticks, and household utensils'. Sometimes they made utterances resembling human speech.[32] What Jeremy Harte has described as a poltergeist - but might as viably be supposed a mischievous fairy, elf or goblin - 'threw Thomas of Ely out of bed in 1389'.[33]

In popular culture in modern times these phenomena commonly have been attributed to the unsettled souls of the human dead. In medieval contexts fairies might be blamed, but in early modern England it was more likely to be demons. It would be a while yet before forces beyond the invisible hand of sentient beings were claimed as possible causes by ghost-hunters and psychologists.

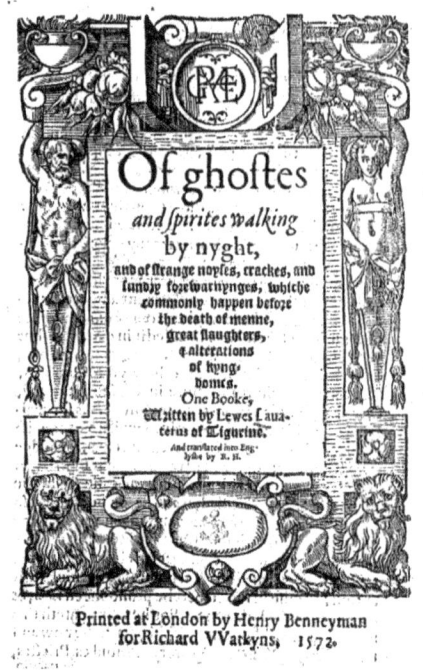

The English edition (1572) of Lewis Lavater's *Of Ghostes and Spirites Walking by Nyght, and of Strange Noyses, Crackes, and Sundry Forewarnynge.*

In 1572 an English translation of a book written by Lewis Lavater (1527-86), printed in Geneva in 1570, appeared as *Of Ghostes and Spirites Walking by Nyght, and of Strange Noyses, Crackes, and Sundry Forewarnynge,* 'perhaps the first book on spiritualism, as we know it, to be published', in Harry Price's opinion, and a source detectable in

---

Paul, 1967), p. 8.
32   S. E. Banks, and J. W. Binns, *Gervaise of Tilbury: Otia Imperlialia* (Oxford University Press, 2002), p. 99.
33   Jeremy Harte, *Fairy Encounters in Medieval England: Landscape, Folklore and the Supernatural* (University of Exeter Press, 2024), p. 20.

the work of William Shakespeare.[34] It starts in the way of subsequent texts on the preternatural, by alerting readers to the likely natural explanation for uncanny events:

> There happen dayly many things by the ordinary course of nature, whiche divers men, especially they that ar timorous and fearfull, suppose to be visions of Spirits. As for example, when they heare the crying of rats, cats, weasels, martins, or any other beast, or when they heare a horse beate his feete on the plankes in the stable at midnight, by and by they sweate for feare, supposing some buggs[35] to walke in the dead of the night.[36]

However, the ensuing discussion of the supernatural includes familiar horrors such as that of the night-time entity walking up and down the bedroom, pinching its slumbering victim, pulling off his bed clothes, sitting on him and, worse still, climbing into the bed beside him. It also provides one of the first unequivocal descriptions of what is now regarded as classic poltergeist activity in a haunted house:

> It hath many times chaunced, that those of the house have verily thought, that some body hath overthrowne the pots, platters, tables and trenchers, and tumbled them downe the stayres; but after it waxed day, they have found all things orderly set in their places againe.

> It is reported, that some spirits have throwne the dore off from the hookes, and have troubled and set all things in the house out of order, never setting them in their due place againe, and that they have marvellously disquieted men with rumbling and making a great noise.[37]

Lavater touched upon other now familiar phenomena including the

---

34 Price, *Poltergeist*, pp. 11-12.
35 Also known as bogeymen, boggarts, bugbears, boggles, bull beggars etc.
36 Lewis Lavater, *Of Ghostes and Spirites Walking by Nyght, and of Strange Noyses, Crackes, and Sundry Forewarnynge* (London, 1572), p. 73.
37 Lavater, *Ghosts*, p. 73.

appearance at night of small fires or candles moving about someone's demon-infested home.[38]

Despite the arrival of Lavater's book, the major Elizabethan and early Jacobean demonologies do not provide much evidence for an equivalent English poltergeist tradition.[39] In 1584 the first major English demonology, Reginald Scot's 560-page long *Discoverie of Witchcraft*, was published in London. Despite its detailed account of instructions on the exorcism of demons, it lacks comment on what might be deemed poltergeist activity. What little there is concerns the activities of terrestrial spirits – fairies, hobgoblins, and the like. These 'jocund and facetious Spirits', he commented, 'are sayd to sport themselvs [sic] in the night by tumbling and fooling with Servants and Shepherds in Country houses, pinching them black and blew' and sometimes carrying them away at night to be found dazed and confused 'lying in some Meddow or Mountain' days, even weeks later.[40] These mischievous household spirits, who might at times reward their human hosts with miraculous gifts of bread, butter and cheese, Scot considered part of the pre-Christian Roman veneration of domestic gods known as 'lars'.

Preoccupied as they were with witches and diabolical pacts, random noises and the movement of objects in haunted houses seem not to have found a significant place in the theological and philosophical debates that concerned early English demonologists. Nor are they found in other major works of contemporary literature – for example, plenty of ghosts (as well as witches and fairy-folk) occur in Shakespeare's plays, but not houses infected by poltergeists.[41]

Poltergeist pamphlets are rare compared to the abundance of witchcraft pamphlets in the late Elizabethan period and beyond. Those concerned with witchcraft usually were founded on cases brought to court; they were, as Marion Gibson has noted, a form of popular crime literature.[42] In poltergeist cases no crimes, in the conventional sense,

---

38   Lavater, *Ghosts*, p. 51.
39   Those published by Reginald Scot (1584), Henry Holland (1590), George Gifford (1593), and William Perkins (1608). King James's famous *Daemonologie*, published in Scotland in 1597, is equally barren.
40   Scot, *Discoverie*, pp. 510-11.
41   In *Macbeth, Hamlet, Richard III, Julius Caesar, Henry VI, The Tempest*.
42   Marion Gibson, *Reading Witchcraft: Stories of Early English Witches* (Routledge,

were likely to be committed. Those few accounts that were produced came instead from the same stable as accounts of other 'wonderful' and unsettling events such as the appearance of a headless bear in Ditcheat, Somerset, and a dragon in woods near Horsham in West Sussex.[43] What early modern poltergeist accounts do have in common with most post *c.*1590 witchcraft pamphlets is a narrative approach in as much as they tended towards a chronological structure as things developed day by day. Episodes of witchcraft, however, could make very good stories, especially when dressed as revenge narratives with readily identifiable causes and effects. They were likely to have clear cut start and end points: a charity-refused event leading to bewitchment and an execution, for example. The random character of poltergeist cases does not lend itself so well to a compelling narrative and, in any case, it is based on hearsay, not the reassuring verdict of a court.

The one substantial record suggesting stories of what are now called poltergeists *were* circulating in this otherwise barren landscape is an account from Oxfordshire at the start of the 1590s, the subject of a pamphlet printed in 1592 and the first of this book's collection of 'Relations'. That it was not unique is implicit in an opening remark describing it as a phenomenon the like of which had seldom been heard of before.

With the exception of a couple of curious cases reported during the era of the devastating English Civil War in the 1640s [Relations 4 and 5], the trail runs cold thereafter until the time when, decades later, news of a spectacular case from France began to filter into English consciousness. This, the most influential publication of a poltergeist account in the English language prior to the Restoration era following the return from exile of Charles II in 1660, concerned the case of a haunted house in southern France in 1612.[44] Many years later, a Protestant pastor, François Perraud, whose home and family were troubled in the town of Mâcon, had his highly detailed account of the haunting printed in 1653, followed

---

1999), p. 114.
43   Anon., *A true and most Dreadful discourse of a woman possessed with the Devill* (London, 1584); Anon., *True and Wonderfull. A Discourse relating a strange and monstrous Serpent (or Dragon) lately discovered* (London, 1614).
44   See Maxwell-Stuart, *Poltergeists*, Chapter 6, 'A Species of Witchcraft?', pp. 97-122, for a full description and analysis.

by a second edition in 1656. In 1658 an English version, translated by Peter du Moulin, was published at the behest of Robert Boyle (1627-91) who was on the way to making a name for himself as one of the most significant scientists and philosophers of his age and the leading light of the London Royal Society when it was founded in 1660.[45] Boyle had first come across the case in Geneva in the 1640s.[46] In his preface, written as a letter of gratitude to Moulin, Boyle declared he had met Perraud in Geneva and received from him a version of his account long before it was printed. His opportunity 'to enquire both after the writer, and some passages of the booke' while he was in Geneva helped him to overcome 'all my settled indisposednesse to believe strange things'. In his dedicatory letter to Boyle at the start of his translation of 'this admirable story', Moulin explained that his (and Boyle's) reason for bringing the story to the attention of English readers was 'to convince Atheists and halfe believers [...] that there are Devills' in order that 'they would believe also there is a God'. Although Perraud was now in his eighties, Moulin was careful to assert 'he writ this relation when it was fresh in his memory, yet did not publish it but 41 yeares after'. Not only did the account reinforce the alarmist mantra of the seventeenth-century demonologist concerned with the alleged rise of atheism, but

The English version, commissioned by Robert Boyle, of the influential Mâcon case

---

45 François Perraud (transl. Peter du Moulin), *The Devill of Mascon: A true Relation of the chiefe things which an uncleane Spirt did, and said at Mascon in Burgundy, in the house of Mr Francis Perraud Minister of the Reformed Church in the same Towne* (Oxford, 1658); Moulin was a tutor to Boyle's nephews.
46 Michael Hunter, *Boyle: Between God and Science* (Yale University Press, 2009), p. 122.

THE RISE OF THE ENGLISH POLTERGEIST

also it served as a template for patterns of poltergeist behaviour.

Perraud's troubles began on 14 September 1612, when he returned, from church business away from home to find 'my wife and her mayd in very great concernation [sic]'. He was told how they had been disturbed in the night after he left by curtains in his wife's bedroom being violently drawn by unseen hands, of blankets being pulled off, of doors that would not open after they had been unbolted, and 'in the kitchen the pewter and brasse throwne about'. The first night after his return he experienced similar phenomena:

Robert Boyle, chemist, demonologist, and member of the Royal Society. Portrait by Johann Kerseboom (1689)

> I heard a great noise from the kitchen, as the rolling of a billet [log] throwne with great strength. I heard also a knocking against a partition of wainscot in the same kitchen, sometimes as with the point of the finger, sometimes as if with the nails, sometimes as with the fist, and then the blows did redouble. Many things also were throwne against that wainscot [wood panelling], [such] as plates, trenchers [boards] and ladels, and a music was made with a brasse cullender, gingling with some buckles that were at it, and with some other instruments of the kitchen.

He arose and searched the place, sword in hand, 'but all in vaine'. 'Then', he concluded, 'did I beginne to know indeed that all this could not proceed but from a wicked Spirit, and so did I passe the rest of the night, in such astonishment as any man may imagine'. The tale then moves on to recount a series of night-time conversations with the demon conducted by Perraud and a range of visitors (and witnesses). These are described in Perraud's account in great detail over several pages. Meanwhile things continued to move about of their own accord including episodes of what was known as *lithobolia* [stone throwing]:

> He threw stones about my house continually [for] tenne or twelve [...] daies from morning to evening, and in great quantity, some of them of two or three pounds weight.

However, no-one was hurt for, as Perraud the good pastor presumed, 'All the time that the Demon haunted my house God permitted him not to doe us any harme, neither in our persons nor in our goods'. Towards the end of his account, in what appears from his remarks to have been at the height of a local witchcraft panic, he related several other demonic/poltergeist episodes in Mâcon and elsewhere, capturing and preserving glimpses of stories that might otherwise not have survived.

'Was not the Story of the Devil of Mascon (attested by the Famous Mr. Boyle) notorious through the whole City?' declared William Freke, many years later, of its considerable impact upon London when the English account was published.[47] If *The Devill of Mascon* was the single most important publication in the emergence of the English poltergeist story in print, the most important event was the Restoration in changing the theological and intellectual landscape. The remarkable scholar, poet and anthropologist, Andrew Lang (1844-1912), in his book on a controversial eighteenth-century poltergeist episode and related matters, *Cock Lane and Common-Sense* (1896), recognized this when he declared:

> Common-sense, and 'drolling Sadduceeism,'[48] came to their own, in England, with the king, with Charles II. After May 29, 1660, Webster and Wagstaffe mocked at boggles, if Glanvill and More took them seriously.[49]

> Before the Restoration it was distinctly dangerous to laugh at witchcraft, ghosts and haunting. But the laughers came in with

---

47   William Freke, *A full enquiry into the power of faith* (1693) in Tony McAleavy, *The Last Witch Craze: John Aubrey, the Royal Society and the Witches* (Amberley, 2022), p. 65.
48   Term, derived from a biblical sect, the Sadducees, who denied the possibility of physical resurrection, used to denigrate sceptics in spiritual affairs.
49   John Webster (1610-82) and John Wagstaffe (1633-77): demonologists who questioned the claims of the less sceptical Jospeh Glanvill and Henry More.

the merry monarch, and less by argument than by ridicule, by inveighing against the horror, too, of the hideous witch prosecutions, the laughers gradually brought hauntings and apparitions into contempt.[50]

From this time on the poltergeist shared centre-stage with other phenomena in the struggle to prove the supernatural.

Although there is a dearth of English poltergeist literature for most of the first half of the seventeenth century, that is not to say there were no cases; those few that have some kind of a record are mostly known through sources printed in the second half of the century. The most detailed account of the spectacular episode in the royal mansion at Woodstock in 1649 [Relation 5] was first distributed in a pamphlet in 1661. Equally spectacular was the haunting of the home of a silk-weaver in Plaistow near London in 1645, recorded in a contemporary pamphlet and also in an eye-witness account which surfaced years later as one of Henry More's contributions to Joseph Glanvill's *Saducismus Triumphatus* [Relation 4]. In 1650 another tale of domestic disturbance was told in *The Strange Witch at Greenwich* [Relation 6].

Henry More, member of the Royal Society, mechanical philosopher, and demonologist.

The rise of the English poltergeist legend with the proliferation of published cases in the second half of the seventeenth century might be explained as the result of serious-minded clergymen determined to prove the reality of spirits. It has been suggested tales of poltergeists, especially when witnessed by multiple people, were 'far more comforting as evidence

---

50 Andrew Lang, *Cock Lane and Common-sense* (Longmans, Green, & Co., 1896), p. 136.

of a spirit-world' than stories of the occasional manifestation of a ghost typically spotted once or twice by a single person.[51] From the start it was an important element in the great resurgence of demonological texts during the later seventeenth century, in defiance of the strikingly short period of time in which age-old beliefs in the certainty of witchcraft and spirits, at least in 'educated' circles, swiftly evaporated.

The historical record for poltergeist cases is skewed by the level of interest they aroused among the ruling class. It is not surprising to find that two of the most detailed accounts, the Tidworth case and the haunting of the New Hampshire home of George Walton in 1682, are the product of the elite networks in which the protagonists were placed. The presence of New England governors at the Waltons' house is surely due to the happy coincidence of their guest and lodger at the time of its haunting being a royal servant. Likewise, John Mompesson of Tidworth was the cousin of Sir Thomas Mompesson of Salisbury and the associate of others with courtly connections. In this instance no less a personage than the king, Charles II, took a keen interest in the news emanating from Wiltshire.

Glanvill, the author of *Saducismus Triumphatus,* was one among many who visited Tidworth in the early 1660s. He was a young cleric with a glittering career ahead of him as a theologian and exponent of mechanical philosophy, and, at the start of 1662, the recently installed incumbent of St John's in nearby Frome Selwood on the Wiltshire-Somerset border. No doubt inspired by Boyle's work in the field and More's pioneering approach to prove certain philosophical arguments by relating case studies in his *Antidote against Atheism* published back in 1653, the disturbances at the Mompesson home offered Glanvill the opportunity to seek empirical evidence for the preternatural for which he had developed a fascination. Whatever else might be said of the affair, it is clear that this was an exceptional case that captured the public imagination. It is reasonable to suppose that, despite precedents, it set off the wave of enthusiasm for the discovery, investigation, and reportage of poltergeist incidents that continues to the present day.

'In the month of February, 1665', Lang declared at the end of the

---

51   Coleman O. Parsons, 'Ghost-stories before Defoe', *Notes and Queries* 3, no. 7 (1956), pp. 294.

nineteenth century, 'there was assembled at Ragley Castle as curious a party as ever met in an English country-house'. Its host, Lady Conway, Lang continued, was 'a woman of remarkable talent and character, but wholly devoted to mystical speculations'.[52] Among those invited to Anne Conway's Ragley Hall home, close to the old Roman town of Alcester on the western edge of Warwickshire, were her teacher and friend, More, and his friend, Glanvill, who had been made a Fellow of the Royal Society in 1664. Boyle was not in attendance but a man very well known to his brother, Lord Orrery, provided the main reason for their gathering. This was an Irish faith healer with healing hands named Valentine Greatrakes who had been summoned to Ragley in the (vain) attempt to cure Lady Conway of her bouts of 'violent chronic headache'. Prior to this he had been part of a group of eminent individuals, which included Orrery and two bishops, who had witnessed, in a room in Orrery's castle in Ireland, the levitation of a butler who had recently had an encounter with 'the good people, or fairies'. No doubt he was pressed to describe it in some detail (it subsequently appeared in Glanvill's works on the supernatural) just as it can be supposed Glanvill was urged to recount his experience of the Tidworth poltergeist. For Lang and his successors this meeting of minds at Lady Conway's was a pivotal moment in the annals of English ghost-hunting:

> Thus at Ragley there convened the nucleus of an unofficial but active Society for Psychical Research, as that study existed in the seventeenth century.[53]

A year later Glanvill published his findings and theories on related matters, for the first time, in *Some Philosophical Considerations Touching Witches and Witchcraft*. An expanded version appeared in 1668 under the title *A Blow at Modern Sadducism in some philosophical Considerations about Witchcraft*. This included an account of the case of the Tidworth affair. The compendium of Glanvill's writings 'concerning Witches and Apparitions', with further additions and much augmented by More, was published in 1681 in the year after Glanvill's death. Its full title is

---

52 Lang, *Cock Lane*, p. 84.
53 Lang, *Cock Lane*, pp. 84-6.

Joseph Glanvill, vicar of Frome in Somerset, member of the Royal Society, and author of the influential demonology, *Saducismus Triumphatus* (1681).

Saducismus Triumphatus, or Full and Plain Evidence, concerning Witches and Apparitions, in two Parts, the First treating of their Possibility, and the Second of their real Existence. The second part, with More's significant contributions, is the single most valuable source for the rise of the poltergeist in early modern England.

The story of the Tidworth demon is, deservedly, very well known, and one that has been exhaustively mined by scholars and others across the centuries since. However, several more cases added by More to the second edition of the *Saduscismus* that fall broadly into the 'poltergeist' category have, by comparison, been overlooked. The maverick historian of the paranormal, Montague Summers, would write, 'There is no more important figure in the history of English psychical research than Joseph Glanvill'[54] while Harry Price considered him the founding-father of the science. The flowering of the English poltergeist story in the second half of the seventeenth century was largely the outcome Glanvill's alliances with like-minded intellectuals: notably his Royal Society mentors and colleagues, Boyle, and More.

In the meantime, another important case came to light in 1671 with the publication of *The Demon of Burton, or A true Relation of Strange Witchcraft or Incantations lately practiced at Burton in the Parish of Weobley in Herefordshire* [Relation 12]. This was followed by *News from Puddle Dock* printed in 1674, and *Strange and Wonderful News from*

---

54 Montague Summers (ed.), *Pandaemonium by Richard Bovet, 1684* (EP Publishing, 1951), p. xi.

Saducismus Triumphatus:

OR,

Full and Plain EVIDENCE

Concerning

WITCHES
AND
APPARITIONS.

PROVING

Partly by Holy Scripture, partly by a choice Collection of Modern Relations,

The Real Exiftence

OF

APPARITIONS, SPIRITS, and WITCHES.

By *JOS. GLANVIL*, late Chaplain to His Majefty, and Fellow of the Royal Society.

LONDON,
Printed for *S. Lownds*, MDCLXXXVIII.
[2d Edition]

Yowell in Surrey in 1681 [Relation 19].

Another Somerset man, Richard Bovet, published his *Pandaemonium, or, The Devil's Cloyster* in 1684, 'being a further blow to modern sadduceism'.[55] Aping Glanvill in various ways, Bovet dedicated his work to Henry More. Although his own set of bizarre 'Relations' is dominated by tales of witches, apparitions and fairies, one concerns poltergeist activity at a house in Bristol in the 1630s [Relation 2]. However, two more demonologies, also closely aligned with Glanvill's, provided more cases of the kind. These are Richard Baxter's *The Certainty of the Worlds of Spirits* (1691), and John Beaumont's *An Historical Physiological and Theological Treatise of Spirits, Apparitions, Witchcrafts, and Other Magical Practises* (1705). Meanwhile, another admirer of the Royal Society demonologists, the author of a set of accounts in *Satan's Invisible World Discovered* (1685), George Sinclair, an Edinburgh academic and associate of both Boyle and More, added some Scottish cases to the record [Relations 7 and 18]. Among other episodes around the turn of the century, a highly detailed early modern poltergeist case appeared as a pamphlet published in London in 1698 which, almost certainly, had been written back in 1682 by a royal secretary, Richard Chamberlain (1648-1706). Under the title *Lithobolia: or, The Stone-Throwing Devil*, it concerns Chamberlain's personal testimony of a haunted house in which he stayed while concerned with state affairs in New England. [Relation 20].

~ ~ ~

THE ENDING OF England's witch craze, which took off in the last decades of the sixteenth century, has long been associated with the publication of Francis Hutchinson's dismissive *Historical Essay Concerning Witchcraft* in 1718. For another hugely influential essayist

---

55 The full title of Bovet's book is *Pandaemonium, or, The Devil's Cloyster being a further blow to modern sadduceism, proving the existence of witches and spirits, in a discourse deduced from the fall of the angels, the propagation of Satans kingdom before the flood, the idolatry of the ages after greatly advancing diabolical confederacies, with an account of the lives and transactions of several notorious witches: also, a collection of several authentick relations of strange apparitions of dæmons and spectres, and fascinations of witches, never before printed.* Pandaemonium was John Milton's name for Hell.

on the subject, Wallace Notestein, it represented the 'final deadly blow at the dying superstition'.[56] Hence, Notestein's own pioneering narrative of the history of witchcraft in England, for this reason, culminated in the year Hutchinson published. Michael Hunter has posited that with the publication of Hutchinson's work 'we have arguably reached a pivotal point in terms of the acceptability of sadducism to the orthodox'.[57] However, as the witch craze came to an end, another spectacular and copiously detailed case came to light. Starting in 1716, the soon to be world-famous Wesley family was plagued by the activities of a poltergeist in their home at Epworth Rectory [Relation 26]. While similar cases before and after were lampooned as fictional and fraudulent, this one was taken very seriously. The subsequent fame of, and respect for, the evangelical Wesley sons, John and Samuel, perhaps played a part in keeping the light of poltergeist faith burning through and beyond the ridicule heaped on the equally well-known Cock Lane case later in the eighteenth century.

Peter Marshall has described the seventeenth-century English demonologists - More, Glanvill, Baxter and company - as the 'unlikely godparents' of the popular English poltergeist tradition. Their incorporation of accounts of the paranormal as empirical evidence in their moral campaigns turned them into 'storytellers in spite of themselves'.[58] By the end of the seventeenth century they had been instrumental in bringing about 'a shift from propaganda to pastime, from indoctrination to literary entertainment'.[59] Just as 'true' poltergeist stories have continued to echo elements of the seventeenth-century template, so too do undisguised poltergeist fictions in modern literature and film.

---

56   Wallace Notestein, *A History of Witchcraft in England from 1558 to 1718* (The American Historical Society, 1911), p. 1.
57   Michael Hunter, *The Decline of Magic: Britain in the Enlightenment* (Yale University Press, 2020), p. 66. A biblical term used in the period to denote non-believers in the supernatural, specifically belief in the afterlife.
58   Peter Marshall, *Invisible Worlds: Death, Religion and the Supernatural in England, 1500-1700* (SPCK, 2017), p. 161.
59   Parsons, 'Ghost-Stories' , p. 293; Marshall, *Invisible Worlds*, pp. 161-62.

An enchanted castle possessed by a monstrous devil.
Richard Bovet, *Pandaemonium* (London, 1684).

2

HAUNTED HOUSES

'The home emerges as a singular entity, something with its own atmosphere, an agency in its own right, it is *more than* the sum of its parts: a charismatic presence excessive of its original creation, taking on a life of its own'

Caron Lipman (2016)[60]

In *The Devil in Tudor and Stuart England* (2010), Darren Oldridge avoided the anachronistic term 'poltergeist' in commenting on the 1662 case of the Tidworth demon. Instead, he invoked the concept of demonic 'obsession' by which 'individuals were tormented by evil spirits' as opposed to 'possession' in which 'they were physically invaded by demons'.[61] Modern analyses of poltergeist cases are likely to emphasise the role of the *person*, the 'focus' of activity. In the opinion of one modern historian of the paranormal, 'The most obvious feature of these cases [is] "Haunted People"', rather than '"Haunted Houses"'.[62] This might be valid for surveys of more recent cases but it is not such a good fit for equivalent phenomena in early modern reportage in England. Although it aligns neatly with elements of some, it is not applicable to many others. The surviving poltergeist narratives from the period reveal a less personal concept of demonic fixation than Oldridge's definition above implies. Perhaps his definition should be broadened to include demonic obsession with *place*, most obviously the 'haunted house'. The

---

60 Caron Lipman, *Co-habiting with Ghosts: Knowledge, Experience, Belief and the Domestic Uncanny* (Routledge, 2016), p. 193.
61 Oldridge, *The Devil*, p. 170.
62 Sugg, *Supernatural Stories*, pp. 12-13.

poltergeist in these stories often behaves in seemingly random, pointless ways and it is as likely to perform for visitors as readily as the family with which it shares its abode. As often as not, its antics are pretty harmless and in some cases it entertains as much as it torments. Servants seem to be as prone to molestation as other members of the household. Much of the time it is active in unoccupied places, making noises and moving things around when no-one is looking. Most of the paranormal activity in these accounts is confined to a single property and the bulk of it occurs indoors. The poltergeist in early modern England was, essentially, housebound – rarely pursuing people from one place to another. While in some of these accounts there *are* individuals who might be construed as the focus of its activities, as well as suspect-witch perpetrators, at the heart of the matter is the entity itself and the house it haunts. Thus, the haunted house demands as much attention as the people occupying it.

Gainsborough Old Hall, Lincolnshire. A complex and impressive late Tudor house. (Photo: author)

Wherever ghosts and spirits loom large in popular culture they are likely to manifest in or around haunted houses: white ladies, perhaps, reflected in the full-length mirrors of venerable mansions, or the plate-glass windows of modern homes. In early modern England they occasionally appeared but, more commonly, were heard: the rustle of ladies' gowns, the scratching and scurrying about of something under the beds of sleepers disturbed in the dead of night. 'That there are haunted houses', Sacheverel Sitwell observed concerning their place in popular culture, 'will be agreed to by all but a minority of sceptical readers'.[63] 'There is no great mystery as to why buildings should have been so frequently haunted', Davies has declared. 'The vast majority of people died inside their homes. It was, therefore, the natural place for their ghosts to return' is a reasonable conclusion.[64] However, the hauntings of houses in early modern England were very rarely attributed to the spectral return of the deceased.[65] We are lumbered with the term 'poltergeist', undermining the case for distinguishing them from regular 'ghosts'. In considering entities causing 'poltergeist-like effects' independently of witches, Gillian Bennett invoked some more satisfactory definitions: 'homely ghosts' and, better still, 'household sprites' and 'housesprites'.[66] The haunted house is the host to its poltergeist-parasite. From the sixteenth century up to the present day, poltergeist cases, in Mâcon in 1612 for example, are likely to occur 'not in a corner, or in a desert, but [. . .] in a house'.[67] It is to the house we must turn if we are to have any chance of unravelling the mystery of the poltergeist.

The spookiness of the candle-lit corridors and multiple rooms of a shrinking, creaking, vermin-infested seventeenth-century house was born of the house itself, not some residual memory of a previous incumbent. Unloved houses – manors left to fade and decay, and, in more recent times, drab utilitarian homes housing tenants with temporary or insecure leaseholds, or, worse still, unoccupied – are especially prone to a

---

63 Sacheverell Sitwell, *Poltergeists: An Introduction and Examination Followed by Chosen Instances* (Faber and Faber, 1940), p. 17.
64 'It was where people mourned the dead and were surrounded by memories of their presence'; Owen Davies, *The Haunted: a Social History of Ghosts* (Palgrave Macmillan, 2007), pp. 46-7.
65 The naming of the Epworth poltergeist 'Jeffrey' or 'Old Jeffries' by the Wesleys, after a man who had died in the house, seems to have been in jest.
66 Gillian Bennet, 'Ghost and Witch in the Sixteenth and Seventeenth Centuries', *Folklore* 97, no. 1 (1986), p. 4.
67 Peter du Moulin, *The Devill of Mascon: A true Relation of the chiefe things which an uncleane Spirt did, and said at Mascon in Burgundy, in the house of Mr Francis Perraud Minister of the Reformed Church in the same Towne* (Oxford, 1658), 'The Epistle *Dedicatorie*'.

reputation for being haunted. Seventeenth-century houses were mostly silent places, certainly when compared with modern homes. Even if we set aside the clatter of radios and televisions, dishwashers and washing machines, to ears accustomed to the ambience of the continuous hum of heating systems, fridges, and distant traffic, these places might seem as silent as the grave. And as impenetrably dark on a moonless night in the complete absence of streetlights, night-lights and the stand-by glow of the numerous gadgets that define domesticity in the twenty-first century. If all that would not make a visitor from the future shiver, the air temperature for much of the year in a seventeenth-century home, while Europe remained in the clutches of what climate historians have dubbed the early modern 'Little Ice Age', certainly would. Add to all this a gale blowing outside and drafts whistling through ill-fitting doors, you end up with houses ripe for haunting.

THE EMINENT HISTORIAN of vernacular architecture, R. W. Brunskill, established a typology for houses according to size: Great Houses, Large Houses, Small Houses and Cottages. There is sufficient contextual information in surviving early modern poltergeist accounts to demonstrate Large Houses frequently provided their setting. Large Houses, Brunskill wrote, included 'the manor house commanding, in partnership with the church, the medieval village street, the house of the unusually successful yeoman, or the highly favoured parson, the small country house of the squire, the imposing farm-house of the wealthy tenant farmer, the house of the clothier or mill-owner'.[68] The first case in England in the collection of relations below, concerns the haunting of a substantial farmhouse in 1591-92; the last (1717-18) is set in a classic 'Queen Anne' style parsonage, a new-build its proud incumbent, the Reverend Samuel Wesley, could ill-afford. If the typical British poltergeist in later twentieth century and early twenty-first-century cases can be considered a 'council-house ghost',[69] those in early modern England certainly were not.

68 R. W. Brunskill, *Vernacular Architecture: An Illustrated Handbook* (4th ed., Faber & Faber, 2000), p. 24.
69 Roger Clarke, *A Natural History of Ghosts* (Penguin, 2012), p. 19.

A significant proportion of these early modern cases concern big men in big houses, men like George Lee, the prosperous farmer of North Aston, excise-man Mompesson of Tidworth, and George Walton, a New England landowner. As employers and representatives of higher authority, they were all potential targets, across the socio-economic divisions of the period, of disgruntled folk in their communities and, conceivably, their homes. Their grand country houses in the seventeenth century were potential playgrounds for human as well as demonic mischief makers. Sir Walter Scott recalled the haunting in 1649 of a former royal residence in Woodstock near Oxford [Relation 5]. Here commissioners of the Long Parliament were plagued by a range of nocturnal disturbances including the tossing about of logs and the movement by unseen hands of pieces of furniture. Again, in contrast to malefic witchcraft it was, in Scott's retelling of the tale, 'of a playful [as opposed to] a dangerous cast'. Following the restoration of the monarchy a decade later, word got out that the instigator was a servant in the house, one Joseph Collins of Oxford, an ardent royalist, who was 'well acquainted with the old mansion of Woodstock' and used 'his local knowledge of trap-doors and passages so as to favour the tricks which he played off upon his masters by aid of his fellow-domestics'.[70] The trials of those at the mercy of the 'just devil' of Woodstock were played out largely across just three rooms of the royal manor house. There were plenty more above and beyond where, behind closed doors, elementals might start their nightly din, and others could hatch their plots. The former senior managers of the property were dismissed but others, maids and the like, some perhaps with different loyalties to the parliamentary commissioners now in residence, remained. Whoever or whatever was to blame, the visitors were not going to receive a warm welcome.

When such houses became haunted they were likely to attract a good deal of attention. Everyone in the neighbourhood, then as now, was likely to take an interest. The growing numbers of visitors to Tidworth irritated Mr Mompesson in the early 1660s and crowds of visitors to other haunted houses are mentioned in several other cases. While godly ministers with serious intent were among their number, Bath and Newton have concluded that for others 'to visit a haunted house [was]

---

70 Walter Scott, *Letters on Demonology and Witchcraft* (Routledge, 1885), p. 300.

a form of entertainment'. Their broad impression of the popularization of haunted houses prompted them to suggest that 'there seems to have been a shift in the later half of the seventeenth century from visits to haunted places being the preserve of the elite to a more democratized attempt to experience the supernatural'.[71] A bold claim, but one for which the contemporary accounts lend a measure of support.

~~~

THERE IS NO reason to challenge Owen Davies's argument that, 'It was from the mid seventeenth century onwards, when Neoplatonism[72] was beginning to crumble, that poltergeist activity assumed considerable importance as a battleground for competing philosophical discourses'.[73] However, this alone does not resolve the question regarding whether it was purely reportage of poltergeist phenomena that was on the rise or whether there were also more cases to report. The absence of cases from the first half of the century compared to their abundance thereafter, even in the annals of those ardent demonologists who hunted for them in the past as well as the present, suggests both explanations are equally worthy of investigation. If indeed there was an increase in supposed poltergeist episodes in the period this begs the further question: why?

While no single cause will be found to explain the take-off of poltergeist reportage by the middle of the seventeenth-century, the fact that it coincides with the completeion of what W. G. Hoskins in a seminal essay published in 1953 described as the 'Great Rebuilding' of England, is probably no coincidence. This 'housing revolution', as he defined it, had started by around 1570 and lasted until c.1640, on the eve of the English Civil War.[74] Subsequent commentators questioned Hoskins's dates: one, for example, found that in the village of Yetminster in Dorset a good deal of rebuilding predated 1570, that chambers

---

71   Bath, Jo, and Newton, John, '"Sensible Proof of Spirits": Ghost Belief during the Later Seventeenth Century', *Folklore* 117, no. 1 (2006), p. 11.
72   Philosophical systems developed in the third century AD and later, influeced by the writings of Plato.
73   Davies, *The Haunted*, p. 80.
74   W. G. Hoskins, 'The Rebuilding of Rural England', *Past and Present*, no. 4 (1953), p. 44.

Anne Hathaway's Cottage in Stratford-on-Avon, built as an open hall farmhouse in 1463, was rebuilt and extended in the early seventeenth century. The original open hall, now with ceilings and an upper floor, is the lower-roofed structure on the right. [Photo: author]

overlaid halls 'and by 1602 we even find cocklofts[75] over the room above the hall'.[76] Most halls had ceilings by the start of the seventeenth century and open hall houses were rarely built beyond 1550.[77] While Hoskins's thesis was challenged and revised by historians bothered by the danger of over-simplifying highly complex subjects through the invocation of such definitive concepts as a Great Rebuilding, from a post-revisionist perspective Hoskins' concept for England of 'a revolution' in the housing of a considerable part of the population in and around the seventeenth century remains persuasive.[78] Brunskill agreed with Hoskins but added, 'the period of the Great Rebuilding varied with location as well as social status; it occurred between about 1670 and 1720 in the northern

---

75 Small upper loft room accessed via the main attic area.
76 R. Machin, 'The Great Rebuilding: A Reassessment', *Past and Present* 77, no. 1 (1977), p. 53.
77 Matthew Johnson, 'Houses, Power and Everyday Life in Early Modern England' in *Constructing Power: Architecture, Ideology and Social Practice*, ed. by Joseph Maran, Carsten Juwig, Hermann Schwengel, and Ulrich Thaler (Lit Verlag, 2006), p.5.
78 Hoskins, 'The Rebuilding of Rural England', p. 54.

counties of England, and later still in parts of Wales', thus concurring with the 'Great Rebuildings' theses of subsequent commentators.[79]

This housing revolution embraced two approaches to house construction: the rebuild of existing structures, and the new build on sites of recently demolished old structures. The building of houses on previously unoccupied sites, Hoskins concluded, 'seems to have been confined almost entirely to cottages' – simpler, more primitive structures that were not part of the revolution in design found elsewhere. Hoskins painted a dismal picture of domestic buildings before the Great Rebuilding in his hugely influential *The Making of the English Landscape* (1955):

> [In] 1550 most English people were still living in the rather dark, squalid and cramped dwellings of their medieval forefathers. These were generally two-roomed houses – a hall and bower – built of a timber frame with walls of reinforced mud, the whole raised upon a rubble foundation. There were no glazed windows, and only one fireplace. The two rooms were not ceiled over, but were open to the rafters and the thatch of the roof. Few houses were built of stone, even in stone country.[80]

All this was about to change as, '[by] the 1560s and 1570s, the wealthier yeomen had built themselves larger and better houses'.[81] The dramatic transition from traditional building practices to modern was due, primarily, to technological developments and the greater availability of cash for investment in the pockets of those above the socio-economic level of cottagers. The Great Rebuilding specifically denotes, to paraphrase Hoskins, the modernization of fifteenth-century open hall houses with the insertion of a ceiling to provide a bedroom-floor above, and the introduction or addition of chimneys and staircases. The house once dominated by its large, communal open hall, turned into a home with multiple smaller rooms with dedicated fireplaces and well-lit with windows adorned with cheaper and improved glass panels. Larger properties developed or were built afresh with corridor passages negating the need to pass through

---

79 Brunskill, *Vernacular Architecture*, p. 29.
80 W. G. Hoskins, *The Making of the English Landscape* (London: Hodder and Stoughton, 1955), p. 155.
81 Hoskins, *English Landscape*, p. 155.

one room to reach another. 'By the mid-seventeenth century', Hoskins declared, 'the typical yeoman's house had three to six rooms, rising to eight to ten among the bigger yeomen'.[82] And these new builds provided the perfect environment for the poltergeist. 'Today, anyone who lives in a very old house finds themselves asked frequently, and quite matter-of-factly, if it is haunted', Susan Owens has observed,[83] yet the houses in which early modern hauntings took place were likely to be ultra-modern builds or state-of-the-art rebuilds of older structures. Beyond its incorporation of an earlier chimney, the Wesleys' haunted home essentially was a new build – a substantial modern house built on the site of the old rectory which had recently been gutted in a suspected arson attack. Where there is sufficient detail in the poltergeist cases of the period this seems to describe the typical context in which it was found. In these the drama takes place in multiple rooms, along corridors, and behind closed doors. As such homes became more abundant so too did the poltergeist tales concerning them.

The new homes of the well-to-do were different both to what came before and to what would follow. The earthen sound-absorbing floors of single-story halls were replaced by flagstone and tile floors, while suspended wooden floors provided platforms for chambers above, and elaborate wooden staircases were introduced to access them. In an age before the abundance of cheap heavily upholstered furniture and wall-to-wall carpets, these were places in which footsteps on stairs and the scraping of chairs were amplified in the soundscapes they filled. There was no triple glazing to baffle unusual sounds from outside. Wilfred Blunt, recalling his visits to the late Tudor abode of William and Jane Morris in the 1880s - the delightful Kelmscott Manor close to Lechlade - remarked:

> Kelmscott was a romantic but most uncomfortable house with all the rooms opening into each other and difficult to be alone in. […] All was uncarpeted with floors that creaked. In the daytime with the sun streaming through the windows the old house was full of happy life, but in the darkness of the night it was a ghostly place full of strange noises where every movement was heard plainly from room to room.[84]

82 Hoskins, 'The Rebuilding of Rural England', p. 55.
83 Susan Owens, *The Ghost: A Cultural History* (Tate Publishing, 2019), p. 7.
84 Fiona MacCarthy, *William Morris* (Faber and Faber, 1994), p. 629.

Nevertheless the houses of the two generations living through this housing revolution, Hoskins noted, 'were infinitely better furnished than those of their fathers and grandfathers'.[85] This is substantiated by numerous inventories and wills from the period. William Harrison in his *Description of England* (1577), Hoskins recalled, described it as 'the great amendment of lodging'.[86] There were more pots, more pewter vessels, more furniture, more hangings – more of everything, in fact, for the mischievous poltergeist to throw about the place.

Humans, instinctively diurnal creatures, are attuned to unseen dangers when night falls. As the sense of sight diminishes, hearing and other senses become more acute. The problem with grand old manor houses and multi-storey town houses is that they have many more unseen places, above and below, and passages and rooms hidden behind sealed doors where all kinds of horrors might lurk. With additional rooms came additional doors and windows to shake, rattle and bang, and, sometimes, to open or close of their own accord. The Epworth poltergeist [Relation 26] seemed to have a particular interest in doors – 'Several nights the latch of our lodging chamber would be lifted up very often, when all were in bed', Samuel Wesley recalled. 'One night', he continued, 'when the noise was great in the kitchen, and on a deal partition, and the door in the yard, the latch whereof was often lift [*sic*] up, my daughter Emilia went and held it fast on the inside, but it was still lifted up and the door pushed violently against her, though nothing was to be seen on the outside'.[87] When they were disturbed by ghostly footsteps and other noises in the garret [attic] rooms above them, the Wesleys, concerned that their children might waken and be afraid, had to get up in the dark, go down via the great staircase into the hall and from there into the kitchen to fetch and light a candle, before heading back upstairs to check on the children in their bedrooms. And

---

85 W. G. Hoskins 'The Great Rebuilding', *History Today* 5, no. 2, (1955), pp. 104-11.
86 Hoskins, 'The Rebuilding of Rural England', p. 49.
87 Samuel Wesley, 'An Account of Noises and Disturbances in my House, at Epworth, Lincolnshire, in December and January, 1716' (transcribed by his son, John Wesley, in 1726 and further transcribed, from this version, by John's brother, Samuel, in 1730); Priestly *Letters,*, pp. 145-6.

poltergeists thrived in these complex houses, especially at night, in the dark, and amid the shadows cast by the feeble light of candles. In such homes, 'Its spaces', Caron Lipman has suggested, 'especially those that are unused or unseen – are granted a dangerous potentiality'.[88]

'Houses', Harry Price remarked, 'often acquire a reputation for being haunted when in reality, they contain nothing more than rats, or an occasional tramp intent on finding shelter'.[89] There was good reason for Susanna Wesley to suppose, initially, the noises in her home were caused by rats. In an age in which 'pest control' for rats denoted the house cat, they could be a significant problem. Although it had been recently built among the ruins of the burned-out rectory it replaced, her house was far removed from the hermetically sealed units of the twenty-first century. Rats and other vermin are most likely to find their way into a house under the rafters and the Wesleys' comfortable home had an additional draw – the family kept sacks of corn, and even had it ground into flour, in the attic space (the 'garrets'). No wonder then that the 'poltergeist' activity was so commonly heard in the garrets, and that their manservant sleeping there seems to have been more troubled by it than anyone else. However, although people in that period might have been generally more 'superstitious' than ourselves, we should not presume they were any more easily deceived: Susanna's husband declared at the time, what he encountered in the house was 'not like the noise of rats, which I have often heard'.[90]

~~~

THE GAME-CHANGER IN all this, the reason homes became complex warrens of multiple storeys, passages and rooms, was the arrival of the chimney. 'Suddenly', Bill Bryson has remarked, 'it was possible to lay boards across the beams and create a whole new world upstairs'.[91]

---

88   Lipman, *Co-habiting*, p. 195.
89   Harry Price, 'My Adventures with Ghosts in Haunted Houses', *Sunday Sentinel*, 19 May 1929, 11, in Sean O'Connor, *The Haunting of Borley Rectory: the Story of a Ghost Story* (Simon & Schuster, 2022), p. 16.
90   Wesley, 'An Account of Noises and Disturbances in my House'; Priestly, *Letters*, p. 146.
91   Bill Bryson, *At Home: A Short History of Private Life* (Doubleday, 2010), p. 113.

Hoskins's Great Rebuilding is, to a considerable extent, defined by the widespread building of chimneys. In early modern folklore chimneys had significance as a place of vulnerability at the heart of the home. They might admit non-human entities (as in the Father Christmas tradition), and the fires in their hearths were sometimes considered especially attractive to demons. Chimneys might also be the means by which malefic spells were conveyed to their intended targets. Contemporary woodcuts portrayed them as a means of egress for witches magically transported to their sabbat meetings.[92] They crop up as a focus of poltergeist activity in several contemporary cases [for example, Relations 17 and 20].

In a recent survey conducted by Brian Hoggard around half of the fifty-one bellarmine jar witch-bottles in his sample[93] were found 'either beneath the hearth stone or within the construct of an inglenook fireplace [...] by far [their] most common location'.[94] Thus, Hoggard has suggested, the witch-bottle and its contents not only served the purpose of countering malefic witchcraft already undertaken, but might also, in some instances (especially when found in a chimney), have been more generally intended to pre-empt any future attempts to harm. In another interesting take on his subject, Hoggard has postulated they might sometimes have been intended as 'spirit traps' luring the demon or witch down the chimney to their doom down the neck and into the belly of a hidden (i.e. buried) anthropomorphic shaped bottle, decorated with the face of a bearded man and filled with urine, human hair and sharp objects such as pins and nails – something akin to sugar-water filled bottles to catch annoying wasps in modern suburban gardens. Whatever their meaning, what is striking in the present context is that the apparent emergence of witch-bottles in the mid-seventeenth century coincides with both the Great Rebuilding in England and the rise of the English poltergeist.

92   David Pickering, *Dictionary of Superstitions* (Cassell, 1995), p. 61; Brian Hoggard, *Magical House Protection: The Archaeology of Counter-Witchcraft* (Berghahn, 2019), pp. 30-1; I am grateful to Chris Groucott, University of Plymouth, for reminding me of the social and cultural significance of the chimney and hearth.
93   Imported stout earthenware bottles decorated on the neck with the face of a bearded man said to be a caricature of Cardinal Bellarmine; frequently found in association with domestic counter-magic in early-modern England.
94   Reckoned to date, in this context, from c.1650-1700; Brian Hoggard, *Magical House Protection: The Archaeology of Counter-Witchcraft* (Berghan, 2021) pp. 13, 15, 18.

The chimney was the key feature in an early modern domestic revolution.
[Anne Hathaway's Cottage, Stratford-on-Avon. Photo: author]

Despite the many shortcomings of open-hearth hall-houses, these at least were spared the potential menace of an open passageway into the heart of the home for malevolent entities flitting about the night sky. Many other concealed good fortune token objects, most commonly shoes, have been found in and around hearths.[95] So long as belief in the certainty of spirits prevailed, as it did well into the second half of the seventeenth century, such things mattered. A fascinating example of witch-bottle counter-magic to suppress a poltergeist is found in the eye-witness account of a haunting in New Hampshire in 1682 [Relation 20].

If chimneys can be construed as funnels or unconventional portals joining the domestic security of the home with a less predictable world outside, staircases too might be considered liminal features in the kind of homes that appeared during the era of the Great Rebuilding. They also feature in the poltergeist stories these spawned – in the Wesley family case, for example [Relation 26], the grand staircase connecting the 'public' space of the entrance hall with the 'private' spaces above, and the staircase hidden behind a door in the nursery leading to the servants' garret quarters beneath the roof, are a particular focus of activity. The sound of unexplained footsteps on stairs has endured in histories of haunted houses.

The arrival of multiple smaller rooms with dedicated roles both fulfilled and fuelled the desire for privacy. 'The merchant in his

---

95   Hoggard, *Magical House Protection*, pp. 31-2, 34-5; in 2013 an old shoe was discovered hidden behind plaster in the chimney breast, predating its rebuilding, of Epworth Rectory, the haunted home of the Wesleys.

Bellarmine 'witch bottle'. Utilitarian vessels of this kind were used in counter-magic practices and sometimes buried in the hearths of seventeenth-century houses. [Author's own collection and photo]

counting-house and the yeoman in his "best parlour"', Hoskins wrote, 'could develop a private life'. Johnson has commented on the 'changing patterns of relations between master and servant through changing patterns of spatial distance and segregation between rooms', together with the development of gender-specific use of space and spheres of male and female activity. Allied to this were technologies and resources such as improved chimneys, window glass, and more abundant supplies of coal which eliminated the 'physical need to herd around the common fireplace in the hall'.[96] Instead, different people engaged in different activities occupied dedicated bedrooms, parlours, and service rooms, in addition to a truncated hall. This kind of house is found in several of the relations in this book; the Cowley home in Welton near Daventry [Relation 8] is a good example: there is at least one bedroom, a parlour to which the family routinely retires, a hall, and buttery [storeroom for barrels, etc.]. 'It is no accident', Hoskins noted, 'that in this period we get the first diaries from the 'middle class', both in town and country'.[97] The same could be said of the proliferation of haunted house stories in the same period.

Concurrent with the Great Rebuilding came a great expansion in the employment of living-in domestic servants. Until the middle of the seventeenth century they were uncommon in the homes of the yeomanry but would become the norm thereafter. An estimated third of households in seventeenth- and eighteenth-century England had domestic servants and, increasingly, these were likely to be female.[98] Servants played a central role in several of the cases. Joseph Priestly, who published the archive of Wesley letters and other materials pertaining to the haunting of Epworth Rectory, put it down to 'a trick of the servants, assisted by some of their neighbours'.[99] The presence of one or more servants is expressly stated in almost half of the twenty-seven haunted house stories under consideration. It has been argued the mere presence

---

96 Matthew Johnson, 'Rethinking the Great Rebuilding', *Oxford Journal of Archaeology* 12, no. 1 (1993), p. 124.
97 Hoskins, 'The Great Rebuilding', p. 110.
98 Anne Laurence, *Women in England, 1500-1760, Women in England, 1500-1760: A Social History* (Phoenix Press, 1994) pp. 135-57.
99 Sarah Trimmer, *The Family Magazine* (London: 1789), vol. III, pp. 42-7, in Davies, *The Haunted*, p. 272.

of household servants undermined the family's psychic security, that their 'liminal status' posed a 'potential threat to order and especially privacy'.[100]

Of great importance in this new domestic set-up was the separation of family spaces from those recognized as the servants' quarters.[101] Poltergeists in seventeenth-century England were likely to intrude on people in their most private spaces and at the most private of times – their bedrooms at night.

~~~

THE CREATION OF complex, less ephemeral, domestic structures in early modern England was, in Johnson's reckoning, 'part of a deep-seated cultural shift of the sort explored by cultural and social historians of the period, particularly those dealing with popular culture and its development through this period'.[102] The proliferation of poltergeist cases, I am suggesting, was among these developments. Furthermore, the Reformation and, in particular, the dismantling of the doctrine of Purgatory in Reformation England, played its part, not just in the rise of the demonic poltergeist but also the houses in which it dwelt, in redirecting money that might otherwise have been spent on the parish church to building, or rebuilding, of a new home.[103]

Structure, fittings, and furniture are not the only elements that define Hoskins's housing revolution. Perhaps even more significant (in this context) is a psychological shift that might be considered both a cause and a consequence of this Great Rebuilding. 'There was not only a revolution in housing, but almost a revolution in human psychology', Hoskins asserted. Owen Davies and Ceri Houlbrook, in their recent study of household apotropaic [counter-magic] traditions, have concluded these developments both 'generated new geographies of privacy' and influenced their incumbents' 'relations with the

---

100 Sheeha Iman, '"Mistress, Look out at the Window": Women, Servants and Liminal Domestic Spaces on the Early Modern Stage', *English Literary Studies*, suppl. Special Issue 29: Door-Bolts, Thresholds, snd Peep-Holes: Liminality and Domestic Spaces in Early Modern England (2020): p. 3.
101 Hoskins, 'The Rebuilding of Rural England', p. 54.
102 Johnson, 'Rethinking the Great Rebuilding', p. 123.
103 Johnson, 'Houses, Power and Everyday Life', pp. 11-12.

HAUNTED HOUSES

Seventeenth-century homes housed plenty of objects for poltergeists to throw around. Note the large 'bellarmine' style jar, bottom right. [Objects in Gainsborough Old Hall. Photo: author]

supernatural or preternatural world'.[104] These houses, with additional doors, floors, hearths, and windows were more *porous*, there were more liminal places where one space passed into another. Such places needed safeguarding. In such places spirits might be found. Johnson broadened the Great Rebuilding discussion by championing a cultural-historical approach rather than the more conventional socio-economic approach.

104 Owen Davies and Ceri Houlbrook, *Building Magic: Ritual and Re-Enchantment in Post-Medieval Structures* (Palgrave Macmillan, 2021), p. 10.

Houses, he surmised, 'can tell us a great deal more about history than has hitherto been assumed'.[105] Bryson has gone a step further in declaring, 'Houses aren't refuges from history. They are where history ends up'.[106] In building my argument for the essential role of the house in the rise of the poltergeist tradition, I fully concur with Johnson's observation that 'buildings might tell us about cultural life: for example, about [...] popular folk beliefs in terms of obvious features such as witchcraft precautions; or the more subtle analysis of the physical and cultural demarcation of inside and outside, wild and tame, cultural and natural'.[107] By looking at houses and their occupants through the lens of the anthropologist, they do, indeed, have many more stories to tell.

---

105 Johnson, 'Rethinking the Great Rebuilding', p. 122.
106 Bryson, *At Home*, p. 18.
107 Johnson, 'Rethinking the Great Rebuilding', p. 123.

3

PARANORMAL ACTIVITY? EXPERIENCES AND INTERPRETATIONS

From ghoulies and ghosties,
And long-leggety beasties
And things that go bump in the night,
Good Lord, deliver us!
Popular corruption of the litany in the Scottish Book of Common Prayer (1637)

THERE IS LITTLE point, many would agree, in attempting to explain what was going on in seventeenth-century poltergeist cases since there is no way of proving the reliability of their tellers' accounts. The parapsychologist can neither prove nor debunk past and present theories in relation to alleged events half a millennium ago. At best we can find parallels and repeated patterns in recent cases where the evidence is more open to scrutiny. The same material, however, presents ample opportunities for the historian seeking historical, if not scientific, explanations.

Poltergeist activity illustrated in a French nineteenth-century magazine, *La Vie Mysterieuse*.

Hereward Carrington, the historian of poltergeists acknowledged by Harry Price, collated a timeline, with outline details, of 375 cases between 355 AD and 1949, 127 of which were British. In so doing he was able to identify a range of typical characteristics:

- [the] frequently noted occurrence of poltergeist disturbances at or about the period of puberty
- [the] outbreak of *fire* in various parts of the 'haunted' house, sometimes in one spot, sometimes in various places at the same time
- [the] phenomenon, in connexion with poltergeist cases, [...] of *stone-throwing*
- objects [...] seen to fall from the *ceiling* - there being no opening through which such objects could have emerged
- objects [...] thrown from some *empty* room
- instances of stone throwing [in which] only very rarely have injuries been inflicted upon the involuntary 'medium', or upon those witnessing the occurrences. Sometimes they have reported that they have been struck very lightly - though the object seemed to be travelling through the air with considerable speed.
- Certainly *some* intelligence is at work, since the manifestations are not merely blind or haphazard. They are directional, even purposeful, in many of their characteristics. Objects are moved or thrown in certain definite directions. Often the 'poltergeist' has replied intelligently, by means of raps or otherwise, to questions which have been put to it.[108]

All of these features typifying poltergeist phenomena can be found in the cases recorded in early modern England and, without exception, in more than a single episode. In most cases several such phenomena can be found. Carrington concluded, 'The *general* character of the phenomena is nearly always the same, and it appears incredible that such coincidental happenings could possibly have taken place in all ages and in all parts of the world, had there not been some genuine manifestations behind

---

108 Adapted from Hereward Carrington and Nandor Fodor, *The Story of the Poltergeist Down the Centuries* (Rider and Co., 1953), pp. 12-15.

these reports.'[109] The importance of this commonality was recognized by the earliest collectors of this kind of material. In his brief analysis of two cases in Joseph Glanvill's *Saducismus Triumphatus*, one from Dorset [Relation 15] and one from Radnorshire [Relation 9], Henry More observed, 'there being that Congeneracy betwixt [the two cases], they mutually corroborate one another'.[110]

Twentieth-century psychology has enhanced analyses of the curious correlation in poltergeist cases, including those from hundreds of years before, of preternatural activity and its supposed child/adolescent focus. When the findings of Freud and Jung were still a novelty, investigators were drawn to the mental states of those affected, particularly the frustration, anxiety, or unhappiness of the pubescent child. Two of these, E. J. Dingwall and John Langdon-Davies, were persuaded disturbances might be explained by both the tricks of the naughty child and psychically induced phenomena that defied simple explanation, while distancing themselves from the supernatural assumptions of the past:

> Nowadays we know too much about the way in which subconscious layers of our personality can act without our conscious selves being aware of it to attribute such things to spirits or outside forces, but is it to be wondered at that 300 years ago such things were supposed even by the wisest to be due to possession by a devil?[111]

Carrington noted the role of pubescent children as the focus of activity and, perhaps, intentionally or otherwise, the cause. A commonplace in modern assumptions is that the poltergeist has a human focus – the person it targets, the person, perhaps, who has somehow conjured it up and released its energy. To an extent this is also a characteristic of early modern cases. Narratives in the Relations below that conform to this principle include the horrific experiences of Old Gast's granddaughters in their bedroom in Dorset in 1677 [Relation 15], and the Glenluce

---

109 Carrington and Fodor, *Poltergeist*, p. 16.
110 Joseph Glanvill (ed. Henry More), *Saducismus Triumphatus, or, full and plain Evidence concerning Witches and Apparitions* (London, 1681, 1688), p. 444.
111 E. J. Dingwell and John Langdon-Davies, *The Unknown: Is It Nearer?* (Cassell, 1956), p. 133.

case in 1654 [Relation 7]. Parallels can be drawn between the case of the 'haunting a Wench' at Greenwich in London reported in 1650 [Relation 6] and the famous haunting of two sisters at Enfield, London, in the 1970s. Another tale details the strange, but not unique, history of the vomiting of indigestible objects by a (bewitched?) young woman / girl, accompanied, on this occasion, by poltergeist activity [Relation 8]. A young female visitor to the home of the Paschall family's London home attracted unwelcome night-time poltergeist attention in 1661 [Relation 10], as did the Mompessons' daughters in Tidworth near Salisbury in 1662-63 [Relation 11], and a young maid-servant at a house in Ewell in Surrey in 1681 [Relation 19]. George Owen, a psychical researcher investigating the Tidworth case, concluded Mr Mompesson's ten-year-old daughter 'was the poltergeist medium – the innocent and unconscious cause of the goings on'.[112]

In the Epworth Rectory case the focus could have been Hetty, one of the Wesleys' daughters who was aged around nineteen at the time of the haunting. Her mother observed, 'It commonly was nearer to her than the rest, which she took notice of, and was much frightened, because she thought it had a particular spight of her'.[113] Hetty's older sister, Emily, reported of the entity:

> it was never near me, except two or three times, and never followed me, as it did my sister Hetty. I have been with her when it has knocked under her, and when she has removed has followed, and still kept under her feet, which was enough to terrify a stouter person.[114]

Harry Price was convinced that correspondence from or concerning Hetty, who he supposed to be the focus of the activity, was suppressed or destroyed for reasons unknown.[115] Was she behaving in ways that persuaded her family she was possessed? Was she subjected to some form of exorcism? Another sister, sixteen-year-old Nancy, also seems to have

---

112 A. R. G. Owen, *Joseph Glanvill and the Demon Drummer* (New Horizons Research Foundation, 1984), p. 11.
113 Mrs Wesley to her son Samuel, January 1716/17; Priestly, *Letters*, p. 127.
114 Emily Wesley to her brother Samuel, *c.* February 1716/17; Priestly, *Letters*, p.138.
115 Price, *Poltergeist*, p. 109.

been singled out.[116] Frequently, even in broad daylight, she claimed it followed her from room to room while she was sweeping floors and seemed to mimic the action and sound of her own sweeping and 'from one side of the bed to the other, and back again'. Most frightening of all, in an episode also strongly reminiscent of the Enfield case (1978-79), while 'she was sitting on the press bed playing at cards' with several of her sisters, the bed 'was lifted up with her on it'. She jumped up, rebuked the demon they had nicknamed 'Jeffrey', and then sat down again, but the bed was 'lifted up several times successively, a considerable height, upon which she left her seat and would not be prevailed upon to sit there any more'.[117]

That children and 'timorous persons' might be found to be the focus in such cases, the target even, of demonic activity, was, Joseph Glanvill concluded, 'because their spirits and imaginations being weak and passive, are not able to resist the fatal invasion; whereas men of bold minds [...] are secure from the contagion, as in pestilential airs clean bodies are not so liable to infection as are other tempers'.[118] However, he warned, 'tis very likely that many of the strange accidents that befall us may be the infliction of evil spirits, prompted to hurt us by the delight they take in their mischief'. It is possible, he thought, that we might feel the 'effects of their malice [...] in more instances than we are aware of'.[119] Conversely, citing Sasha Hindley, Laura Gowing and others, Jacqueline Pearson has suggested the supernatural 'allowed the female and servant voice to be authorised outside of purely domestic concerns', and for 'subjugated knowledge' to be heard in 'the world of its superiors.' 'For low-status men', Pearson continues, 'and, more often, children and women, the suggestive language of the supernatural may also be a way of gaining their own voice'.[120]

---

116   Harry Price, arguing Hetty was the sole focus, mistakenly attributed to Hetty Nancy's experience with the press bed; Price, *Poltergeist*, p. 109.
117   Nancy Wesley to her brother John ('Jack'), September 1736; Priestly, *Letters*, p. 162.
118   Glanvill, *Saducismus Triumphatus*, p. 29.
119   Glanvill, *Saducismus Triumphatus*, pp. 32–3.
120   Jacqueline Pearson, '"Then she asked it, what were its Sister's names?" Reading between the lines in seventeenth-century pamphlets of the supernatural', *The Seventeenth Century* 28, no. 1 (2013), pp. 64–5.

However, there are plenty of early modern English poltergeist cases in which younger family members and children are not identified as playing a particular part. Adults, it appears, were likely to be troubled as much as children by the paranormal in these haunted houses. What *is* striking though is the absence of apparent possession of young people - a common trope, not just in modern poltergeist stories but also in contemporary seventeenth-century English bewitchment cases. In none of the relations, for example, does an adolescent, or anyone else for that matter, say odd things in an alien voice. On the rare occasions a demon is heard to speak [e.g. Relations 7 and 10] it seems to be disembodied or invisible.

Sometimes in early modern England, in accordance with Carrington's conclusions, inexplicable fires broke out in haunted houses [e.g. Relations 25]. Fires broke out in the Campbell family's haunted home in Glenluce, Scotland, on three occasions [Relation 7], and, in 1695 a supposed demon attempted to set Andrew Mackie's house on fire in Galloway [Relation 23]. At Weobley in Herefordshire in 1670, Elizabeth Bridges' disturbances start with lowkey phenomena such as knocking noises and the mewing of unseen cats, and end with a series of unexplained fires [Relation 12]. In Brightling, Sussex, a house was burned to the ground [Relation 22].

Seventeenth-century poltergeists, like their twentieth- and twenty-first-century counterparts, were notorious for hurling projectiles, sometimes aimlessly, sometimes with malicious intent. This is the substance of four of Carrington's list of typical characteristics. In modern examples these might be children's plastic building bricks and other inventions of recent times, in around half of the cases in the Relations below the throwing of rocks, stones, pebbles or brickbats [broken bricks] is recorded. A 1698 pamphlet concerning such a case even takes the technical term, *lithobolia* (the throwing of stones), for its title.[121]

In some instances the stones and pebbles moved unnaturally slowly and often with a curved as opposed to a straight trajectory as they glided through the air. When examined they were likely to be hot to handle. In these early modern English cases, pebbles and other objects were thrown through windows and other openings but, more mysteriously, some reports had them seeming to fall from the ceiling, objects manifesting in

---

121 Richard Chamberlain, *Lithobolia: or, The Stone-Throwing Devil* (London, 1698) [Relation 20].

thin air [Relation 1 is a good example]. Usually they caused no physical harm, touching people very lightly should they make contact. The famous non-conformist minister Richard Baxter recalled, many years later, how, in March 1646/7, when he was staying with an acquaintance in Kirkby Malory in Leicestershire, 'the Neighbours went to see a House in Lutterworth, reported to be haunted'. Here, 'Multitudes flockt to see it, and affirmed, at a certain hour of the day, stones were thrown at those that were present, which hit them, but hurt them not'.[122]

Regarding Carrington's supposed intelligence of the poltergeist, communication with the entity is another central theme in early modern English accounts. The underlying assumption that someone or something must be responsible (an assumption that was central to seventeenth-century concepts of the preternatural) makes this stage almost inevitable in situations in which witnesses to unexplained disturbances have any kind of regard for the supernatural. Samuel Wesley was driven to demanding of the entity haunting his home, 'why it disturbed innocent children, and did not come to me in my study'. Much to his frustration, he failed to persuade his poltergeist to talk and explain its purpose. It would, however, seem to mimic knocks made by members of the family, and, although he 'never heard any articulate voice', on a couple of occasions he fancied he heard it make 'feeble squeaks, a little louder than the chirping of a bird'.[123] In other cases a dialogue, of sorts, was had with poltergeists. The 'Demon of Tedworth' case [Relation 11] is the most obvious example from the period of a more successful communication with a spirit but it is also a feature of many others. In Baxter's recollection of the haunted house in Lutterworth, mentioned above, if 'any one would whistle, it was answered by a whistle in the Room; And no search could discover any Fraud'.[124]

~~~

WHILE INTERPRETATIONS AMONG sceptics and believers are more diverse than ever before, commentators have continued to identify common, even consistent, traits in poltergeist cases over the

---

122   Richard Baxter, *The Certainty of the Worlds of Spirits* (London, 1691), 42.
123   Wesley, 'An Account of Noises and Disturbances in my House'; Priestly, *Letters*, p. 146.
124   Baxter, *Certainty*, p. 42.

past fifty years or so. According to one well-known contemporary British paranormal psychologist, and star of the hit BBC podcast series, *Uncanny,* Evelyn Hollow, poltergeist hauntings, typically, evolve in a series of increasingly alarming stages, an escalation of phenomena from the passive to the active:

> Stage 1: A sense of presence
> Stage 2: Noises
> Stage 3: Moving objects
> Stage 4: Apports and disapports [The unexplained appearance and disappearance of objects.]
> Stage 5: Destruction
> Stage 6: Communication
> Stage 7: Physical violence or threat to life[125]

The suggestion that poltergeist cases build as time goes on is amply attested by the cases detailed below. After over a month of various phenomena, for example, we learn things were 'worse than ever it was before' during three days in April in the case of the Galloway haunting of 1695 [Relation 23]. Some of the cases were documented in sufficient detail to permit us to test Hollow's twenty-first century paradigm in their late sixteenth- and seventeenth-century context. The earliest of these, the North Aston case of 1591-92 [Relation 1], starts at the third of Hollow's hypothetical stages with a bout of unaccountable throwing about of stones. On 29 November 1591 the 'strange accidents', which would grow 'into no little griefe of minde and amazement', began. Stones 'of contrarie bignes', ranging from a pound (0.45 kg) to rocks weighing in at twenty-two pounds (10 kg), started falling from the roof into the open hall. Men were instructed to use ladders to climb up to the roof 'both within and without his house' to search for anything 'amiss in the Tiles or Slates'. Nothing untoward was found and yet the stones continued to drop into the hall; whether they were falling *from* or *through* the roof they could not be sure. In any case, the hall, it transpires, had a ceiling and no mention is made of gaping holes

---

125 In Danny Robins, *Into the Uncanny: A Real-Life Investigation into the Paranormal* (BBC Books, 2023), p. 26.

Mysterious animals, generally construed as demonic, occasionally pop up in early modern English poltergeist cases. This image shows a black dog associated with a haunting in late-Elizabethan Oxfordshire [see Relation 1].

through which the mysterious stones might have passed. Either way it is clear the case had moved on to Hollow's Stage 4, the unexplained appearance or disappearance of objects. Just over a month since the phenomena began, the tale arrives at Hollow's Stage 6 (communication) when a neighbour engages in rudimentary communication with what seems to be the entity causing all the mischief. And so things went on – more stone throwing and new phenomena including appearances of a mysterious great black dog, ghostly footsteps, unaccountable splatters of blood, the throwing about of pillows and invisible tugging of bed clothes.

Returning to Hollow's Stage 1 – 'A sense of presence' – it comes as no surprise that the 'paranormal' activity in most early modern English cases takes place at night when darkness is likely to heighten the senses and increase the propensity for fear of the unseen. Frequently they occur in the winter months when it is dark by late afternoon. It is also, of course, the time best suited to the perpetrator of disturbance who hopes not to be seen. In Puddle-Dock, London, in 1675, the record of the haunting of Edward Pitts' home is spread over around fifteen nights at the tail end of the winter of 1675 [Relation 14]. Sometimes poltergeists in the period announced their presence by illuminating the houses they infested – the house in North Aston in the winter of 1591-92 [Relation 1] was so vividly lit one night it looked as though it was on fire, a phenomenon it shared with the Puddle-Dock case.

Almost without exception these cases begin, and invariably continue, with unexpected sounds such as knocking, just as Hollow would expect (Stage 2: Noises), and as befits a poltergeist/'noisy ghost'. Most famously, the Mompessons of Tidworth hear drumming, and the Wesleys in Epworth rectory are disturbed by phantom knocking on doors, ghostly footsteps, and the rattling of bottles in a cupboard under the stairs. Sir William York too was bothered by unexplained knocking in his house, which also focused on the recess under the stairs hidden behind a locked door [Relation 16]. In a case preserved by Richard Bovet in his *Pandaemonium* (1684), in addition to strange noises, Peter Pain's house in Bristol is also lit up at night as if there are candles or torches burning in every room [Relation 2].

The movement, appearance or disappearance of objects (Stages 3 and 4), as discussed above, occurs throughout the relations detailed below [Relation 20 is a good example]. Even more alarming than the sight of things hurtling through the air of their own accord are the occasions when poltergeists get physical and a case moves to Hollow's final and most frightening stage (Stage 8: Physical violence or threat to life). By and large, the cases under discussion fall short of this but the threat of violence is not entirely absent. 'I have been thrice pushed by an invisible power', complained Samuel Wesley, 'once against the corner of my desk in the study, a second time against the door of the matted chamber, a third time against the right side of the frame of my study door, as I was going in'.[126] In a couple of the narratives knives are

---

126 Wesley, 'An Account of Noises and Disturbances in my House'; Priestly, *Letters*,

thrown by some invisible hand [Relations 8 and 15]. However, accounts of physical injury in these cases, though not entirely absent, are rare. Nevertheless researchers have concluded, 'whether intended to injure or merely terrify people [the behaviour of the poltergeist] was never entirely benign'.[127] This was certainly true of the entity said to have been haunting the home of the Mackies in Scotland in 1695 in which, it was claimed, in addition to several paranormal arson attacks, multiple people were assaulted [Relation 23]. The Deptford demon too, it would seem, was quite capable of causing bodily harm in 1699 [Relation 24].

By and large early modern English poltergeists were not particularly destructive (Stage 5: Destruction). However, there are incidences of petty poltergeist vandalism and, on rare occasions, something worse. With all those stones flying about, it is not surprising to find windows being smashed [e.g. Relations 6 and 20], and a couple of cases from London [Relations 4 and 13] revolve around the wanton destruction of valuable textiles.

~~~

The analysis of the surviving accounts goes some way towards enabling the drawing of broad conclusions regarding phenomena, location, timings, duration and the like. It is certainly reasonable to propose a sequence of stages in a 'typical' haunting akin to those suggested by Hollow: the setting is a house, noises are heard, things get moved and thrown around but no-one is badly hurt, most activity occurs at night, it is likely to continue for many weeks, and there will probably be multiple witnesses. Commentators are unlikely to be able to explain what is going on, but the broad consensus will be that, unless it is fraud, it is the work of a demon. It does not, however, easily fit the witchcraft paradigm – attempts to attribute poltergeist phenomena to the diabolical deeds of witches and their demon-familiars in these stories are rare and almost always, even by early modern standards, unsatisfactory.

The point is, there is a good deal of evidence for us to build a typology of sorts even though, of course, this is an indulgence that falls far short

---

p. 146.
127 Jane P. Davidson and Christopher John Duffin, 'Stones and Spirits', *Folklore* 123, no. 1 (2012), p. 106.

of rigorous scientific enquiry. Nevertheless, it will tell us a lot about the longevity of certain cultural tropes while proving nothing regarding the cause of these weird stories. It will bolster modern believers in such things in underlining the fact that they are not, and probably never have been, alone in their convictions. And, for sceptics, they provide the reassurance that from the time these tales began to be told in print in early modern England they have been challenged in ways broadly in accord with responses to such claims made today.

4

'WHISTLE IF THOU CANST': LIVING WITH DEMONS

'I shall only tell you what I myself heard, and leave the rest to others.'
Emily Wesley to her brother, Samuel, 1717.[128]

POST-MEDIEVAL EXISTENTIAL DOUBTS manifested as fears of witchcraft and reinvigorated concerns about ghosts and demons.[129] Historians are quick to emphasise the 'earth-shaking paradigm shift', as one has recently put it, which was the Reformation.[130] One way in which Protestants distanced themselves from the Catholic paradigm was in their rejection of the tradition that God continued to perform miracles beyond the first century AD, even though, they believed, he had the power to do so. Thus, the seemingly 'miraculous', thereafter, must either be a case of mistaken identity, fraudulent, or demonic. Satan's intervention in the mindset of early modern Protestant intellectuals did not equate to the 'supernatural'. So long as God was omnipotent and had abandoned the working of miracles, demonic interventions had to subscribe to their own laws of the nature of the worlds of spirits from

---

128 Joseph Priestly, *Original Letters by the Rev. John Wesley, and his Friends, Illustrative of his Early History, with other Curious Papers* (Birmingham, 1791), p. 135.
129 Ronald C. Finucane, 'Historical introduction: the example of Early Modern and Nineteenth-Century England' in James Houran and Rense Lange (eds), *Hauntings and Poltergeists: Multidisciplinary Perspectives* (Jefferson: McFarland, 2001), pp. 9–10.
130 Eire, *They Flew*, p. 17.

whence they came. Thus, their activities, from a human point of view, were certainly *preter*natural but not *super*natural.

These late-sixteenth- and seventeenth-century poltergeists must have presented a puzzle for their observers steeped in demonology and the dismal consequences of dark arts and diabolical pacts. They caused mischief, mayhem, inconvenience, and even amusement. But were they guilty of the *maleficia* of demons and witches? Sometimes the boundaries between conventional accounts of seventeenth-century witchcraft and poltergeist tales are blurred. There was, after all, a compulsion for those who found themselves the unwilling hosts of mischievous spirits to find a human hand behind their troubles – a witch in league with the Devil perhaps.

In 1986 Gillian Bennett valiantly addressed 'one curious aspect [of early modern witch scholarship] still left unexplored: that is the mutual influence of the concepts of ghost and witch'. Poltergeists, she argued 'were a frequent accompaniment of witchcraft', citing the Tidworth case as her chief example.[131] A better example from the period is the *Strange and Wonderful News from Yowell in Surrey*, found in a pamphlet published in 1681 [Relation 19]. However, typically, the poltergeist phenomenon in the surviving record is *not* strongly associated with a human progenitor; even the Mompessons' phantom drummer had little more than an oblique, feeble link with the flesh and blood drummer, William Drury, who had his drum confiscated. The attempts to identify Drury as a malefic witch guilty of the weird disturbances in Tidworth were weak and inconclusive, and, for many, probably rang as hollow then as they do now when the story is told. He *was* tried for witchcraft but, according to Mr Mompesson, 'the Grand Jury found the Bill on the Evidence, but the Petty Jury acquitted him, but not without some difficulty'.[132] The Tidworth affair, as in pretty much every other instance of poltergeist haunting in early modern England, lacked the vital element in making a witchcraft accusation stick: no-one was hurt.

'[I]t is a cleere truth', declared Richard Bernard in 1627, 'that the Divell may afflict man or woman, their children and their cattell,

---

131 Bennett, 'Ghost and Witch', pp. 3-4.
132 Michael Hunter, 'New Light on the 'Drummer of Tedworth': conflicting narratives of witchcraft in Restoration England', *Historical Research* 78, no. 201 (2005), p. 327.

without the knowledge, consent of, or association with any Witch'.[133] In various ways poltergeist episodes are less explicable than those of plain witchcraft. In the absence of an identifiable human perpetrator, they baffled those who wrote about them at the time, just as they do those who have written about them since. They simply do not lend themselves readily to those approaches of historians of witchcraft who have been able to hang their interpretations on approaches wrapped up in misogyny, scapegoating, social cohesion, revenge and deviance. The actions of the typical poltergeist are, seemingly, pointless and, thus, all the more inexplicable.

Even so, the poltergeist-as-witchcraft explanation survived the seventeenth century. Although it might have fallen out of favour in more fashionable circles, members of the Wesley family in the eighteenth century, including John, retained their belief in the possibility of diabolical witchcraft. Emily Wesley in 1717 reached the conclusion it lay behind the nightly bangs and crashes that had plagued the family home in Epworth for several weeks:

> I believe it to be witchcraft, for these reasons. About a year since, there was a disturbance at a town near us, that was undoubtedly witches; and if so near, why may they not reach us? Then my father had for several Sundays before it's coming, preached warmly against consulting those that are called cunning men, which our people are given to; and it had a particular spight at my father.[134]

An odd rabbit or badger-like creature, with no discernible head, had been spotted in the house on at least three occasions which Emily suspected to be the manifestation of a transformed witch. The assumption that witchcraft explained the poltergeist, invited accounts of visible demons which may or may not have been independent spirits, witches' familiars, or the transfigured forms of the witches themselves. Several cases feature the manifestation of odd creatures. One of the three servants at Epworth Rectory, Robert Brown, was 'sitting alone by the fire in the back kitchen [when] something came out of the copper hole

---

133   Richard Bernard, *A Guide to Grand-Jury Men* (London, 1627), p. 52.
134   Emily Wesley to her brother Samuel, *c.* February 1716-17; Priestly, *Letters*, p. 138.

Image on a contemporary playing card of devils troubling the Duke of Monmouth's army at the time of his rebellion in 1685.

like a rabbit, but less, and turned round five times very swiftly. Its ears lay flat upon its neck, and its little feet stood straight up'. He chased it with the fire tongs in his hand but it evaded him, not to be seen again.[135]

135 Wesley, 'An Account of Noises and Disturbances in my House'; Priestly, *Letters*, pp. 147-48.

The account of the case at North Aston in 1592 [Relation 1], implies the appearance of a mysterious dog as the manifestation of the demon-poltergeist in the story, a common motif in witchcraft cases of the period. In addition, a horrifying creature, which was like a dog with the face of an ape 'having neither eares, feete, nor taile, [...] glided along upon his bellie' across the floor of an outbuilding. This is the sort of freakish demonic entity familiar in the extraordinary paintings that emanated from the imaginations of Hieronymus Bosch and Pieter Bruegel. These weird, hybrid monsters were also common in English accounts of witches' familiars - imagined if not actually seen. However, in most of the relations considered in this book, the poltergeist is both unaccounted for and out of control. This is what makes it so very frightening and, potentially, dangerous. Where a witch might be hunted down and despatched by judge and jury, the demon unleashed is a law unto itself. Books were written on how to deal with witches, notably Richard Bernard's *Guide to Grand-Jury Men* (1627), but the only recourse to dealing with demons was prayer and righteous living. Family prayers are mentioned in several of the cases. So too, are more mundane approaches to dealing with unwelcome intruders including firearms and the formidable guard-dog of choice in the period, the English mastiff.

Whether or not witchcraft was suspected, the events at Tidworth in the early 1660s [Relation 11] gave rise to much speculation that the Mompessons were being victimised by demons. Multiple witnesses reported various phenomena: cacophonous banging, strange lights, children lifted into the air, furniture moved by unseen hands, Bibles covered in ashes, chamber-pots emptied onto beds, drops of blood found on the floorboards, bedclothes disturbed, banging, the smell of brimstone, and so on, that were swiftly seen as indicative of demonic infestation. Some even claimed to have communicated with the demon-drummer as it tapped out responses to their questions. This poltergeist infestation, like several more in the collection of relations below, shares common ground with the concept of the demoniac: the poltergeist possesses the house just as the demon possesses the demoniac. These parallel concepts are the stuff of horror movies but, surprisingly, while there is no shortage of accounts of what might be considered demonic possession of the person in *witchcraft* accounts in early modern England, they are not a pronounced feature of the major *poltergeist* cases.

THE APPARITIONS IN early modern poltergeist and witchcraft cases, typically, were not interpreted as innocent shades of the deceased, incapable of entirely moving on, but as transvecting witches, Satanic delusions, or demons taking corporeal form. Poltergeists were not, as explained above, to be confused with regular 'ghosts'. Ghosts were generally considered benign entities, either disinterested in the living who might happen to glimpse them in passing, or here to somehow convey messages to the living. However, the noisy, violent poltergeist in early modern interpretations was almost certainly a malevolent, demonic entity which was fundamentally different to the (dead) human sprite.

The surviving poltergeist cases do not strongly support the argument that demonological explanations for such goings-on, especially in the absence of apparitions, were in decline among those who took the time to write about them. It has been proposed by Jo Bath and John Newton that after 1660 'the surety among the elite that all ghosts are, or at least should be, demonic' became a rarity in the interpretation of ghosts.[136] This may be true for apparition accounts but not for poltergeist-housesprites. Where fraud was discounted, the standard resolution in the accounts, from the North Aston case at the end of Elizabeth's reign to the Epworth case at the start of George I's, was to blame a demon. Even if these might be regarded as divine exercises in reminding humanity of the supernatural, as More suggested to Glanvill, this did not negate the role of the demon as propagator.

While the ghost as spectre is, and perhaps always was, usually considered dead (though not entirely departed), the poltergeist, at least in early modern English accounts, is very much alive. Time and again they identify the poltergeist as a demon, a malevolent spirit inhabiting a parallel world, sometimes infesting our own. In the 1630s Sir Thomas Browne eloquently summed up the contemporary educated Protestant position on the matter: 'those apparitions, and ghosts of departed persons are not the wandring soules of men, but the unquiet walkes

---

136 Bath and Newton, 'Sensible Proof', p. 4.

of Devils'.[137] However, as Peter Marshall has noted, even the most influential demonologists could be equivocal regarding the subject. Glanvill confidently categorized spirits as 'intelligent Creature[s] of the invisible World', but Baxter wrote 'tis hard to know by their words or signs, when it is a Devil, and when it is a Humane Soul'.[138] Ghost stories persisted and the concept of the dead returning to the living in spectral form seems to have remained strong.[139] The sixteenth-century Protestant mantra that 'the soules of the faithful are saved, and the soules of the unbeleevers are damned immediately without delay, and therefore there is no Purgatorie'[140] had not succeeded in demolishing this ancient superstition among Protestant congregations. Gillian Bennett highlighted the uncertainty regarding the existence and meaning of ghosts in elite intellectual circles, and, even in the most influential texts, such as those written by Henry More and Daniel Defoe, there is occasional deviation from what we might expect regarding their (other) worldview. In any case, whatever they did or did not think, it would be foolish to presume, as Bennett further observed, they 'may not have been representative of the 'folk' at large'. The stories Glanvill, More and company gathered 'were collected from self-selected informants drawn from a limited group of educated, upper-class people known to the collectors'.[141] This, of course, might help account for the high proportion of poltergeist cases set in substantial houses. However, as Bath and Newton have concluded in their study of early modern English ghost lore, there is no reason to suppose that the broad assumptions in these poltergeist texts deviate much from popular belief in the period.[142]

~~~

IT IS TEMPTING to suppose that the deeply religious, perhaps oppressive, environment of the Wesley household could well have had something

---

137 Cited in Marshall, *Invisible Worlds*, p. 147.
138 Marshall, *Invisible Worlds*, p. 173.
139 Marshall, *Invisible Worlds*, p. 8.
140 Lavater, *Ghostes and Spirites*, p. 156.
141 Bennett, 'Ghost and Witch', p. 11.
142 Bath and Newton, 'Sensible Proof', p. 9.

to do with the psychic turmoil confronting the Wesley youngsters at the start of the eighteenth century [Relation 26]. Experiences of and responses to 'poltergeist' episodes are likely to be determined by each individual's world view. For the arch-sceptic in an increasingly irreligious twenty-first-century England, 'Talking about the paranormal is always a waste of time'.[143] Pat Collins, a Vacentian priest based in Dublin, has argued, in the context of a predominantly Christian heritage, there are three distinct philosophical perspectives underpinning their interpretation:

> First, at one end of the spectrum of belief, there is a naturalistic world view [which] denies the existence of the supernatural realm [...]
>
> Second, at the other end of the spectrum of belief, there is a supernatural Christian world view [which] acknowledges the other-worldly realm of God, good and evil spirits, heaven, hell, miracles and extrasensory experiences [...]
>
> Third, there is a midway point on the spectrum between naturalistic and supernatural belief [which accepts] basic beliefs such as the existence of God and the prospect of an afterlife [but is] sceptical about the existence of many supernatural realities such as angels, miracles, healings, exorcisms etc.[144]

In early modern England, despite the alarmism of the anti-Hobbist[145] brigade, the first of these was yet to take root. However, the evidence of responses to supposed poltergeist activity in the period do support the argument that, at least in intellectual circles, the paradigm shift in Christian England from Collins' second perspective to his third was well underway by the end of the seventeenth century.

---

143 Lucy Mangan, film critic on 'The Hauntings' BBC / Paramount TV series, *The Guardian*, Monday 14 October 2024; in 2021, of the 94% responders to the religion question in the census for England and Wales, 37.2% declared they subscribed to 'no religion'.
144 Pat Collins, 'Things that Go Bump in the Night', *The Furrow* 56, no. 2 (2005), pp. 94-5.
145 Hobbists were admirers of Thomas Hobbes, who was accused of atheism in mid-seventeenth-century England for ignoring supernatuarl possibilities in his philosophical works.

One of the most remarkable things about seventeenth-century English poltergeist cases is how seriously they were taken by the establishment. At grassroots level they were likely to receive the concentrated attention of local ministers, magistrates, and magnates, and some provoked the keen interest of eminent individuals far and wide. Fundamental to the collection and telling of early modern poltergeist stories is the credibility of the sources and respectability of informants, and also the assurance that 'no search could discover any Fraud'.[146] Of all the supernatural cases cited in Joseph Glanvill's *Saducismus Triumphatus* (1681), the Tidworth case was the only one of which he had personal experience. Thereafter he readily accepted the validity of the accounts of respectable people, notably an eminent local magistrate, Robert Hunt, as further affirmation of the reality of spirits—malign and benevolent. 'It will be said by some', he acknowledged, 'that my friend and I were under some affright, and so fancied noises and sights that were not'. However, he contested, 'This is the eternal evasion [but] I know that I heard and saw the particulars I have told'.[147] Then again, as Darren Oldridge has put it, 'what today might be dismissed as 'tricks of the mind' could be readily explained within a belief system that acknowledged demonic visitations as unproblematically real'.[148] Regardless, Glanvill had the evidence attested by 'thousands of eye and ear witnesses, and those not of the easily deceivable vulgar only, but of wise and grave discerners; and that, when no interest could oblige them to agree together in a common lie'.[149] Even now, over three hundred years later, the argument that 'there were simply too many people involved in visiting and watching over a twelve-month period that it seems unlikely an elaborate conspiracy could have gone on undiscovered'[150] is thought-provoking if not persuasive.

Throughout the second half of the seventeenth century and well into the next, the search for 'spirit testimony' was a valid scientific endeavour. Why this mattered so much was plain: although those who denied the existence of spirits were not necessarily atheists, they were 'anti-scripturists' in the sense that they so plainly attested the contrary.

---

146 Baxter on the 1647 Lutterworth case, *Worlds of Spirits*, p. 42.
147 Glanvill, *Saducismus Triumphatus*, p. 330.
148 Oldridge, *The Devil*, p. 62.
149 Glanvill, *Saducismus Triumphatus*, p. 3.
150 Clarke, *Ghosts*, p. 82.

'Credulity, Superstition, and Fanaticism', a print produced by William Hogarth in 1762 - the same year as the notorious Cock Lane poltergeist case and the revival on the London stage of Joseph Addison's comedy *The Drummer, or, The Haunted House* (1716)

Although opinions were forming in educated circles that posed a serious challenge to the supernatural, Glanvill was not a lone voice in his insistence on its reality, and he was not defending it from an antiquated philosophical position. Henry More launched the campaign, a decade before Glanvill started publishing on the subject, with his *An Antidote to Atheism* (1653) in which he declared,

> It is not to be imputed to any vain credulity of mine, or that I take a pleasure in telling strange stories, but that I thought fit to fortify and strengthen the faith of others as much as I could; being well assured that a contemptuous misbelief of such like narrations concerning spirits, and an endeavour of making them all ridiculous and incredible, is a dangerous prelude to atheism itself, or else a more close and crafty profession or insinuation of it. For assuredly that saying was nothing so true in politics, *no bishop, no king*; as this is in metaphysics, *no spirit, no God*.[151]

The story of the 'Demon of Tedworth' became the keystone upon which further arguments for belief in the reality of spirits would be based. Science and its reliance on empirical evidence, Glanvill maintained, was not the enemy of religion but the antidote to atheism. Science might yet prove certain key religious doctrines, notably that of belief in the supernatural. His was, as Stuart Clark has put it, a scientific demonology that was absolutely relevant in Restoration science—he was concerned with the paranormal because of, not in spite of, the mechanical philosophy of the era. Clark concluded that 'At one level, [Glanvill and his allies] were simply compiling a natural history of the demonic'—just one among the several natural histories members of the Royal Society were busy describing.[152]

Glanvill's *Saducismus Triumphatus* provided a model for John Beaumont's *An Historical Physiological and Theological Treatise of Spirits, Apparitions, Witchcrafts, and Other Magical Practises* (1705), a four-hundred page exploration of the principle that a mostly invisible spirit world coexists with the visible natural world, written 'to caution men

---

151 Henry More, *An Antidote to Atheism* (London, 1653), p. 164.
152 Clark, *Thinking with Demons*, pp. 299, 306.

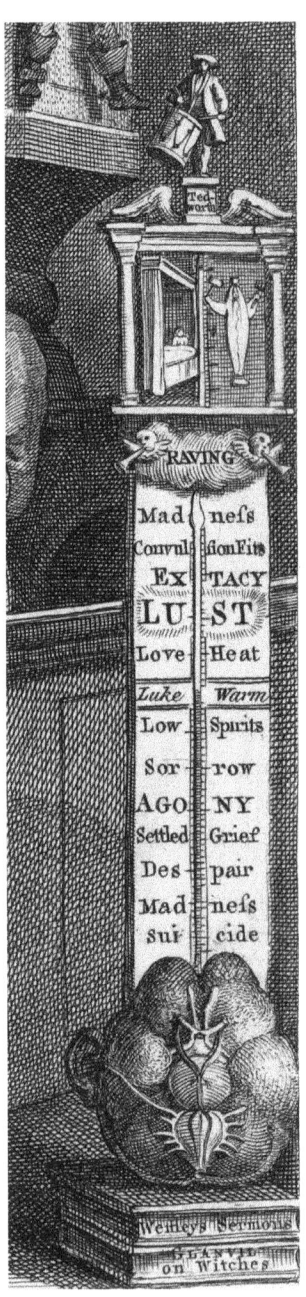

Hogarth, 'Credulity, Superstition, and Fanaticism' (1762), detail showing the 'Drummer of Tedworth' supported by the writings of Joseph Glanvill and the sermons of John Wesley.

not to be over hasty in rejecting things that may seem strange, and do not presently fall within their comprehension'.[153] Among many other relations, the book included a telling of the demon's tale.

Not everyone was convinced. Glanvill's Royal Society associate, the antiquarian and author of *Brief Lives*, John Aubrey, despite his sensitivity towards providential phenomena, considered the Tidworth affair a hoax.[154] He found Glanvill 'an ingenius person' but someone who was 'a little too credulous'. He added that when one Mr Ettrick investigated the case he found requests to make a knocking noise were only responded to when spoken aloud—the 'ghost' would not respond when the request was whispered. When Sir Christopher Wren stayed at Tidworth for a night 'he observed that this drumming was only when a certain maid-servant was in the next room'. Furthermore, Aubrey observed, 'the Devil kept no very unseasonable hours: it seldom knocked after twelve at night, or before six in the morning'.[155] In 1716

---

153 John Beaumont, *An Historical Physiological and Theological Treatise of Spirits, Apparitions, Witchcrafts, and Other Magical Practises* (London: 1705), p. 39.

154 Bath and Newton, 'Sensible Proof', p. 10; regarding Aubrey, Peter Elmer has suggested, 'he fits the profile of the latitudinarian demonologist'; Peter Elmer, *Witchcraft, Witch-Hunting, and Politics in Early Modern England* (Oxford University Press, 2016), p. 151.

155 John Aubrey, *The Natural History of Wiltshire* (London, 1847), Part II, Chapter 18.

Glanvill's famous account was the inspiration for playwright Joseph Addison's comedy *The Drummer, or, The Haunted House*.

Although belief in spirits remained, as Keith Thomas noted, 'a reality for many educated men, however much the rationalists laughed at them',[156] Glanvill and his fellows, in Malcolm Gaskill's reckoning, had engaged in 'an inquisitive and empirical discourse that would talk itself out of existence precisely because of its appetite for truth and proof'.[157] Eventually, As Eire has put it, 'the devil would come to be viewed by many Enlightenment thinkers as the worst of all superstitions and the ultimate proof of the absurdity and danger of all traditional religion'.[158] Satan was indeed, as Eire further maintains, driven from the courtrooms and official records thereafter.

Nevertheless, the Devil and his poltergeists continue to flourish in popular culture. The survival, 'renaissance' even, of the poltergeist tradition in modern times certainly has something to do with the maintenance of core beliefs of Catholicism, and also the trajectory of certain forms of evangelical Protestantism. However, the most important factor could be the dramatic demise in modern England of popular adherence to organized, institutionalised religion, in enabling greater freedom of thought and personal choice in belief. This, however, is the triumph, not of atheism but, of agnosticism. And, more than ever before, these new age agnostics are open to suggestion in matters which seem to defy logical explanation. Judging by the current level of interest in the paranormal in England a quarter of the way through the twenty-first century, disenchantment is not *necessarily* the consequence of what Marshall has called the 'deregulation of the supernatural'.[159]

---

156 Thomas, *Religion*, p. 591, cited in Gillian Bennet, *'Alas, Poor Ghost!' Traditions of Belief in Story and Discourse* (Colorado, 1999), p. 146.
157 Malcolm Gaskell, 'The Pursuit of Reality: Recent Research into the History of Witchcraft', *Historical Journal* 51, no. 4 (2008), p. 1072.
158 Eire, *They Flew*, p. 330.
159 'Ultimately, the disenchantment of the world was a delayed consequence of the deregulation of the supernatural'; Marshall, *Invisible Worlds*, p. 13.

RELATIONS

'[Readers] are best convinced by proofs which come nearest to Sense, such as the following Relations are, which leave a deeper impression upon minds and more lasting, than thousands of subtile Metaphysical Arguments.'
George Sinclair (1685)[160]

'There are a World of well attested Relations in this kind, but all must be Cheat and Imposture with some Men, because, foresooth, they will have it so.'
John Beaumont (1705)[161]

---

160 George Sinclair, *Satan's Invisible World Discovered* (1685), 'Preface to the Reader'.
161 Beaumont, *Treatise*, p. 485.

1
STRANGE AND WONDERFULL ACCIDENTS: NORTH ASTON, OXFORDSHIRE, 1591-92

THE STORY OF the 'Demon of Tedworth' is the most famous of early modern English poltergeist cases but, despite popular claims to the contrary, it was neither the first nor the most spectacular. The 'straunge and woonderfull accidents' in the Oxfordshire home of George Lee predated John Mompesson's troubles by over seventy years and this early case perhaps marks the start of a 'poltergeist craze' in line with that of the simultaneous witch craze in England. It had its precursors, but the anonymous writer, who had the account printed in 1592, was eager to assert that, as a case of its type, it was a 'matter of such especiall weight and consequence, as sildome hath the like bene heard of before'. *A True Discourse of such strange and woonderfull accidents, as happened in the house of M. George Lee of North-Acton, in the countie of Oxford* is an extensive seventeen-page pamphlet – much the most detailed extant account of an English poltergeist case up to this point in time. It really deserves more attention than it has received hitherto.

While the narrative contains elements that might raise eyebrows, especially those passages, as in many subsequent poltergeist accounts, in which a conversation of sorts is had with a spirit who obliges by fulfilling the requests of the investigator, it is rich in the detail of contemporary beliefs. The story also provides the opportunity for the modern reader to enter and follow the ghost hunters around what sound likes a classic rebuilt English hall-house, with a chimney, gallery, and rooms upstairs, that has long since been demolished. We also get other glimpses into late sixteenth-century society such as the popular village sport of quoits played on the green. The appearance of spirit-animals, a commonplace in early modern accounts of the supernatural in England, is equally fascinating.[162]

---

162 Owen Davies cites this case, briefly, in relation to the manifestation of animals;

The Lees of 'North Acton' - Edward, his son George (both referred to from the start as 'Mister' denoting their status, and implying their respectability and thus, perhaps, their reliability), George's wife, and his sister, Anne Lee, lived in a house, or, as described in the pamphlet, a 'Hall', known simply as 'the Farm' in the village of what is now called North Aston between Banbury and Bicester. Its precise location is unknown.[163] John Lee, probably a close relation, was its vicar from 1574 until 1584. Although the 1592 pamphlet describes the place as a town, its total population probably did not exceed a hundred.[164] On 29 November 1591 the 'strange accidents', which would grow 'into no little griefe of minde and amazement' began. Stones 'of contrarie bignes', started falling from the roof into the hall. Twenty-one-year-old George, who was there at the time, instructed men with ladders to climb up to the roof 'both within and without his house' to search for anything 'amiss in the Tiles or Slates'. Nothing untoward was found and yet the stones continued to drop into the hall; whether they were falling *from* or *through* the roof, they could not be sure. In any case, the hall, it transpires, had a ceiling and no mention is made of gaping holes through which the mysterious stones might have passed. Fortunately, no-one was injured but, needless to say, the family and friends were 'greatlie affrighted and terrified' by these unwonted accidents.

George persuaded three or four of his neighbours to stand vigil at the house in the hope that 'they might gather some further knowledge of these strange events'. He and his friends decided to spend the night in an upstairs chamber, but John Yeomans, a brave workman employed by Lee, insisted on keeping watch within the hall, tucking himself into the chimney corner for safety. After sitting there alone and in the dark for three quarters of an hour 'he heard a terrible noise of stones' sounding as if they were falling from the ceiling. He called out for a light and when one was brought, eight or nine stones were discovered scattered on the floor. These were carefully removed and there were no further disturbances for the rest of the night.

Davies, *The Haunted*, p. 35.
163 John Harvey-Lee and Marcus Potts, *North Aston: A Millennium* (Information Press, 2007), p. 16.
164 'Parishes: North Aston', in *A History of the County of Oxford: Volume 11, Wootton Hundred (Northern Part)*, (London, 1983) pp. 6-21.

A TRVE DISCOVRSE

of such straunge and woonderfull *accidents, as hapned in the house of M.* George Lee of North-Aston, in the countie of Oxford, being in truth and matter of *such especiall waight and consequence, as* sildome hath the like bene heard of before.

Which begun the 19. of Nouember 1591. and continued vntill Easter euen last past 1592.

Iustified by the credit of Gentlemen of worship, and others of the Countrey.

¶ Imprinted at London for Edward White, dwelling at the little North doore of S. Paules Church at the signe of the Gunne. 1592.

However, more mysterious stones continued to drop into the hall over the next few days. On 26 December, St Stephen's Night, Lee invited his clerical kinsman, named here simply as 'Giles', who can be identified as Edward Giles, John Lee's successor as the vicar of the parish, together with several of his neighbours to keep him company.[165] After an hour warming themselves by the fire, he produced some playing cards to help his guests while away the time. When they were trying to decide who should deal the cards, Giles provocatively declared this should be the task of 'the first knave' in the hall. Immediately thereafter 'a great stone came flying overthwart the hall, and hit on the wall over his shulder, which greatly amazed both him & the rest of the company'. In response Giles called out, 'the first knave hath dealt here indeede', and another stone was thrown. Under the vicar's direction the cards were put away, knees were bent, and the company turned to prayer in place of gambling. No more stones were thrown for the rest of the night.

It seems that other members of the household had vacated the place shortly after the disturbances began but now George Lee's father, Edward, instructed his daughter, Anne, to return to lodge in the haunted house with a servant-girl, Joan Meisey. Despite being 'verie unwilling', Anne obeyed. However, as they drew near to the gate that opened onto the small court in front of the house, she and Joan were alarmed to hear the sound of stones thrown with great 'strength and violence', ricocheting off the walls; they dared not proceed and they returned to her father. Next, he sent Anne to see Yeomans (the brave workman), together with John Wright, and George Wright, who accompanied the girls back to the farmhouse. Once again, as they arrived at the gate, they heard the din of stones hurled against the walls, but Yeomans, with the same resolution as before, led the party to the front door, unlocked it, and stepped into the hall. Around them stones continued to fall but Yeomans, 'more bold than the rest', addressed, directly, the supposed entity responsible for it all thus: 'If thou bee a good fellowe doe us no harme, for we come not hither to do thee any'. They proceeded across the hall and went up the stairs into the gallery, 'where they durst not abide long', and from there went into a middle chamber beyond. As they did so, two more stones

---

165 'Parishes: North Aston', in *A History of the County of Oxford: Volume 11, Wootton Hundred (Northern Part)*, (London, 1983), pp. 6-21. British History Online https://www.british-history.ac.uk/vch/oxon/vol11/ [accessed 20 April 2024].

dropped or were thrown, 'one lighting upon the postall at the entraunce of the chamber, the other on a Curterne rod of a bedde' which clattered to the ground, striking George Wright lightly on the shoulder as it fell. Whether they dared stay the night in the haunted bedroom is not stated.

On St John's Day (the nativity feast day of John the Baptist, 7 January), as the Christmas holidays proceeded, a member of another local family of some standing, William Whing, with a colleague, Richard Hicks, visited the farm and made some 'very good and godly speeches' on their arrival. However, nothing odd having occurred, 'Whing fell to pleasant jesting', saying, 'Jacke, if thou bee a good fellow, fling us downe a quoit or two, that my companion and I may go to play at the quoits'. Sure enough a thin broad stone - a perfect quoit in form and proportion - fell to the floor. Whing promptly asked 'Jack' for another and, immediately, another was provided. He asked for two more and two more appeared, one of which was recognized by the grass stains on its edges as having 'bene plaid withall on the Greene before the house'. Whing thanked 'Jack' for the four quoits and Hicks now joined the conversation by asking him what more he could do and requesting him to 'fling us downe some other thing'. Immediately a great chunk of mortar, 'as if it had bin puld from some olde wall' crashed with great force to the ground, moldering into powder and turning the onlookers' merriment to fear. 'Come William', Hicks urged Whing, 'let us go hence, I feel it is not good to stand jesting and scorning heer', on which they departed with the quoits and a very odd tale to tell the others.

The following day Edward Lee returned to the farmhouse to sleep 'and took with him two young men to watch, whose names were William King and Thomas Churchill, besides two servant maids, Joan Meisey and Mary Alder'. Mary laid a pallet on the ground for a bed and attempted to get some rest. However, 'As she lay slumbering, a clod of clay fell and hit her on the nose', and she awoke with a start and a shriek. This, in turn, woke Lee who, unable to get back to sleep again, passed the time with the watchers. Thinking the night must soon be over, he thanked the young men for their time and told them they were welcome to leave. On their departure he instructed Mary to call for Yeomans who lived in a little house with his wife at the 'neither [nether] end of the towne'. She delivered the message then returned to the parsonage where the rest of the Lee household was staying.

It was still night-time when Yeomans reached the gate of the little court in front of the farmhouse door. Here 'he espied a great blacke thing, in the liknes of a Dog' standing upright and leaning against the wall of the house as if listening to what was going on inside. Though 'afrighted with this terrible sight', he soon regained his courage and demanded, 'what art thoue in the name of God speake, or I will compell thee'. There being no response, he demanded the coal-black dog to speak a second time and then lashed out at the dumb creature 'three or four times with his staffe', uncertain if he managed to make contact, and it leapt out of the way and cowered in 'a litle corner of the Court, betweene the dore and the Buttery'. John later recalled that, as far as he could

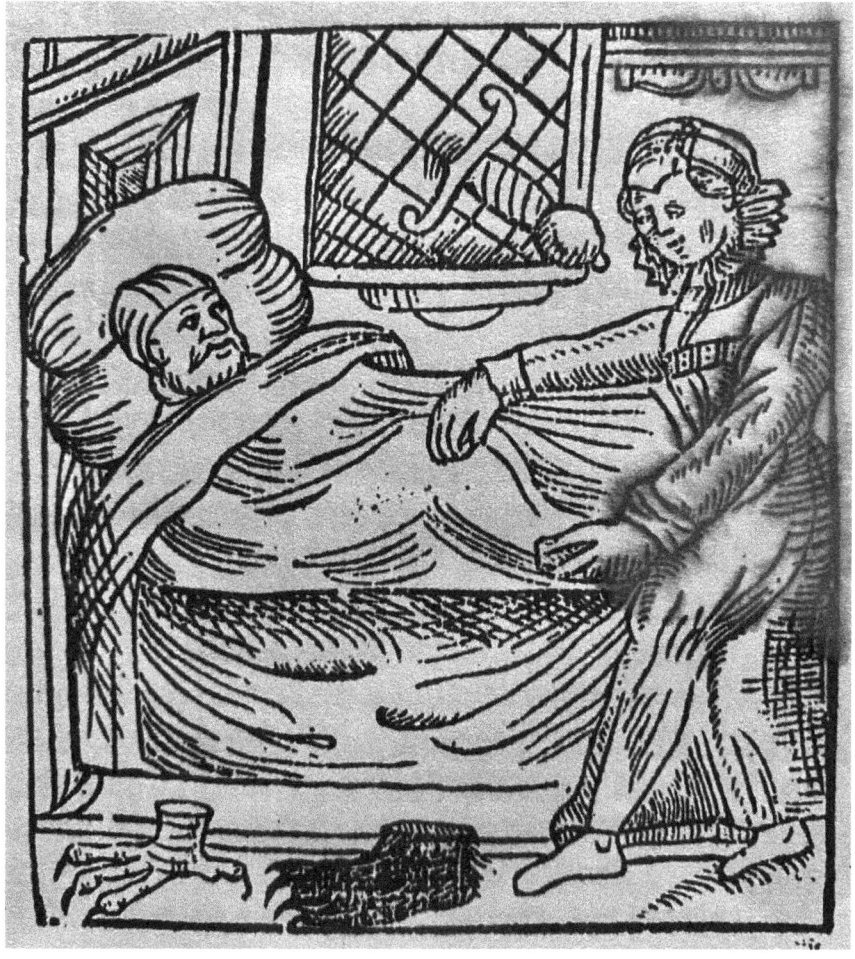

tell, the animal was standing upon a heap of stones - its ammunition, perhaps, for further troubling those who dwelt inside. Undeterred, John continued to strike out at the dog with his staff before it escaped over the garden wall 'and so vanished out of his sight'. He called out to his master inquiring what he should do next and received instructions to follow the creature and search for it in the grounds adjoining the property. As Yeomans set off in pursuit, Mr Lee, thinking it was almost dawn, assumed the danger was past and settled down to get some sleep. In actual fact it was no later than two in the morning - for the second time that night Lee's sense of time had gone astray.

While her master slept, a maid made up a fire in the hearth. She was considering having a nap herself when a stone fell from somewhere above her and hit her on the shoulder. Not wanting to wake Lee she moved away to another part of the room where another stone landed on her. She moved to another spot, this time a chest at the foot of her master's bed. Here she sat leaning her back against the bed, gripping the bed clothes with both hands, too frightened to close her eyes. The flames of the fire began to behave in strange ways, one moment all was dark then, suddenly, they would flash an extraordinary blue and various other colours. Suddenly, to her alarm, she felt the bedcover under which Lee was sleeping being pulled away. Not daring to speak, she instinctively held on to it all the more tightly but still it continued to slide away. Terrified, she cried out 'The gown! The gown!', waking her master who, recovering his bedclothes, asked what was wrong with her. When she explained what had happened he endeavoured to calm her saying, 'Be of good cheer - God is stronger than any devil'.

While the maid was showing Lee the stones that had hit her, she fancied she could hear on the floor of the chamber above them a noise like the trampling of a man's feet. 'Hark master', said she, 'do you not hear somebody walking above?'. Listening carefully, he too heard the sound and agreed it sounded like heavy footsteps. Climbing out of bed he stood and boldly commanded, 'In the name of God, what are you? I charge you, in the name of our Lord Jesus Christ, to tell me what you are! If you are that deceitful serpent, I charge you in the name of the living God, to depart this house, for you have no power here for God is mightier than you!'. Presently the noise ended and they heard it no more.

When day broke, Lee asked his maid to go to the chamber above and have a good look around. She agreed and made her way upstairs. Entering the room she found the shutters wide open and a sword thrust through the window, its hilt held in place by the lattice framework. She called down to her master asking him whether the casement had been closed the night before and whether the sword had been placed, in its sheath, on the bed. He confirmed this had been done and she agreed, declaring, 'They were indeed, for I was the one who shut the casement and the sword was laid on the bed by my own hands'. And then she proceeded to tell him how they now appeared. When he was dressed, Lee inspected the chamber, finding the shutters open and the sword thrust through the window, just as the maid had described. Next, he summoned another serving woman who had also been on the premises overnight who, on being questioned, confirmed she too had seen the casement closed and the sword, in its sheath, lying on the bed.

The same morning other rooms in the house were searched. Joan, the servant, called her master to the great parlour where two of the bolsters from the bed appeared to have been thrown onto the floor in the middle of the room. She insisted she was sure she had placed them on the bed the night before and this was confirmed by another maid. Lee had no doubt that this was the case. 'Fetch me a piece of chalk', he commanded, and when it was provided he drew a line around the bolsters delineating their exact position on the floor. Having instructed the maids to return the bolsters to their place on the bed, they left the parlour for a short time. When they re-entered the room Lee and Joan were amazed to discover the chalk marks had been rubbed out despite the fact that they were the only people in the house and they had all been together since they leaving the room. Lee took up the chalk and reinstated the faded outline of where the bolsters had lain and, once more, left the parlour. After about half an hour they returned and found the chalk rubbed out again. So, for the third time, he made his marks on the floor, this time pressing hard and making sure the lines were broad, dense and crossing over each other where they met. On their return they found the chalk marks unchanged but close by one of the bolsters they found, embedded in the floorboards, what looked like the footprint of a young bear and, close to the other bolster, they also found what resembled the impression of a hawk's talon. These were marks which, the author of the tract remarked, 'continueth there to this day to bee seene'.

That same day the maid saw a hare sitting on the threshold of the door in the small courtyard. Amazingly she was able to walk right up to it without it bounding away, but as she bent down to pick it up it vanished. She told her master but he found her story hard to believe until the next morning when, having made his way from the parsonage to the farm, he saw the footprints of a hare. On another occasion, when she was walking with her master's two spaniels, the maid saw the hare again. Instead of chasing it, the dogs fled, further convincing her this was no natural creature.

These strange occurrences continued from 29 November 1591, when the first falling stones were observed, until the following 6 January after which things seemed to have returned to normal. However, on 15 February, stones began to fall again, this time with more force than before. In the hall of the farm substantial drops of blood, splattered across one end of the long table which had stood there for at least twenty years. Despite attempts to wash them away the spots of blood kept returning. These were seen by many respectable folk. The writer of the account claimed to have seen them himself and that they were still visible.

As in the case of the Tidworth haunting seventy years later [Relation 11], this one attracted the attention of the local elite. Sir Anthony Cope (1550-1614), the Sheriff of Oxfordshire, was one among a party of gentlemen who visited the site of these strange events.[166] Everyone in the house was interviewed and ladders were raised to enable a search of the roof. There was no evidence of mischief-making, at least, not by human hand.

As news of the haunting spread, a party of four, including two young gentlemen - Thomas Power of Wilton and his brother-in-law, Mr Peney, also of Wilton - made a visit. These brave souls declared their wish to stay a night in the haunted house despite Lee's warning they were in for a fright. Nevertheless, seeing how determined they were, he agreed and had some beds made up for them. Between the hours

---

166 Lord Cope is famous for 'Cope's bill and book' – the religious reforms he proposed that earned him a spell in prison in 1587. He was closely associated with Peter Wentworth's puritan faction.

of eleven and twelve o'clock that night something, untold, happened which was sufficiently frightening to cause them to flee from the house and run to the parsonage without once looking back. They banged on the door until someone let them in and they never asked to stay in the haunted house again.

Plenty of other gentlemen and gentlewomen visited the house, many taking away stones as souvenirs. One man, by the name of Albert from the neighbouring village of Somerton, took one away but, on his way home, he suffered a searing pain in his eyes and was blinded in one. He, of course, blamed the cursed stones and others agreed.

Something odd also happened to Edward Lee's wife. One day, when she had five or six workmen labouring in her garden, she instructed her maid to provide them with breakfast. The maid went out to the 'boulting-house'[167] to find enough plates and here, to her alarm, she saw a blanket over the 'boulting tub' moving as if some creature was underneath it. She fled to her mistress who promptly went with her to investigate. When the maid pulled away the blanket they were both horrified to see an ugly black thing creeping over the edge of the tub and fall to the floor across which it slid towards the door. The

mistress started praying to God to protect them while the maid called to the workmen to come and see as it crept into a corner of the washhouse. Mrs Lee took a closer look at the creature before it disappeared from view and declared it looked like a small dog with a broad chest and a bearded ape's face, but without legs, tail or ears. The workmen searched all over but it could not be found anywhere.

167 Boultings were the coarse residue in the process of grinding grain into flour or meal. The boulting tub might be a repository in which to catch the flour in the sifting process separating boultings and flour.

One Mr Wilcocks, a gentleman from Warwickshire, made a visit to witness such marvels. Giles, the vicar, showed him around the farm. They went into the room where the bolsters had been flung from the bed, the place where the chalk circle kept being rubbed out, and, in the small parlour, the bear's footprint and the marks of the hawk's talon. Suddenly, to his great alarm, just as they left the room, a large stone fell at Wilcocks's feet. He picked it up and subsequently asked Mr Lee's permission to keep it. Before he left, he had the vicar sign his name on the stone in order to help verify its provenance when he got home to Warwickshire.

Other weird things were seen and heard around the farmhouse including one occasion when it looked like the place was on fire. However, when the house was searched, all that was found was a feeble fire in the kitchen chimney which no-one could account for.

In 1592 George Lee died and was buried on 22 May. Thereafter nothing untoward was heard or seen again in the house.

THE AUTHOR OF the *True Discourse* offered no explanation for these odd events beyond his assumption they were willed by God to test men's faith and to persuade them to lead less sinful lives. This would become the norm for future accounts of such 'wonderful' occurrences – tales that were worth telling as evidence of divine providence.

2
PETER PAIN'S POLTERGEIST: BRISTOL, 1630s

RICHARD BOVET'S 'FIRST Relation' in his late seventeenth-century demonology, *Pandaemonium, or, The Devil's Cloyster*, falls firmly

MARYLEPORT STREET; 1889.

Medieval and early modern buildings along Mary le Port Street (also known in the past as St Mary le Port Street, Maryport Street, Maryleport Street, and, seemingly, Mary Peol Street) in the heart of Bristol. The street and its church were destroyed by bombing in the Second World War. Artist: Samuel Loxton, 1889 into the poltergeist category of supernatural/preternatural accounts.[168] It concerns the troubling experiences of Peter Pain, a shoemaker living in Mary Peol Street[169] in Bristol in the 1630s. Bovet's informant was a Mr J. R., 'a Gentleman of good Ingenuity, and Reputation' of Bristol who wrote to him in June 1683. J. R. In turn received his information from the son of another respectable Bristolian described simply as 'our late Dean'. The son in question was an apprentice living in the house at the time of its haunting.

The shoemaker was disturbed by unaccountable noises and other unspecified 'stupendous circumstances' in his house for some time. One night, around midnight, 'the usual noise was accompanied with so great a light through the whole House' it seems as if every room must have been lit with burning tapers or torches. Mr Toogood, the then minister of St Nicholas's Church,[170] was persuaded by the Pain family to visit them. He too heard the strange noises. He and the family retired to a chamber at one end of the gallery upstairs, at the other end of which there was a great trunk, so full of lumber it would take four or five men to lift. They closed the door of the room behind them and the minister began to pray on their behalf. Suddenly something was flung against the door 'with extraordinary violence' after which the other noises ceased. When the prayers were finished they went to open the door but found they could not force it open. Terrified, they managed to alert their neighbours who ran to their rescue and found the door was barred by the heavy trunk. This was something, Bovet asserted, the neighbours still living would be willing to attest.

Regrettably the nature of the noises that disturbed the Pain family are not described but one supposes it was the usual poltergeist fare of footsteps, creaking boards, objects being thrown about. In a tantalizing

---

168 Richard Bovet, *Pandaemonium, or, The Devil's Cloyster being a further blow to modern sadduceism, proving the existence of witches and spirits, in a discourse deduced from the fall of the angels, the propagation of Satans kingdom before the flood, the idolatry of the ages after greatly advancing diabolical confederacies, with an account of the lives and transactions of several notorious witches: also, a collection of several authentick relations of strange apparitions of dæmons and spectres, and fascinations of witches, never before printed.* (London, 1684). Pandaemonium was Milton's name for Hell.

169 Probably Mary le Port Street (destroyed in the Second World War), also known as St Mary le Port Street, Maryport Street, and Maryleport Street.

170 Richard Towgood, Vicar of the Church of St Nicholas, 06/12/1626-30/12/1667.

closing remark Bovet speaks of many other 'stupendous circumstances accompanying these noises 'which by reason of the great distance of time, and place, we can have no particular account of' - the lament of all hunters of historic ghosts and demons.

3
EXTRAORDINARY RUMBLINGS IN A GODLY HOME: EDINBURGH, SCOTLAND, c.1635.

GEOFF HOLDER IN his compendium of Scottish poltergeist cases places the earliest of these to around 1632-35. Its narrator, John Maitland, 1st Duke of Lauderdale (1616-82),[171] a controversial and powerful royal adviser who, at the age of around sixteen, married Lady Anne Home in 1632, stated in the account he sent to Richard Baxter in 1660, 'it happened since I was a married man'.[172] Baxter included it in his *Certainty of the Worlds of Spirits* (1691).[173]

The tale was set 'within four Miles of Edenborough'. It concerned an unnamed 'Aged Godly Minister, one that was esteemed a Puritan' and his family, whose 'House was extremely troubled with noises'. These were heard, not just by the family, but also 'many Neighbours', over the course of several weeks. It was especially active on Saturdays, disturbing the minister and his son (his assistant and, subsequently, his successor), prior to the delivery of their Sunday sermons. 'Sometimes', Lauderdale continued, 'they would hear all the Locks of the House, on Doors and Chests to fly open'. Clothing locked in trunks would be found the following morning 'all hanging about the Walls'. On one occasion 'they found all the best Linnen taken out, the Table covered with it, Napkins, as if they had been used, yea and Liquor in their Cups,

---

171 Ronald Hutton, 'Maitland, John, duke of Lauderdale', ODNB (2024).
172 Geoff Holder, *Poltergeist Over Scotland* (The History Press, 2013), p. 15.
173 Baxter, *Worlds of Spirits*, pp. 85-87.

as if Company had been there at Meat'. Meanwhile, 'the rumbling was extraordinary', causing the 'good old man' to call his family to prayer, the effect of which seemed to reduce the racket 'into gentle knocking, like the modest knock of a Finger'. However, as soon as Prayer was over they would hear 'excessive knocking, as if a Beam had been heaved by strength of many Men against the Floor'.

Lauderdale concluded his account by assuring Baxter that his informant, the minister's son, 'is an Honest Man, of good Natural Parts, well bred both in Learning and by Travel into Foreign Parts in his Youth', and that he had heard the story from many other equally reliable witnesses.

4
MAD FROLICS OF WITCHES AND DEMONS: PLAISTOW, LONDON, 1645

THE CONTEMPORARY REPORT of this curious case is reinforced by an eye-witness account, detailed below, that did not appear in print until 1681. *Strange and fearfull newes from Plaisto in the parish of West-Ham, Neere Bow, foure miles from London* was the title of the pamphlet printed in London by 'I. H.' in 1645, the third year of the English Civil War, a time in which, to cite the title of a 1646 ballad printed the following year, life in England seemed to have been 'turn'd upside down'.[174] In the turbulence of it all the ferocious witch hunts associated with the self-styled 'Witchfinder General', Matthew Hopkins, had been unleashed. In winding up his tale of poltergeist activity in the home of Paul Fox, an 'honest', educated and pious silk weaver, the narrator of *Strange and fearfull newes from Plaisto* remarked,

---

174 T. J., *The World turn'd upside down: or, A briefe description of the ridiculous Fashions of these distracted Times* (London, 1946).

it will let be unnecessary for me to perswade your belief any further herein, only let me put you in mind what strange things have been acted by Witches, how many have beene the last Assizes condemned and executed in the Countyes of Essex and Suffolke, all which are already published in print, and are known to be approved at [*sic*] truths and therefore I shall not need further to insist on them

However, the pamphlet does not find evidence of witchcraft in the strange activities, of the 'evill Spirit' infecting the Fox household, 'during the space of one month last past, or more'. At a time, seemingly, of renewed conviction in the region of the reality and capability of witches, this makes these happenings all the stranger still, 'the like never scarce ever heard of'. As in the majority of cases in the period, this spirit appeared to be performing entirely independently of a witch-accomplice. The seventeenth-century poltergeist defied the logic of the seventeenth-century witchcraft paradigm.

The ways in which the spirit haunted the house were certainly bizarre. A sword was found embedded, point upward, in the ceiling of what seems to have been the principal 'chamber' in the house. Subsequently it caused a good deal of alarm when it flew around the place of its own accord. When Fox grasped it by the hilt, he 'had much adoe to keepe it in his hand, the point still turning in his hand several wayes'. It was locked away in another room but somehow reappeared 'and flourished about [...] as before, the doore not opening, nor any signe appearing how it came out of that roome into this.' A walking cane in the kitchen 'came hopping up the staires, giving a tap on every stayre as it came, and presented itself in the Roome, stand[ing] upright upon one end'. For quarter of an hour it danced around the table on which the sword had been placed before lying itself down beside it.

Things settled down for a time thereafter until, one evening, Fox heard 'a strange kind of rapping at the doore'. Before letting it in he demanded who it was knocking on which; 'the Spirit with a soft hollow voice commanded him to open the doore, saying, hee must dwell there'. Fox told it 'to return to Hell Gates, where he thought he might have entrance without knocking'! This seemed to do the trick until one day when Fox, his son, and two servants 'were at their worke, weaving of fine Lace and Ribboning, their worke was cut to peeces in the Loome before their faces' without any sign of a hand or knife. Next 'great stones, Tyles, Brick-bats [chunks of broken bricks], Oyster-shels, peeces of bread, and other things came in at the windows, broke all the Glasse, and frighted young Fox and the two servants out of the roome, but did not any hurt to either of them'.

For a time, Fox, who had already 'sustained great losse in his trade', moved his work elsewhere but the spirit seems to have followed. While his original dwelling was quiet, the work continued to be ruined in the new place. Consequently, he returned home and the demon followed him back there.

Naturally, when word got around, the story aroused a good deal of interest and, as in other poltergeist histories, it attracted a great many visitors to the haunted house, thousands apparently, among whom 'some thinks it is to reveale something that is past and others are of an opinion that it for-shews some things to come'.[175] One day a group of people witnessed a great stone 'tumbling up stairs into the middell of the roome' in which they had gathered. It weighed 'about halfe a hundred weight' (four stone / 25.4 kg), and had lain in the yard for many years. One of Fox's servants returned it to its place but shortly afterwards it came back up the stairs into the room where, after doing a couple of circuits it settled down in the middle once more. Other weird phenomena included members of the household being pinched in their sleep, having their ears tugged and their hair pulled. Some were 'pulled out of their beds', strange noises were heard, open doors were found locked, locked doors were mysteriously opened, books and bread were chucked about, and the cloth in the loom continued to be ruined. On one occasion a pot of porridge Mrs Fox had prepared was emptied over the walls of the room in which it had been set down to cool.

~~~

Henry More heard about this case from an eyewitness, 'Dr Gibbs, a Prebendary of Westminster, and a sober intelligent person', seemingly one of the 'Minsters, Gentlemen & great Scholers' who,

---

175 Anon., *Strange and fearfull newes from Plaisto in the parish of West-Ham, Neere Bow, foure miles from London* (London, 1645).

STRANGE

And fearfull newes from

PLAISTO.

In the parish of

WEST-HAM,

Neere Bow, foure miles fron London, in the house of one *Paul Fox* a Silke-Weaver, where is dayly to be seene throwing of Stones, Bricbats, Oyster-shels, Bread, cutting his worke in peeces, breaking his windowes, stones of fifty wayt comming up the stayers, a sword flying about the roome, Books going up and downe the house.

WITH
Many more unheard of things, fearfull to the amizement of many hundreds of the beholders, both learned men and others; neither can any perceive from whence these strange things come.

WITH
Many more wonders here set downe the like never heard of before.

Printed at *London* by I. H. 1645.

according to the original account, 'have come purpously to see these things and have consulted together to find out the reason or cause of these strange remarkable wounders'. More sent his own account in a letter to his Royal Society colleague, Joseph Glanvill, as accurately as he could recall, about three months after hearing it from Gibbs. Subsequently, He included it in his edited compilation of Glanvill's works, *Saducismus Triumphatus* (1681).[176]

More remembered it in *c.*1680 as having caused a stir some thirty or forty years before. The name of the family occupying the haunted house is not given but ancillary evidence (described in the 'Advertisement' at the end of the account) identifies Paul Fox, the weaver.

Gibbs had cause 'to Travel from London into Essex' and, 'at the request of a Friend', he visited a house in Bow on his way. The reason for his visit seems to have had something to do with a recent tragedy in the house: the death of a young girl who died a few days after being 'pluckt by the Thigh by a cold Hand in her Bed'. Whether he was there to investigate or to offer pastoral support is not stated.

Some weeks later Gibbs happened to be riding by the house again 'but had no design to give them a new visit'. However, 'the Woman of the House' happened to be standing at the door and, exchanging pleasantries, she informed him, 'That though she was in tolerable health [...] things went very ill with them, their House being extreamly haunted, especially above stairs, so that they were forced to keep in the low Rooms'. Objects were being hurled about upstairs and stones and bricks thrown through the windows. Striving to keep a straight face, Gibbs, sceptical in such matters, listened to her tale of what he took to be 'the tricks only of some unhappy Wags to make sport for themselves and their Neighbours'. She suggested that if he stayed a while he 'may chance to see something with [his] own Eyes', and it was not long before an upstairs window in, allegedly, an unoccupied room, opened of its own accord 'and out comes a piece of an old Wheel through it' after which it was pulled shut. A few moments later 'it suddenly threw open again, and out come a Brick-bat'. Determined 'to see what the matter was, and to discover the Knavery' he asked if anyone would venture upstairs with him, 'But none present durst accompany him', so he made his way up

---

176 Glanvill, *Saducismus Triumphatus*, Relation XX, pp. 429-32.

to the haunted room alone. On entering 'he saw the Bedding, Chairs and Stools, and Candlesticks, and Bedstaves,[177] and all the Furniture rudely scattered on the Floor, but upon search found no mortal in the Room'. As he stood there trying to make sense of it all, he was amazed by what he saw next: 'a Bedstaff begins to move, and turn it self round a good while together upon its Toe, and at last fairly to lay it self down again'. He searched for 'any small String or Hair' tied to it, 'or any hole or string in the Ceiling above' but found nothing suspicious. Retiring to the window, he waited a while to see if anything else would happen. Sure enough, 'another Bedstaff rises off from the ground of its own accord, higher into the air, and seems to make towards him'. Convinced by now that he was witnessing 'something more than ordinary', he rushed to the door and fled, shutting it tight behind him. As he made his escape, the door opened 'and such a clatter of Chairs, and Stools, and Candlesticks, and Bedstaves, sent after him down Stairs, as if they intended to have maimed him'. However, and this is an interesting feature of many a poltergeist case, 'their motion was so moderated, that he received no harm'.

Now accepting 'it was not meer Womanish fear or superstition that so affrighted the Mistress of the House', he was talking to members of the family downstairs when 'he saw a Tobacco-Pipe rise from a side-Table, no body being nigh, and fly to the other side of the Room, and break it self against the Wall for his further confirmation'.

Gibbs seems to have been more convinced than the author of the 1645 pamphlet that these phenomena could only be accounted for by 'the mad frolicks of Witches and Demons'. Thereafter, Gibbs reported, in a typical act of counter-magic, a bewitched bedstaff was thrown onto a fire 'upon which an Old Woman, a suspected Witch, came to the House, and was apprehended, but escaped the Law'. Meanwhile the poltergeist infestation continued with such intensity 'in all the Rooms, upper and lower, that the House stood empty for a long time after'.

---

177 Short, moveable, cudgel-like wooden poles placed at the head of the bed to help keep the bolster and other bedding in place.

5
THE JUST DEVIL OF WOODSTOCK: OXFORDSHIRE, 1649

THIS IS ANOTHER one of those rare early cases for which there is more than a single contemporary account. The earliest of these was published in 1649, the year of the events it describes. Entitled *The Woodstock Scuffle*, it is a seventy-two paired stanza ballad spread over five pages.[178] It begins with a general recognition of 'wonders and strange sights' as providential signs of judgement to come for those who continue to 'Tipple, and swear, and Lie, and Whore'. 'But by the Stories which I tell', the anonymous author continues, You'll heare of Terrors come from Hell'.

Fifteen verses in, the story begins. It concerns the arrival at Woodstock Manor, a royal palace eight miles north-west of Oxford, of 'the States Commissioners engaged in the nefarious business of selling off 'the lands of Charles the late'. Charles I had been executed in January 1649. The palace had been severely damaged when it was besieged in 1646. In 1649 it was leased to parliamentarian officers before reverting to the Crown in 1660.

On their first night at the manor house, as soon as the commissioners got to bed they were subjected to some alarming phenomena: 'their Beds were heav'd on high', and invisible fingers seemed to be plucking at their clothing. The following night a 'great Clamor fil'd their Eares', their blankets were pulled, and the bedsheets tightened around their feet where they lay. The night after this the poltergeist started smashing windows: 'the Thing about did flie, and broke the windows furiously'. The book in which the commissioners had been gathering information regarding the tenants on the estate, mysteriously was set on fire. Meanwhile, logs

---

178 Anon., *The Woodstock Scuffle, or, Most Dreadful Apparitions that were lately seene in the Mannor-Hose of Woodstock neere Oxford, to the great Terror and wonderfull Amazement of all there, that did Behold them* (1649).

for their fire were hurled about by unseen hands. Strange shapes of entities resembling a dog and bear were reported, as was a ghostly woman who 'Twas seene, but spak a word to no man, and vanish'd'. The terrified commissioners, meanwhile, had fled, vowing to have nothing more to do with the place.

We are assured in the final stanzas that 'No man can tell the cause of these, So wondrous dreadfull outrages' but the political sympathies of its anonymous author are plain in the closing lines:

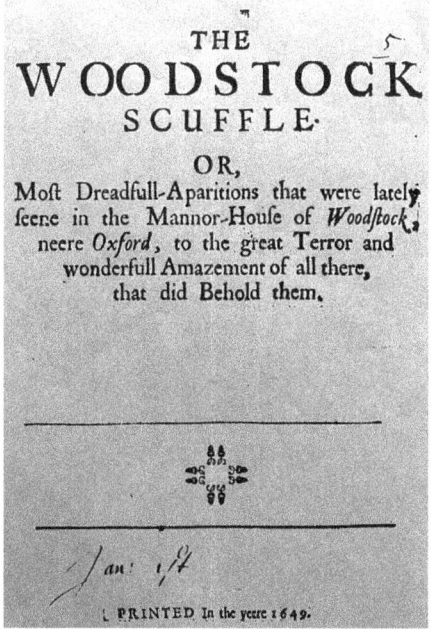

> Yet if upon your sinne you please to discant,
> You'll find our Actions out doe hell's;
> O wring your hands and cease the Bells,
> Repentance must, or nothing else appease can.

This explains why, unlike most of the other publications in this collection of relations, the name of the printer and the place of the print-house are not disclosed.

Interestingly, this is also the case with the another version of the tale, *The Just Devil of Woodstock*, a more substantial thirteen-page pamphlet in prose printed in London in 1660.[179] Although Charles II had recently been restored and the sympathies of its author clearly lie with the Crown, these were dangerous, unpredictable times. Its printer, seemingly, erred on the side of caution by, once again, concealing his name and address. The name of its author is also omitted but it largely comprises, it claims, the first-hand account of Thomas Widows, minister

179 Thomas Widows, *The Just Devil of Woodstock, Or, A True Narrative of the Several Appartions, the Frights and Punishments, inflicted upon the Rumpish Commisioners Sent thither, to Survey the Mannors and Houses belonging to His Majestie*. (London, 1660).

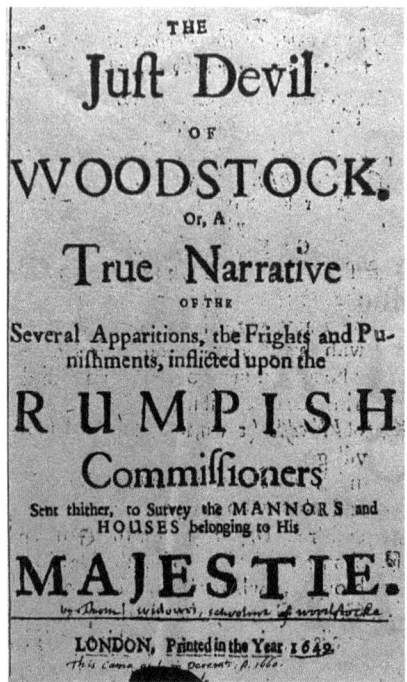 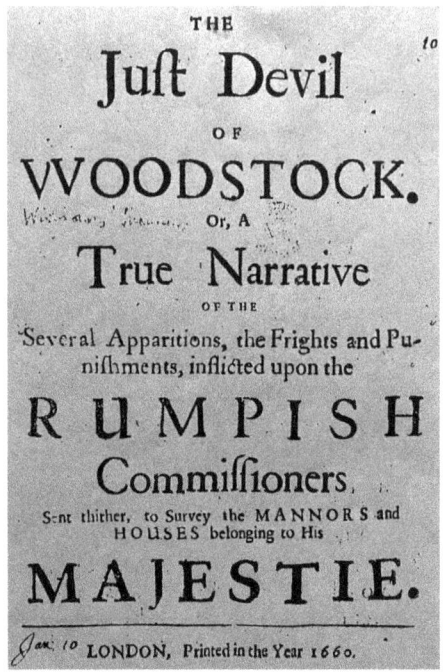

left: Frontispiece of a pamphlet attributed to Thomas Widdows. It is dated 1649, and the core narrative probably dates from 1649, but it was not completed and distributed until the Restoration over a decade later
right: The same pamphlet but this version is dated January 1660/1

and school-master of Woodstock, 'who each day put in writing what he heard' from the mouths of those who seem to have been the target of the poltergeist activity the night before. Thus the pamphlet purports to be an unadulterated rendition of diary entries for the last couple of weeks in October 1649 made by a respectable man 'never thinking that what he had writ, should happen to be made publick'.

A near identical version of this pamphlet survives which is dated 1649 on its front page – the year of the alleged poltergeist episode. However, the evidence of the preface to the main narrative, which clearly post-dates Cromwell's protectorate, reveals this cannot be the case. Regarding this mystery, the author of the preface explains that the reason for why 'this Narrative was not sooner published' is that to have done so at any point between 1649 and 1660 would have been extremely dangerous. Unless another version of *The Just Devil* comes to light which does not obviously post-date 1649, this accident – a disconcerting one for the research-historian reliant on published dates for printed material – makes *The Woodstock Scuffle,* dated 1649, the earlier source. However, there is the attractive possibility that the printer had in fact set-up the front page back in 1649 but he did not risk publishing Widows' account, with a revised editorial, until 1661. The error therefore might be accounted for by the fact that in this alternative version he had simply neglected to update the original 1649 frontispiece.

The pamphlet begins with a list of the individuals mentioned in the narrative and an assertion that the strange events were witnessed by 'many more'. Damage to walls caused by the unexplained throwing about of 'Glass and Stones' it claims could still be seen. The preface that follows celebrates the restoration of the monarchy after 'the tyrannicall times of that detestable usurper Oliver Cromwell'. The events at Woodstock are explained by the clumsy contrivance that the offences of Cromwell's regime were so great that 'the Devil himself dislikt their doings' and was moved 'to drive them [the parliamentary commissioners] from their work'.

The account starts with a summary of the arrival of the commissioners on 16 October. The four of them - Captains Crook, Hart, Cockaine, and Carelesse – had spent the last few days in Woodstock before making their way to the manor. They were accompanied by 'their Messenger Captain Roe, a secretary named Mr Brown, and two or three servants. Their disregard for the house and all it represented was evident from the start as rooms were repurposed at their convenience: the principal bedroom and the 'withdrawing room' now served as both sleeping quarters and kitchen, the 'Presence Chamber' was their office space, the great 'Councel Hall' was turned into a brew house and the dining room became a wood store. To add insult to injury, an ancient and revered tree in the park, known as the King's Oak, was singled out to be dug up by the roots and chopped into firewood. They were, some would say, asking for psychic trouble.

Sure enough, around the middle of the night they were awakened by the sound of knocking on the presence chamber door. They then heard it open and the sound of something walking from there, through the withdrawing room and on into the bed chamber where two of the commissioners, Captains Hart and Carelesse shared a bed. They heard its heavy footsteps pacing about the room for half an hour before it seemed to crawl under the bed itself where, as far as they could tell in the dark, it began biting and the gnawing at the bedcords.[180] And then the terrified men felt the mattress on which they lay being heaved by the entity beneath. This continued, on and off, for another half hour before, after going under a servant's bed where it 'did the like to them', they heard it walk out of the bedroom and back into the drawing room where the rest of the group of men had their beds. There it treated them in the same way, and, 'having welcomed them for more than two hours', it walked out 'and shut the outer door again, but with a clap of some mightie force'. Although they were 'in a sweat', the visitors managed to get back to sleep, and didn't discuss it until the morning. Talk was had of the possibility of a dog at large in the room or something 'more akin to the likeness of a great Bear'. An untouched 'quarter of beef' on the floor pointed to a visitation by something more mysterious than a regular nocturnal carnivore, pet or otherwise.

The next night they were awoken again, this time by what sounded like the 'great clefts of the King's Oak' in the presence chamber being 'thumpt down' and rolled across the floor, and chairs and stools tossed from one side of the room to the other. This continued for about an hour before the entity walked into the withdrawing room where the two captains, the secretary and the two servants slept. Here it seemed to pause for a while, as if taking a breather and making a 'hideous tone' as it did so, before moving on into the bedroom. Once more it seemed to go under the captains' beds where they lay and shook them with such vigour they had to grasp the bedposts to prevent themselves being thrown out. This lasted for around half an hour before it returned to the withdrawing room where it seemed to stand at the foot of the men's beds and then heave them up until they were almost vertical before dropping them down again. This also went on for about half an hour before it left them alone, departing 'with a great noise'.

In the middle of the next night the men in the bedchamber were awakened by someone or something stomping so heavily across the floorboards the whole room seemed to shake. It then went into the adjoining withdrawing room 'where it took up a brass warming-pan, and returning with it into the bed-chamber', made a great din with it as

---

180 Ropes stretched across the bed frame to support the bedding.

loud and unsettling 'as a ring of five untuned Bells rang backwards'. The following morning the captains, 'not to seem afraid', made light of the matter 'and jested at the Devil in the pan'.

On the fourth night more objects were thrown 'with some great force' around the rooms and from one room into another. Captain Hart was rudely awakened by the sensation of 'being taken by the shoulder and shaked until he did sit up in his bed' assuming he had been disturbed by one of his companions. However, when he was hit on the head with a trencher [serving board] 'it made him shrink down into the bed-clothes'. With three dozen trenchers now flying about 'all of them in both rooms kept their heads at least within their sheets'. When Hart 'ventured again to peep out to see what was the matter' he soon retreated as more trenchers 'came so fast and neer about his ears'. Meanwhile, walls and doors were banged with such ferocity it sounded as if 'several Smiths had been at work'. The next morning they found trenchers, pots and spits scattered all around. Nevertheless, the captains refused to be distracted from their work and braced themselves for another night at the manor.

This time the disturbances began about midnight with 'great knocking at every door' which then 'flew open'. Something very large

Woodstock Palace in a print from *c.*1700.

'they knew not how to describe' entered the withdrawing room. The floorboards shook with every step as it moved towards the curtained bed in which Captains Crook and Carelesse were lying. It paused for a moment and then 'The bed-curtains at both sides and feet were drawn up and down slowly, then faster again for a quarter of an hour, then from end to end as fast as imagination can fancie the running of the rings'. It shook the beds violently before moving into the bedchamber and repeating the performance. Next it hurled eight pewter dishes around the room but left others on which food had been placed. At the same time they heard the sound of 'weightie things', presumed to be great logs hacked from the King's Oak, being thrown about in the presence chamber.

The following day, 22 October, the commissioners had business away from Woodstock but when they returned on the 23rd their troubles continued. In the middle of the night those in the withdrawing room were awoken by what sounded like 'the cracking of fire' in the bedchamber next door. Also hearing groans coming from within, they promptly sent their servants to investigate. They found the men all asleep but without any bedcovers. These they found, together with their clothes, boots and all, stuffed in the corners of the chimney breast. Following instructions to build up the fire, they were alarmed 'when the firebrands flew about their ears so fast, that away ran they into the other room, for the shelter of their cover-lids'. Hiding under their bedsheets they could hear something that had followed them into the room which stamped about angrily and, as before, hurled trenchers, platters and the like about. After a couple of hours it left them alone but only after it had 'stampt again over their heads'.

The company was away again on 24 October and when they returned on the twenty-fifth they were joined by Crock's brother, a lawyer, sent by officers Captain Parsons and Major Burler to replace the king's man, one Mr Hyans, as deputy-steward of the manor. The commissioners made a great fire of logs from the King's Oak to welcome him to the lodgings he and his servant would be sharing with his brother in the withdrawing room.

In the middle of the night 'a wonderful knocking was heard, and into the room something did rush, which coming to the chimney-side, dasht out the fire, as with the stamp of some prodigious foot'. This was followed by loud thuds which the occupants of the room took to be the sound of the great 'clefts and roots of the chopped up oak tree being thrown to the ground with such force the house 'shook with it'. Cockaine and his bed-fellow immediately arose and drew their swords. The noise immediately ceased as they made their way to the bed in which the Crook brothers were lying. To their consternation the brothers gave no answer when Cockaine called out. Calling again, more loudly, there was a faint, nervous reply and he did what he could to reassure the terrified lawyer on his first night in the haunted house. After a while without any further disturbances, they decided they might as well go back to bed. When Cockaine returned to his he was perplexed to find it appeared someone had made the bed in the short time since he had got up. When he pulled back the bed clothes he was even more surprised to find 'three dozens of trenchers were orderly disposed between his sheets'. As soon as he and his bed fellow started removing them, a great noise erupted all around. They quickly jumped back into the bed with the remaining trenchers for company. The racket continued for a further half hour.

The following day Deputy-Steward Crook declared the matter 'the Devil's law-case' and vowed to leave immediately. Only after a good deal of persuasion did he agree to stay put for another night. This time the party took care to build up the fires and light more candles in the hope of keeping their tormentor at bay. Once more however, around midnight, it returned, dashed out the candles and walked about the room making a weird unnatural noise. As before, it tugged the bed curtains back and forth and shook the bedsteads with such vigour those lying on them clung to each other to prevent being thrown out. A strange, more subtle, sound was heard as if coins were being dropped into the room from above. When Cockaine lit a candle to investigate 'he perceived the room strewed over with broken glass, green, and some pieces of it were broken bottles' – a cruel trick to play on barefoot sleepers in the black of night. Suddenly Cockraine's candle went out and pieces of glass started flying about the room, prompting the Captain to make 'haste to the protection of the Coverlets'. Meanwhile 'the noise of thundering rose more hideous [than] any time before'. The following morning the maid was instructed to sweep all the glass into a corner where 'many came to see it'. For Richard Crooks, the lawyer, it was all too much and he refused to stay a day longer. Stopping briefly in Woodstock, he was heard to declare 'that he would not lodge amongst them another night for a Fee of £500'. The rest of them, however, felt they must stay until their work was done.

That night the commissioners prepared to sleep 'with pistols charged, and drawn swords laied by their bed sides'. In the middle of the night they were awakened by the opening and closing of windows. When they sat up to see what was going on 'stones flew about the rooms as if hurled with many hands', hitting the walls and bedheads, accompanied by bouts of a 'thundering noise'. And so it continued for a full two hours.

The following morning eighty or so stones were swept up into the corner where the glass had been swept the day before. All of those sherds of glass, however, had, in the meantime, mysteriously disappeared. Many came to view the stones that now filled the space in the corner, and some maintained the stones were not of the kind found locally. Accounts spread of loud noises emanating from the manor, some resembling canon fire or thunderclaps that could be heard in Woodstock.

The following night Captain Hart, lodging in the bed chamber, was awoken by the sound of Captains Roe and Brown groaning. Finding he 'could not now stir himself' the bed-bound Hart called out to Captains Cockaine and Crooke for help. Bizarrely, though he heard the call, Cockaine found he was unable to answer or even look around: 'something he thought, stopt both his breath and held down his eye lids'. Struggling against these feelings he thrashed about in the bed and kicked Crooke awake who, half asleep, uttered comments sufficiently insulting to be worthy of a duel. However, these helped bring Cockaine to full consciousness and, recalling Captain Hart's calls for help, he ran to the other room where he found him 'sadly groaning'. Searching the chimney hearth in the dark he found a candle and material to light it. He had not gone two steps before something blew the candle out and threw him into a chair at Hart's bedside. Presently Captain Careless began to call out 'with a most pittiful voice, come hither, O come hither brother Cockaine, the things gone of me'. Although he was 'scarce yet himself' Cockaine managed to rouse Careless, Hart and 'the other two' (presumably, Captain Roe and Mr Brown) and get them sitting up in their beds. No sooner had he done so than he heard Captain Crook in the bedchamber 'crying out, as if something had been killing him'. Cockaine grabbed a sword and rushed into the other room to save him. Whatever had been oppressing Crook immediately released him and Crook bound out of bed. Crying out 'Lord help, Lord save me' he threw himself into Cockaine's arms, thanking him profusely 'for his deliverance'.

After all this commotion the whole party, deeply unsettled, gathered together to pray while 'there was such stamping over the roof of the house, as if 1000 horse had been there trotting'. Meanwhile it was observed that the pile of stones swept into the corner of the withdrawing room the night before had mysteriously vanished.

As the night of 29 October approached, the commissioners took further precautions. In addition to lights and candles they persuaded 'their Ordinary keeper' to lodge with them and to bring with him his guard-dog, a mastiff. These measures seem to have worked: that night they experienced no disturbances whatsoever.

They went to bed with greater confidence on 30 October until, around midnight, something banged loudly at the door as if with 'a smiths great hammer' – so loud they thought it might break. And then something large, heavy-footed and bear-like entered the room, walked about it and stomped its way into the adjacent bedchamber. Here 'it dasht against the beds heads some kind of glass vessel, that broke into sundry pieces'. These were hurled around the bedroom and into the room next door. Meanwhile the entity hammered on tables and walls, and for the next two hours or so it created such a din the occupants felt 'as if the roof of the house were beating down upon their heads'. It slammed the doors with great violence as it left, and in the morning they found sherds of glass strewn all over the place.

The commissioners discussed whether or not they should dare stay there a night longer but, since their business was nearly done, they decided to take the risk. It was now 31 October, All Hallows' Eve, and they had been the manor's unwelcome guests for a fortnight. That night they took to their beds once more with fires and candles burning. The 'Ordinary keeper and his bitch, with another man' joined them. They were awoken around midnight by rapping on all the walls around them. The dog barked as the door seemed to open, followed by a thing that hit a table so hard it cracked, smashed a warming pan against a wall with such force it was flattened, and then boxed the heads and ears of those cowering under the bed clothes. Captain Careless was whacked on the head with a horse's shoulder-blade, and Brown sustained a severe blow to his leg. They were pelted with stones and deafened by what sounded like a cannon firing. All the windows were smashed. As the commotion died down 'the thing walkt up and down' and Cockaine and Hart, in the bedchamber, demanded of it, 'In the Name of the Father, Son and Holy Ghost, What are you? what would you have? what have we done that you disturb us thus?'. There was no reply and the noise ceased.

Hart and Cockaine got out of bed, built up the fire among the embers of which he retrieved their smoking 'Book of valuations' which some unknown hand had transported there from the table nearby where it had been left. They placed one great candlestick close to the door between the two rooms so that it's light could be seen from both. However, as soon as they had got back to bed the commotion started up again, louder than ever before. Suddenly the candle and candlestick were dashed against the ceiling as if they had been given a mighty kick by an invisible horse, and the fire went out. And then, as they lay in their truckle beds, the men were soaked with foul-smelling water, 'worse than any earthly stink could make'. Meanwhile something crept beneath their beds and launched them, commissioners and all, up towards the roof, before falling apart as they crashed back to the ground. Defeated at last, they fled from the haunted rooms and ran down the stairs until they reached the Council Hall. They spent the rest of the night beside the fire in the Presence Chamber, wrapped up in what garments and blankets they could find, saying prayers and singing psalms by candlelight. Meanwhile, although 'no noise was in that room', it was heard 'most hideously round about, as at some distance'.

It later transpired that other witnesses to the disturbance included six poachers setting traps for hares and rabbits. On hearing the bizarre noises emanating from the house, 'they were so terrified that like men distracted away they ran, and left their Haies [hares] all ready pitched ready up, and the Ferrets in the Cony [rabbit]-burrows'.

Now the commissioners, 'more sensible of their danger', resorted to one Mr Hossman, the esteemed minister of Wotton, for guidance and prayers. Perplexed by the whole affair, Hossman in turn rode off to seek the advice of Mr Jenkinson and Mr Wheat, both justices of the peace. As for himself, Hossman also declared he would not spend a night in the haunted house even if he was offered £500 to do so. The commissioners shared his conviction that returning to lodge there would be unwise and so, instead, they had their goods removed to the chambers above the gatehouse and made this their base for their next and final night at Woodstock Manor. After another troubled night, details of which they decided to keep to themselves, they left early the next morning. However, it was soon 'well-known and certain, that the Gate-keeper's wife was in so strange an agony in her bed, and in her bed-chamber such noise (whilst her husband was above with the Commisioners) that two maids in the next room to her, durst not venture to assist her, but affrighted ran out to call company, and their Master, and found the woman (at their coming) gasping for breath'. No-one sleeping in the manor after the departure of the commissioners suffered any kind of further unnatural disturbances.

~~~

THE JUST DEVIL provided the bulk of the material regarding the case that was printed in Robert Plot's *The Natural History of Oxford-shire* (1677), and, subsequently, as one of Henry More's additions in his editing of Joseph Glanvill's *Saducismus Triumphatus* (1681).[181] Plot, More and Glanvill were all members of the Royal Society. Plot claimed he had received several accounts of the episode including one written by 'a Learned and Faithful Person then living upon the place, which being confirmed to me by several Eye-witnesses of many of the particulars'. These, apparently, included one of the commissioners. Somewhat reluctantly since, generally, Plot did not hold 'such kind of Stories' in high esteem, certain that many of them were 'perform'd by Combination', he felt this one was sufficiently odd to be worth sharing.[182]

In 1696 John Aubrey, another Royal Society fellow and one who had challenged the veracity of both Robert Boyle's 'Devil of Mascon' and Glanvill's 'Demon of Tedworth' stories, published yet another account of the case which he claimed he had received in a letter sent to him by John Lydall of Trinity College, Oxford, on March 11 1649/50.[183] This version,

---

181 Robert Plot, *The Natural History of Oxford-shire* (Oxford and London, 1677), pp. 210-14.
182 Plot, *Natural History*, p. 210.
183 John Aubrey, *Miscellanies* (London, 1696), pp. 70-1.

intended neither for publication nor profit, is far less extravagant in its claims. Unlike the highly detailed pamphlet narrative, this one, like so many more from the period, is dominated by the mysterious throwing of stones phenomenon. It is evident from Lydall's closing remark that these paranormal events were construed at the time as having something to do with the chopping down of the 'King's Oak'. It sounds like he wrote his letter in response to a query from Aubrey himself regarding the fate of the tree and subsequent events at the manor. It is sufficiently succinct to warrant transcribing in full:

Mr. Aubrey,
Concerning that which happen'd at Woodstock, I was told by Mr. W. Haws, (who now lives with Sir William Fleetwood in the Park) That the Committee which sate in the Mannor-house, for Selling the King's Lands, were frighted by strange Apparitions; and that the Four Surveyors which were sent to Measure the Park, and Lodged themselves with some other Companions in the Mannor, were pelted out of their Chambers by Stones thrown in at the Windows (but from what Hands the Stones came they could not see) that their Candles were continually put out, as fast as they lighted them; and that one with his Sword drawn to defend a Candle, was with his own Scabbard in the mean time well Cudgell'd; so that for the blow, or for fear, he fell Sick; and the others were forc'd to remove, some of them to Sir William Fleetwood's House, and the rest to some other places. But concerning the cutting of the Oak, in particular, I have nothing.

Your Friend, To be commanded to my power,
John Lydall.

Christina Hole in her *Haunted England* (1940), was sympathetic to the theory that the mischief at Woodstock was caused by royalist objectors, more likely alive than dead, to the presence of parliamentary commissioners lording it over a royal estate. Her source was George Sinclair's *Satan's Invisible World Discovered* (1685) in which a version of the pamphlet, probably derived from *Saducismus Triumphatus*, also was included.[184] The story inspired a novel by Walter Scott, *Woodstock, or The Cavalier. A Tale of the Year Sixteen Hundred and Fifty-one* (1826).

Nothing remains to be seen of the haunted mansion which once stood in the landscaped grounds of what became Blenheim Palace.

6
A VIOLENT GHOST AND A WILY WENCH: GREENWICH, 1650

T*he Strange Witch at Greenwich, (Ghost, Spirit, or Hobgoblin) haunting a Wench, late servant to a Miser, suspected a Murtherer of his late Wife* is a twenty-eight-page pamphlet printed in London in May 1650. It starts with an account of odd things occurring in Greenwich that year and points an accusatory finger at a young servant girl who is deemed a witch and the perpetrator. Most of the pamphlet is dominated by a philosophical and theological discussion of witchcraft, informed by an abundance of allusions to biblical and other texts regarding such matters as miracles, Satan and exorcism.

There is a telling ambiguity in the title of this pamphlet concerning the cause of the domestic disturbances it relates. The most fundamental question in any complex poltergeist case – 'Who or what is causing this?' – is ages old. It is addressed by its author with the pen-name of 'Hieronymus Magomastix', the surname meaning something along the lines of 'enemy of the magi (magicians)'. He identifies himself as having been the incumbent of St Bride's in Fleet Street, a place by then closely connected with London's printing industry. The long serving vicar of St Bride's, James Palmer (d. 1659), took up the post in 1616 but was persuaded to resign in 1645 at the height of the Civil War, partly because of his old age but also, it seems, for not being sufficiently hardline to

---

184 Christina Hole, *Haunted England: A Survey of English Ghost-Lore* (1940, 1949; Fitzhouse Books, 1990), pp. 164-66.

satisfy London's ascendant puritan community. A succession of at least seven temporary incumbents/occasional 'lecturers' followed between then and the Restoration.[185] He is almost certainly its author.

Told with levity and humour from the start, his is the story of 'a strange witch or ghost now at [...] Greenwich', haunting the house of one Meriday/Merryday playing 'pranks' such as 'throwing stones at the glasse windowes', moving chairs, stools, 'other utensills' and items of clothing, and throwing books. One of these, a Bible, ended up in the fire thus proving itself to share the same distaste for scripture, in the author's opinion, as 'a new Enthusiast, Papist, or an Atheist'. These 'mad merry pranks' he summed up were 'as strange as ever Hobgoblins, pinching Fairies, and Robin Goodfellow acted in houses in old Times amongst Dayry Wenches, and Kitchin Maids'. Nothing new then by the sound of things, even though such tales, up to this point, are scarce in the surviving record.

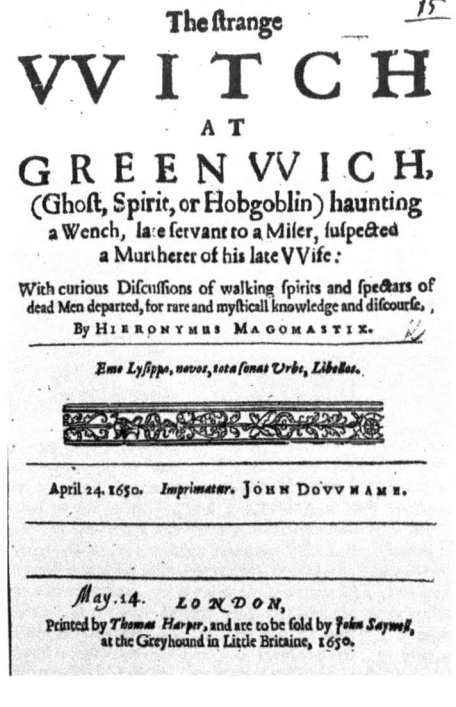

The clerical author claims to have received his information directly from Merryday's wife, son and daughter, and also one 'Master Halfpenny and his Wife, who saw a Laundyren [laundry iron] of it self without any visible mover leap out of the fire, [and] a Candlestick skippe up into the chamber'. Other neighbours claimed to have heard 'strange noises and ratlings, as of Carts or Waynes rumbling up and downe the house when the doors have been lockt, and except a Cat or a Rat, no visible Creature within.'

185 Walter H. Godfrey, 'History of St Bride's: The seventeenth century to the Great Fire', in *Survey of London Monograph 15, St Bride's Church, Fleet Street* (London, 1944), pp. 24-8. British History Online http://www.british-history.ac.uk/survey-london/bk15/pp24-28 [accessed 4 February 2024].

The disturbances seem to have drawn a good deal of attention including that of the narrator when he and his daughter were joined by 'much company' when they arrived one night to take a tour of the house. They were rewarded with a stone 'throwne at my Daughters heeles'. This is his/Palmer's account of a subsequent visit:

> as I went into the Garden a knife was throwne after mee, which I tooke up and with vehemency there back againe to the very place from whence it came, daring the Witch or Spirit to throw it at mee againe, and conjuring it in the name of that Jesus which is terrible to Divells [,] to speake unto mee, and to reveale the reason why it haunted the house, and to returne to its own place, but I had no reply, neither by voice or gesture.

The mystery is, in part, explained by the supposed antics of a fourteen-year-old 'wily Wench', allegedly contriving to appear haunted or bewitched in order to draw attention to her former master ('a Miser') who she suspected of murder. It is reasonable to suppose she had recently escaped from service in a dysfunctional household in which we discover her mean-spirited employer was rumoured to have killed his wife, 'the Dame' - her mistress. These suspicions, compounded by the odd happenings at the Merrydays, had even led to the exhumation of the woman's body to check it over for signs of death by unnatural causes.

The reason we find her in the Merrydays' house in Greenwich seems to be that this 'bold faced brazen brow'd wench' was in fact the Merryday daughter mentioned above. She had told Palmer that one day, about three weeks after the alleged murder, she was in her mother's garden when 'a stone was throwne at her, and hit her on the back, none being near her, nor within her sight'. She picked up the remarkable stone and studied it closely, pacing up and down the garden. For some reason – urged by Satan to do so according to the account – she hurled it at her mother's (bedroom?) window! As well as, no doubt, breaking the glass, this broke the ice between her and the devil leading her astray with the consequence that forty more stones thrown, according to her confession, by invisible hands, (and all counted thereafter) continued the battery of the house. This was the start of the rest of the trouble, of 'stools, cushions, candlesticks' and the like thrown about either by her or the demon she had unwittingly unleashed. Another suspect in all these matters was also a member of the household who is identified as 'the old Wife' and 'her Mother in Law' – presumably the girl's grandmother on her father's side. She was said to be 'not so good as shee should bee'. The mystery remained unsolved with some concluding 'its probable the Wench acts all her self with her owne hands by legerdemaine [sleight of hand]', others inclined to believe a witch was manipulating the girl, and many local townsfolk, untroubled by the rejection of belief in ghosts in educated circles, supposed it was 'the Ghost or Spirit of the dead woman her late Dame which walkes'.

The logic in all of this is convoluted to say the least, but, in this context, superfluous. It does not in any way undermine the veracity of the account as evidence for how people in mid-seventeenth-century England supposed genuine spirit-poltergeists behaved. Already, at this very early stage in the extant record of the telling of poltergeist stories, we have several key elements in place: the claims of multiple witnesses to the seemingly impossible movement of objects, and the identification, self-identification too perhaps, of a traumatized young teenage girl as the target or conduit of poltergeist activity. It all bears a striking resemblance to the famous events at Enfield in the 1970s.

7
'SATAN IS MY FATHER': GLENLUCE, SCOTLAND, 1654

THE TALE OF the haunting of the home of Gilbert Campbell, a Galloway weaver, appears in an unlikely context – George Sinclair's *The Hydrostaticks* (1672), a scientific study of the physics of 'fluid bodies'.[186] It is one among several miscellaneous 'Observations'

---

186 George Sinclair, *The hydrostaticks, or, The weight, force, and pressure of fluid bodies, made evident by physical, and sensible experiments together with some miscellany observations, the last whereof is a short history of coal, and of all the common, and proper*

tagged onto the end of his main text, its inclusion justified as a further proof of the reality of demons and what are now identified as poltergeists. In so doing he was inspired by 'several Writers [who] have remarked such strange accidents, and have transmitted them to posterity, which may serve for good use'. It is reasonable to presume he had in mind, in particular, Robert Boyle's ground-breaking English version of the story of the Mâcon devil, and Joseph Glanvill's recently published account of the 'Demon of Tedworth' haunting. He had met Boyle in London in 1662[187] and in emulating the work of these eminent members of the Royal Society, Sinclair aimed to cement his own reputation as a natural/mechanical philosopher. His Glenluce case study completed the trilogy of the most influential English / Scottish poltergeist narratives of that period. Its inclusion in Henry More's enlarged 1682 edition of Glanvill's *Triumphatus Saducismus*)[188] was Sinclair's ultimate reward. Soon after, Sinclair published 'The Devil of Glenluce enlarged with several Remarkable Additions' in his own derivative demonology, *Satan's Invisible World Discovered* (1685). In addition to transcriptions of the Mâcon, Tidworth and Woodstock accounts,[189] his own set of 'relations' included two further Scottish cases with poltergeist elements.[190] In his 1672 version of the haunting, eighteen years after the events described, Sinclair was careful to emphasize its reliable provenance:

> the true information, which is here set down, as it was Written, at the desire of a special Friend, by Gilbert Cambel's own Son, who knew exactly the matter, and all the circumstances

In the enlarged 1685 version Sinclair lent further credibility to his source in declaring he was 'a student of Philosophy in the Colledge of Glasgow' when he provided his information concerning the haunting

---

accidents thereof, a subject never treated of before (Edinburgh, 1672), pp. 238-47.
187 McAleavy, *The Last Witch Craze*, p. 15.
188 Glanvill, *Saducismus Triumphatus,* pp. 489-98.
189 Sinclair, George, *Satan's Invisible World Discovered* (Edinburgh, 1685)' Relation X, 56-75; Relation XXXI, pp. 193-9; Relation VI, pp. 32-9.
190 Sinclair, Satan's Invisible World, Relation XXI, 'Touching Isabel Herriot', pp. 144-54; Relation XXXII, '*Anent* Margaret Wilson', pp. 200-2.

George Sinclair's *Satans Invisible World Discovered* is the principal source for several paranormal tales from Scotland.

of the family home. Henry More subsequently asserted the validity of the account, remarking 'the very abruptness of its ending shews it to be fresh writ, while the thing was doing, and that Matter of Fact was the measure of the Writer's Pen'.

As Tony McAleavy has noted, the Glenluce demon had much in common with those identified at Mâcon and Tidworth.[191] The disturbances are presumed to be linked to an itinerant mischief-maker, in this instance 'one Alexander Agnew, a bold and sturdy Beggar' who, we learn, was subsequently hanged at Dumfries for blasphemy. The protagonist has reason to avenge himself upon the family, this time because of the familiar scenario in multiple witchcraft cases from the period – the family's refusal to fulfill presumed charitable obligations. Just as the disgruntled drummer in the Tidworth case is construed as he who conjures the demon, so is the beggar in the Glenluce case. Nevertheless, in both they play a peripheral role: in this instance, as the spotlight falls on the poltergeist, Agnew is mentioned just once at the very start and then disappears from view. These stories are studies of demons – demonologies – as opposed to studies of witches.

Campbell's troubles began in October 1654. He 'was oftentimes hindered in the exercise of his Calling, all his Working-Instruments being some of them broken' by unknown hands. According to Sinclair's later version, this was preceded by bouts of unexplained whistling, 'such, as children make, with their small slender glass whistles' and a threatening young female voice heard by the 'Gentle-woman', Jennet Campbell. Around the middle of November, he began to be plagued by that familiar feature of early modern poltergeist cases: stone throwing. Stones were thrown 'in at Doors and Windows, and down thorow the Chimney-head, which were of great quantity, and thrown with great force'. However, in common with several others in this collection of relations, 'by God's good providence, there was not one person of the Family hurt, or suffered damage thereby'. At this point Campbell began to share his hitherto secret troubles with his neighbours and the local minister. More wanton vandalism followed: 'for not long after, he found oftentimes his Warp and Threeds cut, as with a pair of Sizzers, and the Reed broken'. Members of the household found their clothing, 'their

---

191 McAleavy, *The Last Witch Craze*, p. 86.

Coats, Bonnets, Hose, Shooes' cut in the same manner 'even while they were wearing them', but without injury to the wearer.

At night they were kept awake by something pulling off their bed covers 'and leaving their bodies naked'. Chests and trunks were opened and the contents strewn about. Tools and loom parts were moved and found hidden, if found at all, in out of the way places. No household goods or the tools of Campbell's trade were off limits and he was obliged to store everything in a neighbour's house. For the time being, work upon which his family relied came to a halt.

He was persuaded at one point by certain 'not very judicious' individuals to try moving his children out of the family home on the assumption that one of them was probably the focus of the demon's attention. Things quietened down for four or five days but after the last of his children, Thomas, who had been lodged furthest away, returned home 'did the Devil begin afresh'.

Things now took a very serious turn when, the following Sunday, the house was set on fire. Fortunately, with 'the help of some people, going home from Sermon', the blaze was brought under control and the house was saved. The household spent the following Monday 'in privat Prayer and Fasting' but, around nine o'clock on the Tuesday morning, another fire broke out. This too, with the help of neighbours, was put out before much damage was done.

Suspecting his son Thomas was somehow the cause of it all, Campbell had him rehoused in the minister's home. Nevertheless, their problems continued unabated:

> the persons within the Family, suffering many losses, as the cutting of their Clothes, the throwing of Peits [measures of peat cut for fuel], the pulling down of Turff, the Feal from the Roof, and Walls of the House, and the stealing of their Apparel, and the pricking of their flesh and skin with Pins.

A presbytery meeting was held at the haunted house for the purpose of a 'solemn Humiliation' and Campbell was persuaded to bring his boy, Thomas, back home. Thomas claimed a voice had forbidden him to do so and he was sufficiently tormented thereafter to necessitate sending him back to the minister.

And so the weeks and months passed. On Monday 12 February 1655 'the rest of the Family began to hear a voice speak to them'. While Thomas was still lodging at the minister's, a conversation of some kind was had by other members of the Campbell household 'with the Devil'. The following day the minister arrived with Thomas and 'accompanied with some Gentle-men',[192] and, 'after Prayer was ended', an extensive dialogue was had with the spirit which evolved into a biblical debate and slanging match. In the local brogue it identified four or five Glenluce inhabitants as witches, one of whom Campbell declared 'was dead long ago'. The terrified boy, Thomas, was warned 'that if he did not depart out of the house, he would set all on fire'. The party searched vainly for the source of the voice, some suspecting it came from one or more of the other children in the family who were by now in bed. The 1685 account declared 'Several times hath he beat the Children in their Beds'.

'I am an evil spirit, and Satan is my Father, and I am come to vex this house' the demon declared before a partial manifestation of an entity was observed – 'there appeared a naked hand, and an arm, from the elbow down, beating upon the floor, till the house did shake'. The demon declared it was not his own but that of his 'father', Satan. By now much of the night had passed and the visitors decided it was time to depart. 'Let not the Minister go home', pleaded the demon, 'I shall burn the house if he goes'. They left but, shortly afterwards, the minister returned to sit with Campbell and his family who he forbade to refrain from engaging in further conversation with the demon but to pray instead. The demon was incensed:

> What? Will ye not speak to me? I shall burn the house, I shall strike the bairns, and do all manner of mischief.

Things settled down for a while and, from April until July, Campbell 'had some respite and ease' but thereafter 'he was molested with new assaults: and even their Victuals were so abused, that the Family was in hazard of starving'. In desperation he applied to the Synod of the

---

192 Named in the 1685 version: 'James Bailie of Caroline, Alexander Bailie of Dunraged, Mr. Robert Hay, and a Gentlewoman called Mistris Douglas, whom the Ministers Wife did accompanie'.

Presbyterian Church for guidance. A meeting was convened in October 1655 to discuss whether or not the family should be advised to abandon their home altogether. In February 1656 a committee was formed to meet at Glenluce which advocated prayer as the way forwards. This seems to have quietened things down before starting up again in the summer:

> the Devil began with new assaults, and taking the ready meat that was in the house, did sometimes hide it in holes by the door-posts, and at other times did hide it under the beds, and sometimes among the Bed-cloaths, and under the Linings; and at last, did carry it quite away, till nothing was left there, save Bread and Water to live by. After this, he exercised his malice and cruelty against all the persons of the Family, in wearying them in the night time, with stirring and moving thorow the house, so that they had no rest for noise, which continued all the moneth [sic] of August after this manner. After which time, the Devil grew yet worse, and began with terrible roaring, terrifying voices, so that no person could sleep in the house, in the night time, and sometimes did vex them with casting of stones, striking them with staves on their beds

On 18 September, at around midnight, a loud voice was heard declaring, 'I shall burn the house'. Three or four nights later one of the beds was set on fire. '[A]nd so', the account ends, 'he continued to vex them'. In 1685 Sinclair's addendum brought the tale to a more satisfactory conclusion:

> The Goodman lived several years after this in the same house: and it seems, that by some conjugation or other [an exorcism?], the Devil suffered himself to be put away, and gave the Weaver a peaceable habitation. The Weaver has been a very Odd man, that endured so long these marvelous disturbances.

8
STRANGE VOMITING AND A HAUNTED HOUSE: WELTON, NORTHAMPTONSHIRE, 1658

THE RECORD FOR this case, reproduced in Joseph Glanvill's *Saducismus Triumphatus* (1681), is a letter dated 22 May 1658, written by a Mr G. Clerke and sent to 'Mr M. T.'[193] Clerke was Gilbert Clerke, an eminent mathematician and presbyterian theologian ordained at Cambridge University. Clerke sent his letter from his home at Loddington, close to Kettering in Northamptonshire and twenty miles or so from Welton which is a mile north of Daventry. It is here that the haunted house in the story was to be found. Judging by his opening remark, Clerke sent his account because he was aware Henry More was interested in collecting such material: '[it] would fit Mr More gallantly' he wrote. The 1658 date indicates More's interest in collecting preternatural case studies long predated his contributions to Glanvill's posthumous work. Clerke declared he had 'first heard the story related to Sir Justinian Isham, by a Reverend Minister, of his own experience'. Isham (1610-75), a baronet, Member of Parliament for Northamptonshire in 1661, and scholar, would become an early member of the Royal Society soon after it was established in 1663. The previous year Clerke had dedicated a book on natural philosophy, *Tractatus de Restitutione Corporum* (1662), to Isham. He was keen for Clerke to visit the place but he was unable to do so at the time. However, a short time later he heard about the case again, this time from a friend he was visiting who happened to live near to Welton. The 'principal Man concerned in the story' one of his friend's relations and also someone Clerke himself was acquainted with. Since this friend needed to visit the man's home regarding some business concerning 'some Deeds of land', Clerke decided to go along with him in order to find out more about the case in question. He arrived at the

---

193 Glanvill, *Saducismus Triumphatus* (London, 1681), Relation XXII, pp. 434-7.

house on, or close to, May Day (1 May) 1658, less than a couple of weeks before he wrote his letter.

Having clarified his sources, Clerke proceeded in his letter to tell the tale. The 'principal Man' was named Moses Cowley, a respectable landowner in Welton. He and his wife, we are assured, were 'very civil and orderly people'. He lived close to his mother, Mrs Cowley, a widow who shared her home with her widowed daughter-in-law, 'Widow Stiff', and her two daughters. The account makes references to its hall, parlour, buttery, and at least one bedroom. It was in this house that the troubles began with a spectacular, but not unusual, account of what is sometimes termed 'strange vomiting' – the throwing up, in this instance by the younger of the two daughters, of indigestible material: five hundred or so 'Stones and Coals' over around a fortnight. Some, allegedly, were quite substantial, weighing up to 'a quarter of a pound'.[194] In the meantime this classic sign of supposed bewitchment in seventeenth-century England was accompanied by phenomena more akin to patterns of poltergeist behaviour.

Cowley told Clerke that they would find the bedclothes in an empty room thrown off the bed, and no sooner had he remade the bed and returned to the parlour 'they were off again'. When he resorted to placing a Bible on the bed, the bedclothes were pulled off again and the Bible was found hidden under the bedclothes in another bed. A 'strike [bundle] of Wheat standing at the Beds feet' was persistently knocked over, and items of furniture, 'Coffers and things', were moved about in such disorder 'as they could scarce stir about the Room'.[195] Meanwhile similar things were occurring in the hall when the family was in the parlour: 'things would be transposed in the Hall, their [spinning?] Wheel taken in pieces, and part of it thrown under the Table'. Elsewhere, 'In their Buttery their Milk would be taken off the Table, and set on the ground, and once a Panchion [large bowl] was broken, and the Milk

---

194 For more examples and my analyses and interpretations of 'strange vomiting' episodes see Andrew Pickering, *Witches of Selwood: Witchcraft Belief and Accusation in Seventeenth-Century Somerset* (The Hobnob Press, 2021); Andrew Pickering, 'Great News from the West of England: witchcraft and strange vomiting in a Somerset village', *Magic, Witchcraft and Ritual* 13, no. 1 (2018), pp. 71-97.

195 Strike of wheat: a measure of grain, probably, in this instance, contained in a measured bushel (bucket) and levelled at the top by a strike (stick).

A seventeenth-century woodcut illustrating the 'strange vomiting' phenomenon found in multiple seventeenth-century English accounts of the paranormal.

spilt'. Their beer was ruined when someone or something mixed sand into it, the salt was 'mingled most perfectly with Bran' and, mysteriously, a 'seven pound weight, with a Ring, was hung upon the Spigot [tap of a barrel]' by unseen hands. Even when she tried locking it in a box, Cowley's mother kept finding her flax thrown about. Cowley himself saw a loaf of bread fall off the breadboard of its own accord, and one of the women's pattens [wooden shoes] 'rose up in the House, and was thrown at them'. On another occasion 'He heard the Comb[196] break in the Window, and presently it flew at them in two pieces'. Even more disconcertingly 'A Knife rose up in the Window, and flew at a Man, hitting him with the Haft'. A glass ink bottle was also seen to fly through the window, its stopper following moments later. Following

---

196 Probably a part of the opening mechanism.

these incidents 'every day [an] abundance of Stones were thrown about the House which broke the Windows'. A 'great many People' witnessed in one of the rooms, perhaps the bedroom with the 'strike of Wheat' at the foot of the bed, 'the Wheat thrown about amongst them'. Strangely, as in other poltergeist cases before and since, despite all this, 'no hurt was done' to any of those witnessing these phenomena in broad daylight.

When Clerke visited, he was shown broken windows and the places 'where the several particulars were done'. Attempts were made to find the perpetrators and 'some that had long been suspected for Witches were examined, and one sent to the Gaol' but, seemingly without making a confession or receiving a guilty verdict.[197] Regardless, Clerke was convinced of the truth of the affair, 'it having so much of sense, and of the day time, so many and so credible Witnesses beyond all cavil and exception'.

9
MR LLOYD'S STORY: BLEDDFA, POWYS, C.1659.

THIS CASE IS one that Henry More appended to John Glanvill's 'Relation XXIII' concerning the haunting of 'Old Gast's House' in Dorset [Relation 15 in this collection] in *Saducismus Triumphatus*.[198] More found it 'in Mr. Glanvill's Papers' in the form of a letter. Glanvill assured his recipient that 'he may rely upon it for truth' for he had it 'from a Person of Quality and Integrity in those parts', namely, 'the Parish of Blethvaugh, in the County of Radnor'. Here, 'some Two and Twenty years ago', the house of one Walter Meyrick was infested by a poltergeist. In his letter, Glanvill called it 'Mr. Lloyd's Story' after the justice of the peace from whom he received it. It was, we are assured,

---

197 Although Ewen listed the case in his famous compendium, he found no court or gaol delivery record to substantiate it; C. L'Estrange Ewen, *Witchcraft and Demonianism* (Heath Cranton, 1933), p. 456.
198 Glanville, *Saducismus Triumphatus*, pp. 443-44.

based on eye-witness testimonies Lloyd had of those 'that dwelt in the house'.

Radnorshire, part of Powys since 1974, is the name of the historic county in mid-Wales which borders the English counties of Herefordshire and Shropshire. Bleddfa (Blethvaugh) is about seven miles south-west of Knighton and lies amid the barren, mountainous slopes of Radnor Forest. In the brief account of the haunting of Mayrick's house we come across further instances of lithobolia: 'there were Stones flung down out of a Loft of great weight', and 'Men were struck down with Stones'. That they were not hurt in the process, More argued, 'shews plainly they [the stones] were not flung but carried'. This was another noisy entity which was capable of 'strange Tunable Whistlings in the Rooms, where none was seen to Whistle', and making a tinkling noise at night that sounded like the tapping of a frying pan 'with a little piece of iron'. When the family returned from church they found 'the Doors bolted or barred against them on the inside' despite 'nobody being within'. A purse containing 'two Gold Rings and Six and Four-pence' went missing, but, 'the Party complaining thereof' reappeared, dropping down 'from the top of a Room, which had no Room over it'. Most of the valuables had gone, 'only Four-pence' remaining. A pickaxe was used by unknown hands on a coffer containing 'a Bag of Money'.

This Welsh poltergeist was rather more prone to violence than most of its English counterparts. A woman 'sitting at Supper, was struck flat to the Ground' by 'an invisible Force', 'a Trencher was struck out of the hand' of a maid-servant, 'and a smart Box on the Ear given to another, no visible thing being near that did it'. One unfortunate man was 'beaten with two Staves black and blue, but none to be seen that thus belaboured him' even though it happened in broad daylight. Another man was 'struck down with a Stick by day, while he tended the Goose roasting, which this invisible Striker seemed to have a plot upon'.

Sadly, that is pretty much all More had to share with his readers, and I am not aware of any other more substantial version of this very interesting story of an unusually avaricious and violent poltergeist.

10
ANDREW PASCHALL'S TROUBLESOME SPIRIT: SOPER LANE, LONDON, 1661

THIS STORY WAS told by a man 'of Judgement and Integrity', Andrew Paschall (1631?-96), a Somerset clergyman (from 1663), academic and correspondent of the Royal Society who had a particular interest in the creation of a universal language.[199] It is another one of those Relations in Joseph Glanvill's *Saducismus Triumphatus* (1681) added by his friend and posthumous editor, Henry More, who declared 'This narrative, though it was not among Mr Glanvil's [sic] Papers, but I found it by chance in mine own Study'.[200]

It is an eye-witness account dating from 1661 when Paschall, at the time a fellow of Queen's College, Cambridge and university preacher, was at his parental home in Soper Lane in the heart of the City of London.[201] Here his mother and father lived with Paschall's eldest brother, one of his sisters, the sister's 'young Maiden Gentlewoman Bedfellow', and at least one servant – a maid who slept in the same room as the two young ladies. This 'young Maiden Gentlewoman' seems to have been the focus of the poltergeist's attentions, or, in Andrew Lang's terminology, the 'medium', and by Paschall's own reckoning, the person 'who seemed to be principally concerned' in the poltergeist activity that followed.

One night she was disturbed by the sound of what seemed to be 'one walking in the Chamber' and 'by a noise made as of a long Gown, or some trailing Garment brushing and sweeping up and down the

---

199 A. J. Turner, 'Paschall, Andrew', *Oxford Dictionary of National Biography* (Oxford, 2004).
200 Glanvill, *Saducismus Triumphatus*, p. 448.
201 Soper Lane was badly damaged in the Great Fire just five years later (1666). Its church of St Pancras was destroyed and not restored but the lane itself was rebuilt and renamed Queen Street.

Room'. This was followed by 'a noise of clattering their Shoes under the Bed, with a scratching and tugging of the Mat under the bed likewise'. Awakened, either by the noise under the bed or by her bedfellow, Paschall's sister also heard the strange sounds beneath them and soon the servant was awake and listening, terrified, in her own bed. All this commotion, probably exacerbated by anxious whispers and gasps of alarm, was enough to bring Paschall's mother into the room from her parents' adjoining bedchamber. Although it was night-time she had not gone to bed herself since, we are told, they needed 'to prepare a Chymical water which required their being up all night'. Paschall's brother was also still awake and, hearing the disturbances in the rooms above his own, he too went up to find out what was going on. When a candle was brought into the room the noises ceased but, after the mother and brother had departed, 'the Chamber door (which shuts with difficulty) flew to with a great bounce, it being wide open before, it shook the Room, where [his] Mother was busied about the aforesaid Preparation'. This was followed by the hurling 'with a mighty force' of a shoe over the bed across the room. As a consequence, Paschall's brother agreed to stay with them in their room for the rest of the night.

The following evening, Paschall continued, 'as we sate at Supper, we all heard a great Noise above in the Chamber, at the end of the House, as it were flinging of Chairs and Stools about the Room, or removing of great Trunks'. Everyone went up to investigate but the noise had abated, and everything seemed to be in its regular order. Pashall's sister and her friend went to bed but he and his brother were resolved to stay up awhile in anticipation of further disturbances. Sure enough they were soon alerted by the girls knocking in the room above. On this signal they joined them to hear that the same sort of noises they had heard the night before had returned and, worse still, 'the Bed-cloaths upon them were often tugged and pulled, insomuch as they were fain to hold them hard with their hands to keep them from being pulled off'. The light of a candle once again quietened things down but, Paschall went on, 'we were no sooner out of the Chamber with the candle, but the noise under the bed, tugging of the Mat, pulling of the Bedclothes began again'. And then they heard a shriek – the alarm of the young gentlewoman who fancied something 'little and soft like a Mole' had got onto the bed and run across her. When the brothers returned with their candle, all, for the time being, fell quiet.

The next manifestation that night was the sound of 'a low whispering noise', mostly around the head of the bed. By now the parents had arisen and heard the same odd noises as their children. In the dim candlelight they reckoned they could see something, under the sheets, 'continually moving and stirring in one part or other of the Bed'. In a passage strikingly reminiscent of Glanvill's own subsequent investigation of a bedroom poltergeist a couple of years later [Relation 11], Paschall continued:

> [...] we frequently saw it heave and lift up the Cloths upon the Bed towards the Feet, in a little Hill or rising, which both my Brother and I often clapt our hands upon, perceiving it to move, and withal to make a little clacking noise, which cannot any more than the former whispering be exprest in Writing. We could not perceive any thing more than the Cloths, as often as we saw them so moved and heaved up.

As a precaution, the shoes in the bedroom - potential projectiles - had been placed on what is described as the 'Bed Tester' which implies it was a four-poster bed with a canopy. While they were talking, one of these flew off and hit Paschall lightly on the head, and 'another came presently tumbling down after it'. Meanwhile their young visitor, in the bed, continued to complain of the sensation of her mole-like intruder crawling over her. The moment the brothers left the room she cried out after them having felt something tugging 'a Mantle about her'. Paschall returned into the room to assist, and he too felt the mantle being pulled by some unseen force. Both brothers sat by candle-light in the room for the rest of the night. Despite their presence, the bedclothes, periodically, continued to move about the young guest's feet, the mat under the bed was pulled about, and the mysterious whispering sound was heard. Paschall summed up, 'There was scarcely any of us, especially she her self, that did not Conjure that Whisperer, by the most Sacred Names, to speak out and tell us its intent, but nothing was to be seen, nor any answer made'.

The following night the family's young visitor 'resolved to change her Chamber, to try if the disturbance would follow'. Paschall's sister joined her and the two brothers, as before, remained downstairs listening out for any noise from above. Sure enough, they soon heard loud knocking summoning them back upstairs. This time there had been a clattering noise around the bedroom door followed by further clattering sounds under the bed, more pulling of bedclothes, and spooky whispering. The brothers, once again, stood guard for their sister and her companion through the night. Towards midnight 'that thing which came into the Bed before, came now so often, with such ungrateful skippings up and down upon her, that she often shreekt and cryed out'. She claimed to have had the horrible experience, several times, of this 'cold and very smooth' entity climbing into the bed near her feet then running, all over her, all the way up to her head. Once, in this most intimate of settings, lying in bed in the dark, she asked Paschall to 'clap [his] hand upon her back near her shoulder Blade, as feeling it just then come thither'. He felt what seemed to be 'a cold blast or puff of Wind' blowing on his hand as he did so. Meanwhile more whispering was heard at the head of the bed and further vain attempts were made to get it to get it to talk and explain its purpose. When Paschall 'spake to it very carefully to speak out or whisper louder [...] it hissed out, much louder than before, but nothing intelligible to be heard'. Eventually Paschall's mother joined them from her room next door, to do what she could, by praying at her bedside, to calm the terrified girl. This proved to be what was called for: 'it pleased God within a short time after to remove all those noises, and that which disturbed her'. 'After that night' Paschall concluded and as far as he was aware, 'there hath [not] been any thing of that nature heard in the House'.

More in his review of the case, declared, 'This troublesome Spirit I suspect to have been the Ghost of some party deceased who would have uttered something, but had not the knack of speaking so articulately as to be understood'. Clearly, despite the theological repudiation of the concept of Purgatory in Protestant England, belief continued in the possibility of the spirits of the dead lingering in the present,

11
MR MOMPESSON'S GOBLIN: TIDWORTH, WILTSHIRE, 1662-63

IN THE WINTER of 1662–63, the vicar of Frome in Somerset, soon-to-be Fellow of the Royal Society, Joseph Glanvill, in the company of one Mr Hill, visited the home, thirty-four miles away, of John Mompesson at North Tidworth (then sometimes known as Tedworth) on the edge of Salisbury Plain, a few miles north-east of Amesbury in Wiltshire. Here he spent a night during which he witnessed various forms of what would now be called poltergeist activity associated with the so-called 'Demon of Tedworth', the most famous episode of its kind in early modern England. These events caused such a stir at the time that the king, Charles II, had it investigated by a royal committee. The evidence for this case is exceptionally abundant. Glanvill's experiences, and those of his companion, were first published in his *A Blow at Modern Sadducism in some philosophical Considerations about Witchcraft* (1668), and another early version of his account, probably written around the time of their visit in January 1663, survives in the State Papers. Michael Hunter has concluded, that, since it ended up in the State Papers, the implication is that 'it was sent to court, perhaps with a view to arousing interest in the affair there'. Hunter continues, 'Although the author of the paper is not identified, and although the extant copy is not in his handwriting, a strong candidate for its authorship is none other than Joseph Glanvill, since various aspects of the author's experiences in the children's bedroom as reported in this paper recur in almost identical autobiographical terms in Glanvill's published account of the case.'[202] Better still, a remarkable, extensive contemporary correspondence and related papers concerning the case, mostly written by Mompesson, survives. These have been, collated, expertly analysed, and published by Hunter.[203]

---

202 Hunter, 'New Light', p. 325.
203 Hunter, 'New Light', pp. 311–53.

The earliest of numerous subsequent printed works concerning the case appears to be a ballad by Abraham Miles, *A Wonder of Wonders; being a true Relation of the Strange and Invisible beating of a Drum, at the House of John Mompesson, Esquire, at Tidcomb in the County of Wiltshire*, of which a single copy is known to have survived, and for which Hunter has provided a publication date of February 1663.[204] In April that year it was also reported in two journals, the *Mercurius Publicus* and *The Kingdom Intelligence.*[205] The information it contains, Hunter has proposed, probably came from recent 'oral testimony'.[206] Appearing in the days or weeks immediately after Glanvill's visit to Tidworth, it indicates he and his travelling companion were just two 'Gentlemen of quality' among 'many hundreds who have gone from several parts to hear this miraculous Wonder' – the phantom demon. They also came in the hope of seeing 'Stools and Chairs [dancing] about the Rooms'. Providential as well as entertaining, the ballad presents the Tidworth 'wonders' as a sign that 'Dooms-day' is nigh, a common sentiment in the literature of this deeply unsettled time. A 'hellish Fiend', presumed to have an association with some obscure unidentified witch, is blamed for the disturbances, the most shocking of which is that of the Mompesson children pulled out of bed by the hair by an unseen hand.

The story begins in the middle of March 1662 when Mompesson was visiting the neighbouring village of Ludgershall. Mompesson was a landowner and he had certain responsibilities as both an excise officer and an officer in the militia. His affairs had taken him to the bailiff's house in Ludgershall and there he heard the beating of a drum. His enquiries revealed the drum belonged to one William Drury, a local man from Uffcott, about fifteen miles to the north in the Vale of the White Horse beyond Marlborough. Drury, it seems, had been making a nuisance of himself, making a racket with his drum, after he had been refused a hand-out to which he claimed he was entitled. He had first approached the parish constables for money, presenting them with official-looking documentation in support of his claim which the bailiff suspected was forged and, so far, no payment had been made. Mompesson now intervened, instructing a constable to bring Drury to

---

204 The ballad sheet, in accord with the Julian calendar, is dated February 1662.
205 Hunter, 'New Light', pp. 314-15.
206 Hunter, *Decline*, p. 90.

him. The drummer was picked up in a nearby alehouse and, drum slung from his shoulder, set before Mompesson. On what grounds, he demanded, and by whose authority had he claimed payment in the parish? Drury duly produced his pass and a warrant signed and sealed in the names of local dignities, Sir William Cawley of Burderop and his supposed captain, Colonel Ayliff of Grittenham. These individuals were real enough but, alas, Mompesson, who knew them well, saw at once their handwriting was not that on the papers he now had before him. Commanding Drury to take off his drum, he instructed the constable to present him to a local magistrate at the earliest opportunity. Drury promptly confessed to his subterfuge and that he was not the colonel's drummer, and that he had had the warrant forged. He begged Mompesson for the return of his drum, the means, presumably, by which he scraped together a street performer's meagre living. Mompesson informed him he would have the return of his drum only on condition that the colonel, whose drummer he pretended to be, could vouch for his previous good character. He then departed, leaving the drum with the bailiff and the drummer in the hands of the constable who, subsequently, let him go.

The 'Drummer of Tedworth'.
Abraham Miles, *A Wonder of Wonders; Being A true Relation of the strange and invisible Beating of a Drum, at the House of John Mompesson, Esquire, at Tidcomb in the County of Wilt-shire* (London, 1663)

About a month later, in mid-April, shortly before Mompesson made a trip to London, the bailiff sent the drum over to his house in Tidworth. His business in the capital kept him away from home for a couple of weeks or so. When he returned on 4 May he was alarmed to hear his wife's account of a recent great disturbance in the house when, in the middle of the night one can presume, the household was awoken by crashing noises that sounded like the work of thieves. Whether they came from within or outside the house is unclear, but no unwanted intruders were discovered and, it seems, nothing was taken or damaged. Most importantly, no-one was injured or otherwise harmed by whoever, or whatever, had been the cause.

For the next three days and nights all was well but on the night of 7 May loud noises, this time hollow sounding thumps, were heard again. Mompesson rose from his bed and, armed with a brace of pistols, searched his property but found nothing. One thing he was sure of however - this was not how a regular thief behaved. He must seek some other explanation.

From this point on the thumping noise was heard more frequently and in a regular pattern. For five nights running they would be disturbed by loud thumps outside. After three nights of quiet it would return and the cycle would be repeated with such regularity they were able to predict when it would start up again. The perpetrator of the noise had an irritating habit of setting to work just as Mompesson and his wife were going to sleep, whether they went to bed early or late. This surely was not the random effect of gusts of wind on barn doors or the like. Someone surely was observing them, waiting for bedtime candles to be gutted. Someone, perhaps, with inside knowledge of their evening and night-time activities.

So it continued for the rest of the month until, in early June, it began to be heard inside the house. And the room in which it was first heard was Mompesson's mother's, the very room in which Drury's drum had been stored. It is not clear if the strange hollow thuds that kept the family awake at night had already been linked to the drum but, from this point on, the association is unequivocal. There can be no doubt whatsoever that the drum really was heard in the house in 1662: it was a favourite plaything of Mompesson's children who had plenty of fun bashing it, indeed, it was for this very reason that their grandmother, who enjoyed their company, had it in her room. The distinctive hollow thumps continued to be heard for four or five nights in seven, sometimes for two hours at a time and making such a din the windows and beds would shake. As before it would start off half an hour or so after they had retired to bed but now its arrival was announced with what Mompesson described as 'a perfect hurling in the air over the house'. Wild weather however cannot explain the drumming that would wrap up its nightly performance by beating out the pattern played by the drummer when the guards were dismissed. As a militia man, Mompesson admired the skill of his unseen drummer.

The drumming continued to emanate from his mother's room throughout the rest of June and July and on into August. Mompesson made his bed in his mother's room in order to keep an eye on the drum during its two-hour long performances. Did the skin of the drum flex as it reverberated? Probably not, for the sound was not always confined to the room in which the drum was housed. By way of an experiment, on several occasions family members prayed together in the room to see if it would have an effect and, while this did not prevent the drumming it did, at times, seem to coincide with a shifting of its music a short distance from the drum itself.

As summer moved into autumn the drumming moved beyond the grandmother's chamber to rooms above it. Other curious noises were also heard - the clatter of dried pease on floorboards, the sound of the shoeing of a horse, sawing noises, and more. Mercifully, as Mrs Mompesson went into labour before the birth of a further child, the disturbance lessened and then abated for the next three weeks while she regained her strength. For a time the family could even trust it was gone for good.

All this while, no doubt, Mompesson continued his search for the cause of the disturbances. We can presume he discussed the matter at length with his wife and mother, interrogated servants, and obliged all to be vigilant. Natural causes, no doubt, were considered for some of the noises but the drumming sound, which he was convinced by now was that of a tutored hand, called for the discovery of a perpetrator. If these drum rolls were indeed being produced *within* the house that perpetrator, surely, was among them. One of the children? A servant? Suspicion, perhaps even accusation, must have heightened tensions between members of the household.

Their troubles began again around the end of October, some three weeks after the child was born, and this time they were even more dramatic. On previous occasions the boom of the drum had been great enough to rattle windows and shake beds and now the bedsteads in which his the youngest of his other children slept became the focus of these phenomena. These shook with such violence that it seemed they must break, and yet, though the adults grasped the bed and

The haunting by demons of the Mompessons' home, 1662-63. Detail from William Fairthorne's frontispiece for the second part of Joseph Glanvill's posthumous *Saducismus Triumphatus* (1681), containing his collection of Relations.

felt it shudder as if struck by some mighty hand, none felt the blow directly. Meanwhile, for an hour at a time, the drum would sound out perfect renditions of marches Mompesson knew well: 'Roundheads and Cuckolds go digge, go digge' and other 'points of Warre'. This would seem to rule out the possibility of earthly tremors. Was someone playing a drum in an adjoining room? Did the beds shake because someone was beating the ceiling of a room below? Perhaps, but at around this time, if not before, it is clear Mompesson himself had abandoned the search for such rational, natural explanations. Ominously a new noise was now heard, seemingly coming from beneath the beds in which his children lay: the scratching sound, he suggested, such as something with iron talons might make. This thing, whatever it was, he considered the cause of the odd and alarming way in which the children seemed to be heaved up in their beds. Worse still, it followed the terrified children even as they fled from room to room. He knew what a demon looked like and they had iron talons; he had seen them before, perhaps in chapbooks relating accounts of witchcraft or, possibly, in surviving Doom paintings on the walls of churches before Cromwell's men had them whitewashed.[207] The sceptical modern mind turns to rats scurrying around under floorboards in creepy candle-lit bedrooms, the seventeenth-century mindset sympathetic to the possibility of corporeal manifestations of the Devil himself, was one more open to a demonic explanation.

The Mompessons' home stands no more. The detail of its design and construction is unknown but it is reasonable to suppose it was not far removed from that which graces the William Faithorne's famous illustration in Glanvill's *Saducismus Triumphatus* (1681) in which the best-known version of the story of the phantom drummer was preserved. This shows a conventional mid-century gentleman's home - a stolid stone and brick built three- or four- storied structure with four chimneys. Its eighteen front windows suggest a fairly substantial dwelling, one large enough and grand enough to house a gentleman, his wife, mother, several children, and a small retinue of live-in staff, with reception rooms, even guest bedrooms, to receive visitors. And Mompesson was to have a great many of these once word got out regarding his poltergeist.

Since the disturbances up to this point were mostly associated with the bedrooms in the middle part of the house, Mompesson decided to make up temporary beds in a garret room in the loft space above for the children who, one can suppose, were too scared to get much sleep in their haunted room below. Unfortunately, as so often seems to be the case with poltergeists, the entity seemed to be bound to the children it had latched onto as opposed to the room in which they formerly slept. On the fifth of November, early in the morning, while the children were in bed, loud noises were heard emanating from the loft. One of Mompesson's servants, perhaps sleeping in a neighbouring garret, was

---

207 The spectacular Doom painting at St. Thomas's in Salisbury, very close to Mompesson House where John Mompesson's eminent cousin lived in Cathedral Close, Salisbury, was whitewashed in 1593 and not revealed again until 1881.

soon on the scene. Here, he claimed, he witnessed the impossible. In the room he observed two boards of some description that were standing edge long rather than lying flat on the floor. Rather more remarkable was the fact that they seemed to be moving of their own accord. By now preternatural phenomena in the house were regarded among the household as the work of some invisible entity and, accordingly, the man spoke to it, commanding, 'Give me that board!' Amazingly it moved towards him but stopped short a yard short. 'Nay', he said as if training a dog, 'Let me have it in my hands!' and this time it came the remaining yard. The man then shoved it back across the floor and the routine was repeated, not just once, but twenty times. When the game was over the spirit departed, leaving behind an offensive sulphurous smell as it did so.

When he was told of this strange business Mompesson does not seem to have questioned the truth of the matter but instead chided his servant for being over-familiar with the unknown entity. The vile smell was Mompesson's greater concern and, for the first time, he wondered if he could continue putting up with his unwelcome visitor. After all, the stink of sulphur - fire and brimstone - was a pretty convincing sign of something diabolical.

The loft-bedroom plan having failed, the children were reinstated in their chamber below. The spirit, making a din, followed. That same night, having more of an idea of what he was dealing with, he called on the services of Mr Cragg, the local minister - probably John Cragg, a Cambridge-educated cleric. He led the household, together with many of the Mompessons' neighbours, in seeking solace and divine assistance in prayer at the children's bedsides. During their prayers the thing departed back into the loft where, presumably, it continued to be heard, but as soon as the prayer-group dispersed it returned to the bedroom and carried on making mischief. Now it put on probably its finest show yet, doing the things one would expect of a regular poltergeist - chairs moved, and the children's shoes were tossed over their heads. A bedstaff was thrown at Cragg yet when it hit his leg he hardly felt a thing.

Following these dramatic events, Mompesson sent his youngest children to lodge with his neighbours. The eldest daughter, aged about ten, was moved into her parents' bedroom which, for a month now, had ceased to be a focus of the disturbances. However, the moment she got into bed that evening the sound of the drum returned. And so it continued through the rest of November and on into December 1662. The intelligent spirit now communicated directly with the family by imitating their own raps and playing, on demand, any of the familiar drum tunes they might request.

At the start of December, the youngest children returned home. Wondering where best to accommodate them, Mompesson decided to make up beds for them in the parlour where the family tended to dine - one of the remaining rooms not yet plagued by the poltergeist. The drummer however followed them into their new bedroom. Knocking noises were accompanied by the more alarming sensation of having their night clothes tugged and their hair pulled. Convinced by now that 'the Devill has most malice, where there is most innocence', Mompesson was running out of options as to where he might find a safe haven for his children.

Despite Mompesson's prayers and commands, the demon would not show itself. Perhaps, he thought, Drury, the drummer, might be persuaded to speak on its behalf. Despite the fact that he was now incarcerated in Gloucester gaol on a charge of stealing pigs, Mompesson suspected he was somehow instrumental in the bizarre events in faraway Tidworth. This was more than a mere haunting, this looked like a case of witchcraft, a conclusion he shared with clerical men like Cragg and other 'persons of judgement'. As soon as he was released and returned to Wiltshire, Mompesson would pay him a visit. What puzzled and troubled Mompesson was the meaning of it all. Was it divine retribution on sinful men or a test of their faith in a providential God? He took courage from the fact that although the Devil was at large in his home, the mighty hand of God, so far, had prevented him from destroying his family. He remained steadfast in his determination to stay put and see it through, wherever providence might lead.

On 6 December 1661 Mompesson completed his account of events since the day he first heard Drury's drum back in March, and sent it to his wife's Wiltshire relation, William Creed, a Doctor of Divinity and, from 1660 until his death in 1663, a professor of Christchurch College, Oxford. Although a native of Reading, he acquired the rectory of Codford St Mary in 1645, twenty miles to the west of Tidworth, and from 1658 he held the neighbouring Stockton living. Another ardent royalist, the Restoration brought him rewards: in 1660 he was made an archdeacon of Wiltshire and a prebendary in Salisbury Cathedral. The Mompessons had met up with Creed fairly recently and now he seems to have requested a full account, amounting to over two thousand words, of the whole business. Mompesson asked Creed to show it to another Oxford man, Thomas Pierce (1622-91), the President of Magdalen Hall, who had recently purchased an estate in Tidworth. Mompesson hoped these learned associates and experts in philosophical and religious affairs might be able to provide answers to the grave questions that troubled him. He also shared the information with his worthy and recently knighted kinsman, Sir Thomas Mompesson of Salisbury, to whom the letter was initially sent. Sir Thomas read it carefully before having it posted to Dr Creed in Oxford. A postscript added a few more details including levitation episodes. Unnamed servants in the house, it seems, had claimed that they had had the frightening experience of being lifted at night to great heights, bedstead and all, and then let down gently back to the floor. Sometimes they felt a great weight on their feet as they lay in bed, candles failing to burn, and dogs failing to bark in response to sudden, loud and inexplicable noises. Sometimes the cacophony emanating from the house was so great it could be heard in the fields around and even woke the Mompessons' neighbours. Still, at least the poltergeist had taken to keeping reasonable hours - it was quiet at night but made an early start, drumming the household awake at five each morning. Almost as irritating as the spook was Mompesson's stream of uninvited visitors 'which have troubled me half as bad as the spirit'.

Sir Thomas's response to Mompesson was kindly and encouraging. He admired his 'Christian courage' and it is evident he had already offered John alternative accommodation (it is unclear as to whether his reference to 'my house' in relation to this referred to his own Salisbury home or another property in his possession). It is evident the case was already the talk of the town, or Sir Thomas's part of it at least, and he reiterated the common opinion that this was indeed the outcome of witchcraft, assuring him he was 'sorry to see what trouble that witch hath given you'. His acquaintance, Sir Edward Nicholas (1593-1669), had come across the like before when he was living in exile in France during the Interregnum. He was from Winterbourne Earls, just to the north of Salisbury and about ten miles south of Tidworth. A powerful and influential man, Nicholas had been among young Thomas Mompesson's guardians, and he served both Charles I and Charles II as Secretary of State. It was he who on 8 September 1658 gave Charles II and his court in Brussels the news everyone was waiting for: the death of Oliver Cromwell. It was on his advice regarding how to deal with a witch that John Mompesson seems to have based his next strategy.

As Christmas Day approached the mysterious drumming was rarely heard but, in its place for a short time, was the sound of what Mompesson described as 'jingling' in the next letter he wrote to Creed on 26 December 1662. One day at noon a neighbour had visited and had a chat with Mompesson's mother. Soon their conversation turned, of course, to the supernatural and the neighbour commented on stories of fairies she had heard regarding such things as their habit of leaving money in 'Maydens shooes'. Unfortunately, the Mompessons' fairy, or whatever it was, showed no such signs of benevolence, though, as Mrs Mompesson assured her guest, 'I should like that well if it would leave us some money to make us satisfaction for the trouble and charge it putts us to'. And that very night, in jest it must have seemed, the spirit started up its jingling noise – 'a Chinking of money all about the house'. 'We thought', Thomas wrote, 'we should have found all the house strewed with half Crownes in the Morning'. This noise too soon subsided but further 'unlucky trickes' lay ahead. On Christmas Eve, about an hour before daybreak, one of the Mompessons' little boys, got out of bed to go the toilet. As he did so, the pin securing the latch of door was pulled out and, as the door swung open, it hit him 'in a sore place of his heel' causing him to cry out. In the night on Christmas Day all of Mompesson's mother's clothes were strewn around her room and her Bible was hidden among the ashes in her hearth.

Prior to this, and in line with Sir Thomas's recommendation, John, one of Mompesson's serving men, 'a Clowne of great Courage but no great Witt, but of good conversation and sober', had offered to sleep in the most haunted room in the house. Mompesson gave him a sword to keep beside his bed and settled himself down to sleep in an adjoining room. Of this experiment Mompesson reported, 'there is scarse a night but there is a Conflict' between John and the spirit, 'sometimes John hath the best of it, and sometimes the Goblin'. The demon flung John's breeches and doublet around the room and hurled his shoes at him. John, with sword in hand, recovered his things but the spirit menaced him again as soon as he fell asleep, lying across him so heavily that he was unable to move for as long as a quarter of an hour at a time. Only after great excursion was John, now 'in a great sweat', able to free his hands in order to beat off it off. The noise of these nightly struggles was sometimes enough to awaken Mompesson sleeping in the room next door who sometimes sent for assistance despite his proud servant's determination to take on the spirit single-handed.

Visitors to the house reported similar occurrences. Some had the nightmarish experience of an invisible hand grabbing their own as they reached in the dark for the chamber pot. This essentially nocturnal visitor however desisted from further mischief in daylight.

Although Mompesson had had Drury's drum burned long before these developments, the drummer continued to bother him. Following the sessions at Gloucester, he interviewed him again, this time near Marlborough at Drury's Broad Hinton home, in the hamlet of Uffcott. He was particularly interested in Drury's alleged relationship with one Woolston Miller, the recently deceased vicar of Berwick Bassett. Miller, he discovered, had been investigated for magical practices, particularly those pertaining to the recovery of lost goods. Drury had been 'a reteyner to his house' and continued to call in on his widow after his death and consulted Miller's collection of 'gallant Bookes' from which he learned such things as fortune-telling.

By now Mompesson was considering moving out of his home due to the visits by that 'great concourse of people' that 'almost devoure me', the 'unrulynesse' of his servants who were taking advantage of the fact that Mompesson knew they would be hard to replace given the house's reputation, and his reluctance to leave his wife, children and mother to attend to important matters that might necessitate being away from home. However, refusing to be driven out by the devil, he determined to stay put. One of his recent visitors was a man in the service of Thomas Pierce who also wrote at least one letter concerning the affair to Mompesson around Christmastime 1662.

Meanwhile the demonic disturbances showed no sign of abating. Indeed, simultaneous episodes had convinced Mompesson the house was a rendezvous of more than a single spirit 'for there have been three at work at one time'. His sole consolation was that the Devil, that cunning entity so good at hiding his tracks and causing those of an atheistic inclination to doubt his existence, had revealed himself to those strangers who dared visit Tidworth's infamous haunted house. '[It] is strange to me that the Devill should have no more witt', he concluded in the letter he wrote to Dr Creed on 26 December, commenting that he had received a further three letters from 'persons of great quality' requesting opportunities to visit his home.

The latest phenomena included a 'tinging' sound in the chimney presaging the entity's arrival, and the appearance at night of a blue light. Mompesson's wife heard what sounded like someone coming up the stairs without shoes before she saw the light in her bedroom which glimmered for the best part of a minute. It was also seen four or five times in his children's room. Doors were seen opening and closing of their own accord and the rustling of what sounded like a silk dress was heard. One night his serving man was so terrified by the blue light that 'his haire stood on end'. The following night he persuaded a neighbour to sleep in the same room and he lit a candle in the chimney for further reassurance. Within a quarter of an hour the burning candle had parted company with its candlestick, never to be seen again.

Mompesson continued to be plagued by visitors. In a letter written on 4 January 1663. he mentioned a recent gathering that included Sir Thomas Chamberlain of Wickham in Oxfordshire (c.1635-82), and Giles Tooker, the son of a local Member of Parliament. One of the gentlemen in the party addressed the spirit as follows: 'Satan, if the Drummer set thee on worke, let us understand so much by giving three knockes and no more'. Three distinct knocks were heard soon enough but when the gentleman knocked again without an instruction in order to see if the entity would imitate him as it had done in the past there was no response. However, when he repeated his former question, this time inviting the spirit to respond with five knocks instead of three the assemblage was duly rewarded 'and then [it] ceased from knocking that night any more'. Whether or not this phenomena convinced Mompesson's visitors of the diabolical nature of the haunting is open to question. Mompesson admitted 'This I suppose is no evidence to a Jurie' and he fully appreciated the scepticism of those who had not witnessed the extraordinary phenomena.

Certain gentlemen who had travelled some distance to visit the haunted house were rewarded with mysterious knocking sounds which prompted them to search for 'any secret Angles or holes where any body might be put to make noises to deceive them, but found none'. To Mompesson's consternation his excitable visitors began calling on Satan to 'Doe this, and that, and Whistle if thou canst, or let us see where thou canst tell money, or make chaires dance'. Other than continued knocking they witnessed nothing out of the ordinary. However, two minsters who were also visiting the house 'assured them they had seen the motions of the chaires and stoles as reported'. They remained dubious, spoke of pulling up floorboards in search of the perpetrator of the knocking, and, in their discourse with the ministers, 'declared their diffidence of the being of Spirits' to the dismay, no doubt, of these men of the cloth, 'and so departed with some kind of suspicion that what they heard was onely a cheat or a fancy, all but one, who seemed to be well satisfied upon a particular observation he had made'. This episode encapsulated the thrust of the debate that would run through and beyond the era of the Restoration as learned believers and sceptics wrestled furiously with one another in numerous printed pamphlets and books regarding the legitimacy of their conflicting views of the world. Clearly Mompesson was unimpressed by both their behaviour and their scepticism, remarking, 'They were the onely persons that ever I observed went away with so much dissatisfaction, and whose carriage was of that nature, that I shall be more carefull how I admit strangers for the future'. There is no doubt regarding where *he* stood in relation to the argument regarding the certainty of spirits. The ministers on the other hand were his very welcome guests who supported him and his family in their prayers and fasting. There was some consolation at least in his conviction that the impious conduct of those 'uncharitable and misbelieving people' was an affront to God and they must expect 'an irreparable damage to their Estates' as a consequence. And such a conviction should be enough to convince others that he at least would not risk divine retribution by daring to invent tales of supernatural phenomena.

Another visitor around this time was one William Maton who seems to have lived in the neighbouring village of Belford according to evidence traced by Hunter. In a letter, dated Wednesday 6 January

1663, he wrote to his nephew, Francis Parry, 'a Scholar in Corpus Christi College in Oxford', he described his own experiences of the poltergeist. He affirmed he had heard it many times 'Drumming, Scratching, Threshing'. The previous Sunday, the day before Mompesson wrote of his recent and unwelcome guests, a voice was heard to say, repeatedly, 'A witch, a witch'. Maton also confirmed the spirit's willingness to act on command and that 'it will heave up the beds two foot from the boards' although whether he personally witnessed this, or for that matter, the ghostly voice, is unclear. What he saw and heard, including the discovery of Mrs Mompesson's Bible in the ashes of the hearth, were, as far as he was concerned, 'enough to convert an Infidel'.

Parry seems to have been in the area at the time and might well have visited the house at some point before, according to Mompesson, he returned to Oxford on Saturday 10 January. Mompesson's detailed record of events from 10 to 21 January, untitled and undated, is held in the Corpus Christi College collection, sent, one might suppose to one or both of the Oxford academics – Dr Creed and Francis Parry – who had taken such an interest in the matter. Early that morning, before daybreak, Mompesson was disturbed by the sound of drumming outside his bedroom which then moved on 'to the other of the house, where my Cosen St John of Lediard and Mr. Pleydell lay' another distant relation by marriage. Here the drummer played at their door and 'in the Aire four or five 'tunes' as opposed to, one supposes, random thuds. It sounds like the drummer, phantom or otherwise, was trained in the art.

The following day, Sunday 11, a smith was lodging at the house, sharing a room with 'my man', as Mompesson described him, probably the chap who had bravely taken on the spirit in single combat through the night on previous occasions (and an obvious suspect for those looking for a flesh and blood mischief-maker). The smith had a most disturbed night with the unpleasant recurring sensation of having his nose pinched with one of his own tools, 'a pairs of Smiths Pincers'. When his room-mate arose and reached for his hat an invisible force flung it to the other side of the chamber.

The next evening Mompesson's maids found they could not relight the candle that had gone out in the children's bedroom. Every time they struck the steel and flint, 'the Spirit sitting at the bedshead' mocked

Frontispiece to Thomas Addison's comedy *The Drummer: Or, The Haunted-House* (1716).

them in some unspecified way before they eventually succeeded.

The spooky night-time visitor left them alone through the night of Tuesday 13 January, but when Mompesson arose early in the morning to prepare for a trip to Sarum (Salisbury), as he dressed, he heard 'a great noise below where my Children lay'. He seized a pistol (one can suppose he kept one with him at all times under the present circumstances) and went immediately to his children's chamber 'where there was a voice crying a witch, a witch, as once before, and the chaires jumbling together'.

On the Wednesday night all the house except the cockloft was quiet. The following night, when Mompesson and his wife had just gone to bed, 'the chaire at my beds feet rocked very hard up and downe, and it knocked very hard upon the boards'. As soon as Mompesson got up and lit a candle, the disturbance ceased. The demon was back again on the Friday. One of Mompesson's daughters, who seems to have had a bed in her parents' room at the time, became the poltergeist's target while her father was visiting a neighbour. In the dim candlelit chamber the 'bedtick' – a bag containing bedding of some kind – was seen to move about as if something animate had climbed inside, the entity was heard to move from one side of the bed to the other, and the young girl lying there was heaved upwards. This commotion lasted for around two hours. Perhaps the most frightening manifestion was the accompanying sound of panting 'like a dog out of breath'. At some point Mompesson returned and swords were drawn but the danger of hurting the child prevented the watchers from cutting down the invisible demon in its tracks as it dashed around and under the bed.

On Saturday 17 January, when their daughter went to bed, she was accompanied by a female bedfellow, either a sister or a young maid-servant, who had been briefed to alert them to any disturbances by knocking on the floorboards with a bedstaff. The moment the panting was heard again the girl knocked twice before the staff was grabbed out of her hand and hurled across the room. Her parents, downstairs with some neighbours at the time, ran up to investigate. As soon as they entered the room, Mompesson recounted, 'we […] smelt a bloody, hot, ill smell, and the roome though without fire was very hot, and the children in the bed in a great sweat that it run down their faces, and sweat so violently that we durst not remove them out of the bed, and the greatest heat was about their bed and in it'. They heard panting and scratching sounds which seemed to emanate from the bed and witnessed the 'heaving up of bedclothes' during the next hour and half before 'at last it went into the next chamber where it knockt a little and seemed to rattle a chaire'. Over the next two evenings the performance, bar the 'ill smell', was repeated. The following night, on Tuesday 20 January, the objectionable stink returned together with more quiet panting, by now sometimes resembling 'the palpitation of the heart', and the frequent sensation 'we could plainly feel' of the room seeming to shake.

On the Wednesday things calmed down and little was heard. But 'the last night', by which Mompesson seems to have meant Thursday 22 January, further over-night guests – Mr Bennet of Salthrop in Wroughton, Wiltshire, his serving man and another gentleman – experienced various spooky happenings once in bed including the rattle of the drum, the rustling sound of a silk dress, ghostly words spoken, and the hiding of a silver spoon. Most startling must have been the discovery that 'every thing in the chamber' was 'piled up in the chimney'. Altogether the poltergeist 'was very troublesome to Mr. Bennet' perhaps 'because he spoke so ill of the Drummer'. Incidentally, the drummer, William Drury, had been an occasional employee of Bennett's father, Sir Thomas, on his Salthrop estate.

~~~

GLANVILL'S VISIT TO Tidworth in 1663 can be fairly precisely dated by the evidence of a letter Glanvill wrote to the learned divine (and demonologist), Richard Baxter, on 21 January: 'I came yesterday from Mr Mompesson's house at Teidworth.'[208] His account, in its final form as it appeared in *Saducismus Triumphatus,* has been transcribed and transposed on numerous occasions from the later seventeenth century to the present day. It too, like the consideration of the case here, was

---

208 Hunter has noted: 'Although it lacks a year, the letter is addressed to a house where Baxter resided only in January 1663'; Hunter, 'New Light' pp. 311–53; Geoffrey K. Nuttall and N.H. Keeble (eds), *Calendar of Correspondence of Richard Baxter, Vol 2: 1660–1696* (Oxford: Clarendon Press, 1991), letter 710, 'From Joseph Glanvill 21 January 1662/3'.

built, for the most part, on Mompesson's letters concerning the affair.[209] It is of such pivotal importance in the history of the rise of the English poltergeist, it would be perverse to decline from relating, once more, Glanvill's own experiences in the haunted house.

The story of the 'Demon of Tedworth' is the first of Glanvill's relations in *Saducismus Triumphatus* and is told across seventeen pages.[210] The first seven pages sum up the history of the case up to the time of Glanvill's visit with his colleague, Mr Hill, towards the end of January. By now 'It [the poltergeist] had ceased from its Drumming and ruder noises before I came thither, but most of the more remarkable circumstances [...] were confirmed to me there by several of the Neighbours together who had been present at them'. Mompesson took Glanvill and Hill upstairs to his children's bedroom, where the poltergeist had taken to bothering them as soon as they went to bed. They had been alerted to the latest disturbance by a maid-servant at about eight o'clock. As the three of them went upstairs Glanvill heard 'a strange scratching' noise and, on entering the room, he 'perceived it was just behind the Bolster of the Children's bed, and seemed to be against the Tick [bedding fabric]'. This scratching he described as sounding like someone with long nails might make. At eight o'clock on a winter's night the room, presumably, was dark and dimly lit by candles.

In the bed lay Mompesson's daughters who were aged between around seven and eleven. Glanvill could see their hands above the bedclothes and was certain 'they could not have contributed to the noise that was behind their heads'. With their father in the room, and, by now, having grown accustomed to it, 'they seemed not to be much affrighted'. Glanvill went up to the bedhead and thrust his hand behind the bolster where the sound seemed to be coming from. Immediately it ceased but then started up in another part of the bed. When he removed his hand from behind the bolster it began there again. Next, Glanvill decided to see if he might be able to communicate with whatever was in the room with them. 'I had been told', he recalled, 'that it would imitate noises, and made trial by scratching several times upon the Sheet, as 5, and 7, and 10, which it followed and still stopt at my number'. He and

209 'the bulk of Glanvill's later account was based on Mompesson's letters to Creed'; Hunter, 'New Light', p. 326.
210 Glanvill, *Saducismus Triumphatus*, pp. 321-38.

Hill 'searcht under and behind the Bed, turned up the Cloaths to the Bed-cords, graspt the Bolster, sounded the Wall behind' but discovered nothing. Thus, Glanvill declared, 'I was then verily persuaded, and am so still, that the noise was made by some *Demon* or *Spirit*'.

After half an hour or so of scratching, it now seemed to go 'into the midst of the Bed, under the Children, and there seemed to pant like a Dog out of breath very loudly'. When Glanvill placed his hand on that part of the bed he felt it 'bearing up [...] as if something within had thrust it up'. He felt among the bed clothes and searched under the bed for a dog or a cat, or some other living thing in the room, but found nothing. The 'panting' noise continued and with such intensity 'that it shook the Room and Windows'. For the next half hour, while Hill and Glanvill remained in the room, this vibration effect continued and, they were later told, for at least as long after they had returned downstairs. Meanwhile Glanvill reckoned he saw something like a rat or a mouse 'moving in a Linnen Bag that hung up against another Bed that was in the Room' but he could find 'nothing at all in it'. 'There was', he confirmed, 'no body near to shake the Bag, or if there had, no one could have made such a motion, which seemd to be from within, as if a Living Creature had moved in it'.

That night Glanvill and Hill slept in the room 'where the first and chief disturbance had been'. They slept well but were both awoken early in the morning 'by a great knocking just without our Chamber door'. This is Glanvill's account of what happened next:

> I askt who was there several times, but the knocking still continued without answer. At last I said, *In the name of God, who is it, and what would you have?* To which a Voice answered, *Nothing with you.* We thinking it had been some Servant of the House, went to sleep again. But speaking of it to Mr. Mompesson when we came down, he assured us, that no one of the House lay that way, or had business thereabout, and that his Servants were not up until he called them, which was after it was day. Which they confirmed, and protested that the noise was not made by them.

Mompesson went on to tell them that the regular evening disturbances 'would be gone by the middle of the night, and come divers times early in the Morning about Four a Clock'. This was, Glanvill observed, probably around the time they had been awoken by the banging on their door.

Later that morning Glanvill was informed by his own servant that his horse 'was all in a sweat, and looks as if it had been rid all night'. On the ride home to Frome, he continued, 'after I had rid him a Mile or two, very gently over a plain Down from Mr. Mompesson's House, he fell lame, and having made a hard shift to bring me home, died in two or three days, no one being able to imagine what he ailed'. In the wake of his recent weird experiences in the haunted house, Glanvill concluded, 'This I confess might be accident, or some unusual distemper, but all things being put together, it seems very probable that it was somewhat else'.

Although the haunting would exercise both Mompesson and Glanvill for years to come, not least in the defending of their respective reputations regarding their claims, Glanvill's and Hill's visit marks the end of the chronology in terms of more or less dateable preternatural occurences in the Mompessons' home.

Meanwhile, early in 1663, Drury had been arrested again on a charge of stealing pigs and was sentenced to transportation. However, he managed to escape from the convict ship and acquired a new drum. Mompesson had the vagrant seized once more and the drummer found himself charged with witchcraft as well as pig-stealing. Drury was alleged to have admitted to a visitor while he was in prison that he was responsible for the disturbances, but the witchcraft charge could not be proved. For the pig-stealing he was transported to Virginia.

12
THE DEMON OF BURTON: WEOBLEY, HEREFORDSHIRE, 1670

In 1671, one 'C. W.' had a five-page pamphlet printed in London entitled *The Demon of Burton, or A true Relation of Strange Witchcraft or Incantations lately practiced at Burton in the Parish of Weobley in Herefordshire.* The frontispiece declared it had been 'Certified in a Letter from a Person of Credit in Hereford', dated 1 March 1670 (i.e. 1671) and attributed to 'J. A.' who claimed to have received his information 'from eye Witnesses of unquestionable credit, and reputation'. P. G. Maxwell-Stuart, who drew on John Ashton's *The Devil in Britain and America* (1896) in his summary of the episode, concluded 'we may be entirely justified in suspecting fraud as the source'.[211] The same, of course, could be said of any poltergeist cases recorded hundreds of years ago. However, this particular one has much in common with numerous other episodes across time and place. One striking feature is the orderliness of the spirit in neatly rearranging household objects – an unusual, but not unique, characteristic of poltergeist cases. Whatever was the cause of the mysterious apportments, it was not the work of a 'noisy ghost' – things were moved around behind locked doors in the dead of night without the crash and bang of other poltergeist tales. In accord with other cases of the sort there is an escalation in activity in this one from the trivial the more destructive. Since this is a seventeenth-century episode it is not surprising to find witchcraft was presumed to be the cause of the 'Hocus pocus Minor' and the ensuing *hocus pocus* 'Major'.[212] Alternatively, the phenomena can be interpreted as a series of unrelated events: the petty mischief of a resident poltergeist or domestic servant, the unfortunate disease of livestock, and malicious acts of arson.

The story is set in a farmhouse leased by Mrs Elizabeth Bridges who moved in, with at least one servant (a maid), around February 1670. The farm had recently been acquired from Thomas Tompkins, described as 'a decay'd yeoman', by William Briggs, a London linen-draper, and, presumably, a close relative of Elizabeth. Its exact location is unknown; extant old farmhouses from the period in the vicinity include Lower Burton Farmhouse, around three miles north of Weobley and

---

211 Maxwell-Stuart, *Poltergeists*, p. 144; Ashton, *The Devil*, pp. 60-64.
212 It has long been thought that the phrase 'Hocus Pocus', used to mimic a magical incantation, is derived from the sacred words *hoc est corpus* ('Here is the body') as stated by Catholic priests in the Eucharist ceremony, the sacred Holy Communion that focused on the miracle of transubstantiation: the transformation of bread to flesh and wine to blood.

six west of Leominster. Built in the seventeenth century, the listing for Lower Burton Farmhouse describes a (rebuilt?) timber-framed two-storey structure with brick and rubble infill with two storeys and a jetty.[213] Elizabeth's place however sounds like a largely unmodified 'hall-house' with open hall and hearth (and no mention of rooms above), and adjoining chambers with dedicated roles – a cheese room, a buttery, and so forth. On the other hand a reference to burned coals found on the premises implies it had a chimney. Outside there is an orchard, a vegetable garden, and a dairy. Soon after her arrival Elizabeth began to be disturbed by knocking at her door at dusk and early in the morning by someone or something that was not to be seen when she opened it. From the start of the account it was presumed to be the work of a demon-familiar acting on the whim of a witch. In the night she was troubled by the mewing and screeching of unseen cats and on successive mornings she found the stools and benches, tucked under the table the night before, placed neatly round the fire. When she baked several loaves and left them on the table overnight they too were found to have moved, seemingly of their own accord since she had locked up the house before going to bed. Somehow they had found their way into another room where they turned up in tubs and under bundles of clothes. Her cheeses and meats also moved from one room to another and, despite locked doors, sometimes being discovered outside in the orchard. The cabbage plants in her garden were pulled up and placed

---

213   Lower Burton Farmhouse, listed 1953, Grade II.

neatly in the shape of crosses and fleur-de-lis. She 'caus'd them to be set again' by whoever she had working in the garden. She also made sure the soil around the cabbage patch was finely raked but, despite the plants being pulled up on two further occasions, no tell-tale 'track or footstep' could be found.

Meanwhile, in her 'Cheese chamber', where she had several cheeses and a bag of hops, further curious things were happening. Somehow, overnight, and behind the room's locked door, 'the Cheeses were all laid in the Floor in several formes and the Hops all strewed about'.

Another night there was mischief in the buttery where 'several dishes of cold Meat left upon a hanging Shelf' were found, the next morning, neatly laid on a tablecloth on the floor, with one of Elizabeth's silver spoons beside each. Most of the meat appeared to have been eaten but at least none of the silverware had gone astray.

One morning Elizabeth's breakfast plans were ruined when the half of the roasted pig she called for was found to have been stripped to the bone. On another occasion a bowl of strawberries she had bought and 'set up in a pewter dish in her Buttrey' one Friday around midsummer disappeared overnight. She and her maid searched for the dish and strawberries all the following day without success. However, on the following Monday morning, when she got up, Mrs Bridges found the dish, empty, at the foot of her bed. Other irritating happenings included the unaccountable mixing of fresh milk with 'a quart of Vinegar in a Bottel' she had recently bought and left in the dairy. The vinegar had turned the milk and made 'a perfect Posset'.[214] And so it continued, with something odd happening most nights, for a month. Fine ash was spread around the floor around the locked doors of rooms but, as was the case with the finely raked soil in the cabbage patch, no footsteps of intruders were found.

Things took a more sinister turn when Elizabeth's cattle started dying of mysterious causes. A sow fell down dead after an episode of leaping about 'in several unusual postures'. And then, for several months, life on the farm seems to have returned to normal. Then, 'one night as the Tenant and her Maid were going to bed, and passing by the Hall', they were alarmed to find ablaze the 'the green boughs, tyed on the Posts,

---

214   A dish made with curdled milk.

after the Countrey fashion'. The fire was soon put out but it's cause remained a mystery; no candles had been lit and 'no fire had been made in that Room of a fortnight before'. Several neighbours had been alerted who came in and kept watch on the house for the rest of the night. Soon after a hay loft was set alight and most of the hay was destroyed as the barn burned. A while later a store of grain and 'a Mow [stack] of Pulse and Pease' were set alight, seemingly by the 'dead burnt Coales' discovered thereafter in the middle of the mow. Everyone agreed, we are told, that they 'could not be convey'd thither but by Witchcraft' although there is no evidence 'the Hagg' presumed to be responsible was ever identified.

These 'dreadful fires' were tackled and brought under control by the neighbours, afraid that they might spread through the whole village. As for Mrs Bridges, she had had enough and left. A 'valiant' Welshman who lived in the village, John James, decided to spend a night in the haunted house, armed with a basket-hilt sword and accompanied by a large dog. He was awakened in his bed in the middle of the night by 'a great knocking at the door' through which as 'many cats as he conceived came into his Chamber, broke the Windows, and made a hideous noise, at which the Mastiff howll'd and quak'd'. John's candle went out and, in a cold sweat, he fumbled about in the dark until he found the door 'and ran half a Mile without ever looking behind him, protesting next day he would not lye another night in the House for a hundred pounds'.

As had been the case at Tidworth ten years before, the haunting seems to have aroused a good deal of interest: 'hundreds of people, both Ministers, Gentlemen, and others, came to the House to see and hear the passages'.

13
THE RIDDLE OF A HOUSE DISTURBED: LONDON WALL, 1674

STRANGE AND WONDERFUL *News from London-Wall* is a five-page pamphlet printed in the city in 1674.[215] The setting once again is a haunted house – this time the home of 'a Gentlewoman of good credit and conversation' in an alley by London Wall. Here this well-to-do woman lived with her several 'very little children' and her sister. On 3 March 1674, her troubles began when she discovered 'several pieces of Linnen cut and mangled'. One of the children – a boy aged about five – was blamed and punished by being tied by the arm 'to a place in the kitchen' where his mother could keep an eye on him. However, when she went to one of the rooms upstairs she found 'several more thing cut and spoiled', seemingly *since* her little boy was confined in the kitchen. Realising he was not to blame, she set him free and made sure all the doors were kept open 'that she might (if possible) catch the party that did her this mischief'. Nevertheless a fine pair of gloves with a gold fringe, kept in a locked box, was found cut into tatters, and, before the following night more linen in the property went the same way. The following Sunday more of the same happened and, that night, 'a Gown, and other Apparel, both hers and her Sisters' were ruined 'and most of her Chairs all slasht to pieces, as with a knife'. Clothes locked away in chests and trunks were found 'laid in the same order they left them in, only cut in several places'.

On the Monday morning a washerwoman arrived to help clean the house. Three knives she had placed in a drawer of a dresser had

215 Anon, *Strange and Wonderful News from London-Wall, being A Fulland True Relation of a House miserably disturb'd ever since Friday the Third of the Instant April, where Bedding, Linnen, Apparel, and Household-stuff of great Value, have at several Times, both in the Day and Night, been Cut to Pieces by Invisible Means; Knives Removed out of a Drawer in the Kitchin, and scattered in the Chambers and Garret, and things fast lock't upon Trunks and a chests, Cut and Spoiled in an unheard of Manner* (London, 1674).

disappeared when they were looked for at dinnertime. After an extensive search, one of them turned up in the garret, one in another room, 'and the third they at last discovered in an excellent Bed, which cost above Ten pounds, and had scarce been used, on which it had done very mischievous execution, having cut three or four holes quite through the Clothes and Ticking, down to the very Feathers, every one as large as the Crown of a Mans Hat or bigger, and the pieces flung up and down the Room'. In addition, 'a pair of Stockings which the Sister had just finished, but not taken the Knitting-Needles out of them, were cut all along the very Toes up to the top, only hanging together there by one single thread of Worsted [wool], which was not cut'. It was noted at the time that this was a repeated behaviour: the care seemingly taken, except in the instance of the bed, to refrain from leaving the damaged items from being cut into separate pieces. Prized items, including 'much pure Linnen', 'rich Laces', and 'silk Petticoats' went the way of the stockings. Neighbours spoke of hearing weird noises emitting from the house on occasion, to which the woman and her sister were oblivious.

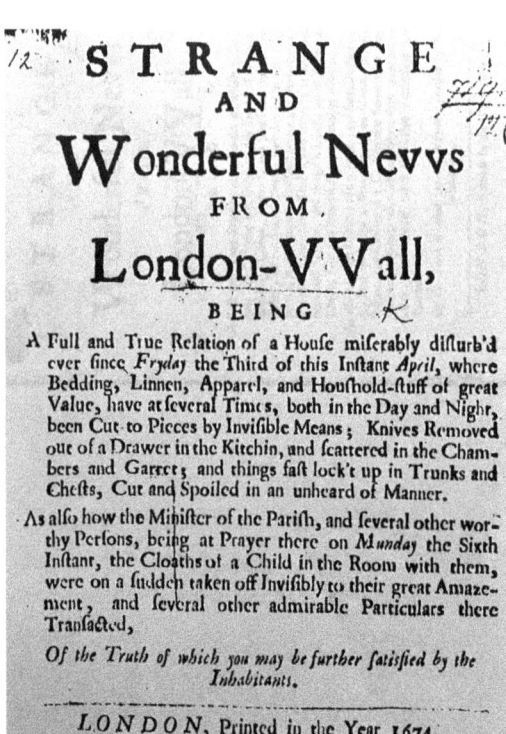

The mistress of the place turned to a local minister for support. He seems to have carried out what was, in effect, an exorcism: 'like a true Christian Pastor [he] came towards the evening with several other able persons to the House, and went to prayer'. In accord with many a modern horror movie their actions incurred a paranormal response. In this instance 'a little Child being in the Room with them, on a sudden all its Headcloaths were hurried off, and scattered up and down amongst them, and yet the Child never stirred its hands towards the Head, nor did any Creature touch it'.

It sounds like the exorcism might have worked since no further disturbances are recounted. Nevertheless, the woman's sister chose not to live in the property a moment longer and the woman herself had her best bedding and other items moved into an unoccupied house close by that she appears to have held in her possession. Meanwhile, everyone, including 'the several Persons of worth and credit' who visited her one Monday night to hear 'this Relation from her own mouth', remained perplexed as to how, despite locked doors and windows shut fast, these uncanny events might be explained – as the anonymous author of the pamphlet concluded: '[it] still remains a Riddle'.

14
'WHAT ARE YOU?': PUDDLE DOCK, LONDON, 1675

News from Puddle-Dock in London, printed in London at the end of March 1675, is a six-page pamphlet recalling the haunting of the home of Edward Pitts.[216] The available surviving copy is torn across the pamphlet at the bottom left of the front page and part of the text throughout is missing as a result – a casualty of the passing of time but not fatally so in as much as most of the document has survived. No doubt others of an ephemeral, throw-away, short print-run nature have not.

Puddle Dock, an important dock site on the Thames in its heyday, is now reduced to a single street bearing the name, an echo of times past, in the Blackfriars area of the city of London. The account begins

---

216 It is dated 1674 in accord with the unreformed calendar; Maxwell-Stuart gives it a 1676 date which seems unlikely since it does not tally with the 1674 date on the printed pamphlet, even after the change in dating systems is taken into consideration, however, the different versions of the Woodstock case of 1645 [Relation 5] highlight the danger of taking print-dates at face value; Maxwell-Stuart, *Poltergeists*, p. 145.

with the bold declaration 'If ever any year might justly be termed *Annus Mirabilis* or the *Wonderful year*, this will certainly deserve that Title'. These wonders it goes on to describe as unnatural occurrences in the natural world: the birth of abnormal babies and beasts, extreme weather events, and 'the Devil himself [...] let loose amongst us'. Natural disasters with supernatural causes that a sinful people should take heed of. The year described covered the period from the end of March 1674 to March 1675, the month of the events in which the haunting occurred. 1674 had started with severe floods and blizzards in parts of Britain. A bad harvest designated it a 'famine year' and there were further great floods, this time in the Midlands, in May. The gales in some parts in December were exceptionally severe and the New Year coincided with an earthquake in Alrewas in Staffordshire (4 January 1675).[217] Meanwhile, London had been hit hard by a smallpox epidemic in 1674.[218]

In the manner of the typical poltergeist case, this one starts with low-key episodes of oddity which, over the course of '15 or 16 Nights', swiftly build to the more dramatic. The fact that Pitts is referred to throughout as 'Mr. Pitts' implies he was 'respectable' – a 'gentleman' perhaps but one of modest means. His house is comfortable but, as one might expect in the cramped conditions of the City, not large, and seems to have comprised a parlour and kitchen on the ground floor and two bedrooms upstairs. There is no reference to servants. Each night, after his wife and children had gone up to bed, he made sure the doors to the parlour and kitchen were shut tight before retiring himself. The first development was the discovery each morning that the doors to the parlour and kitchen had opened, seemingly of their own accord, during the night. His attempts to secure the doors by taking a rope and fastening it 'to the handle of the door, and from thence to a nail on the stairs' appears to have been ineffectual in preventing the allied and even more disconcerting phenomenon of 'his Goods in these Rooms' being 'removed from one place to another in a most strange manner'. The pewter ware stored on shelves in the kitchen would be found elsewhere

---

217   J. M. Stratton, *Agricultural Records, A.D. 220-1977* (John Baker, 1978), p. 55.
218   Olga Krylova, David J. D. Earn, 'Patterns of smallpox mortality in London, England, over three centuries', *PLOS Biology* doi: 10.1371/journal.pbio.3000506, 27, accessed 11/03/2024.

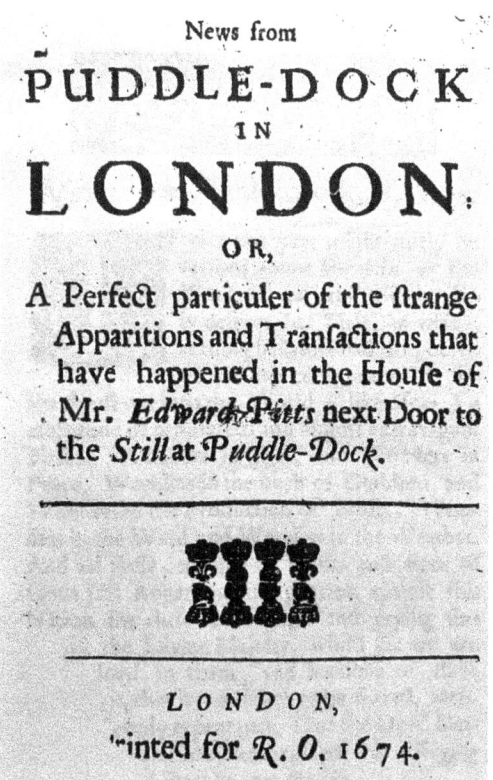

News from
PUDDLE-DOCK
IN
LONDON:
OR,
A Perfect particuler of the ſtrange Apparitions and Tranſactions that have happened in the Houſe of Mr. *Edward Pitts* next Door to the *Still* at *Puddle-Dock*.

LONDON,
Printed for R. O. 1674.

in the room, and the contents of a box of candles would be found similarly scattered, some placed in candlesticks, others laid in patterns, two by two.

After a couple of weeks of these disturbances, the Pitts were in for an even greater shock. One Sunday evening the family prepared for supper in the kitchen. The fold-up table 'was brought to the fire side; upon which the Meat was set'. Edward took a loaf of bread from the dresser and placed it on the table. As he began cutting it he noticed for the first time, on the same dresser, 'a great thing like a Catt'. Surprised and 'a little affrighted', he called out to his wife, 'here's a Catt, I never saw a Catt in this house before'! The cat, or whatever it was, equally alarmed one might suppose, 'seemed to slide off the Dresser, giving a thump on the Boards, and so vanished away'. Pitts' fifteen-year-old daughter was the only other member of the family who saw it. Nevertheless, by the time this part of the story reached the pamphleteer, it was said to be 'as bigg as any Mastiff Dog' and onlookers 'could not perceive that it had any Leggs'. An expanded shaggy cat story with a perfectly rational explanation perhaps. The mysterious cat episode though is an appendage, and one without any obvious connection to the poltergeist activity on which the story is built.[219]

---

219 Maxwell-Stuart's single sentence reference to the case starts with the cat element and delegates the rest to 'some poltergeist phenomena' which skews the significance of the latter but probably reflects accurately how the seventeenth-century reader/listener would be most likely to recall this one among so many other tales of poltergeist

That night, at midnight, they heard the night-watchman call out 'Have a care of your light!' alerting the locals that someone in the neighbourhood had left a candle burning in the city which had been devastated by the Great Fire just eight years before. Certain they had extinguished their own candles before going to bed, the Pitts assumed it was someone else's fault but, since they were already awake given that this was 'the time of the night that they used to be disturbed with what it was that haunted the house', Edward decided he should get up and double-check. However, as he related to the author of the pamphlet, he found 'he had no power to stir'. Assuming he was too scared to go downstairs to investigate, his wife offered to go with him, but he assured her he could not rise, much as he wanted to. That night, he went on to tell the narrator, he saw 'a great light in his Chamber 6 several times' which 'diminished by little and little till all his Room was dark, and then of a sudden he had as much Light if it been a clear day'. The next morning, as usual, he rose and made his way downstairs to see what had occurred overnight. He found the door to the kitchen wide open and 'his Parler door was off the Latch a little ajar, barricadoed with a great 2 handed Chair'. Thrusting the chair aside he opened the door and went into the room. Inside 'upon the Table there he found a great Wooden Sand-box, upon which was 2 snuffs of Candles burnt to Ashes'. A third candle alongside the box had caused it to char as it burned, without, thankfully, setting it ablaze. This explained the smell of burning Mrs Pitts had noticed in the house before her husband's discovery. Most mysteriously, 'This Sand-box Candlestick Mr. Pitts had never seen before, nor had he ever been master of such a one in his Life'. Even more disconcerting must have been his finding, on the table upon which the sand-box had been placed, 'two Splinters of Wood' carefully laid in the shape of a crucifix. The three shorter ends of the cross were cleft and in each a piece of paper with religious acclamations printed on both sides. A chair was found, drawn up beside the table and the texts, which suggested someone had sat down and studied them closely.

'This night, March 16', the pamphlet ends, 'Mr. Pitts intends to have some people to sit up, that may speak to any thing that shall appear, and to demand in the name of the Father, *what are you?*'.

---

activity; Maxwell-Stuart, *Poltergeists*, p. 145.

15
OLD GAST'S GHOST: LITTLE BURTON, DORSET, 1677

Relation XXIII in Henry More's compendium of Joseph Glanvill's demonological texts, *Saducismus Triumphatus*, concerns a poltergeist episode near to a place called Leigh.[220] It details the haunting of 'Old Gast's House of little Burton' and Glanvill received the account in 1677 from James Sherring, an eye-witness. The precise location of these places is not provided but More concluded in his editorial commentary on the case, 'it was in the very County in which Mr. Glanvill lived' – in other words, Somerset.[221] As More knew, 'there are Burtons more than one here, and also Leighs'. Tantalizingly, there is a Leigh Common close to Glanvill's former living at Frome, and, within a couple of miles of this is the village of Bourton. These places are in the immediate vicinity of the infamous accounts Glanvill had received from the local magistrate, Robert Hunt, of the Selwood Forest witch covens and sabbat meetings with the Devil in the immediate vicinity of the Somerset towns of Bruton and Wincanton.[222] However, his supposition seems to have been incorrect. Close scrutiny of place-names and people's names in Sherring's account, in conjunction with maps and parish registers, reveals, beyond reasonable doubt, these events took place, not in Somerset, but in the neighbouring county of Dorset.[223] Little Burton lies within the parish of Long Burton, now known as Longburton, three miles south of Sherborne and four miles north of Leigh. The parish records list both Gasts and Sherrings, including a James 'Shirring', son of James, who was baptized in Long Burton in 1680, three years after the account of the case was written by his namesake. William Sherring, also with a father called James, had been baptized there back in 1665. James Sherring of

220 Glanvill, *Saducismus Triumphatus*, pp. 438-42.
221 Henry More, 'Advertisement', Glanvill, *Saducismus Triumphatus*, pp. 442-44.
222 Glanvill, *Saducismus Triumphatus*, Relations III-VI, pp. 345-72.
223 S. D. Tucker places it in Somerset; Tucker, *The Hidden Folk*, p. 241.

Long Burton married Alice Cuffe in Henstridge on 26 January 1663/4. This then is a Blackdown Vale history, the setting for much of Thomas Hardy's *Tess of the d'Urbervilles*, rather than a part of the history of its neighbour, Selwood Forest. It does, however, reinforce the argument that this part of England was of central importance in the struggle to prove the existence of (demonic) spirits in the second half of the seventeenth century.[224]

Old Gast shared his seemingly haunted home, in which things 'were thrown about and broken, to their great damage', with his two granddaughters, 'one of them about twelve or thirteen years, and the other about sixteen or seventeen'. His house seems to have been a humble one with a hall downstairs and at least one chamber above. There is no mention of servants or additional family members beyond the granddaughters. On the first night Sherring was at the house he had the company of two men, Hugh Mellmore and Edward Smith. The first odd thing to occur was the apport of a bowl of soapy water that somehow made its way from the kitchen, through the room they occupied, and on to a room upstairs. The first indication they had that it had been moved was when they heard the sound of splashing water and, on going up the stairs to investigate, a couple of wet cloths were thrown at them. In the chamber above they found the bowl of water, 'some of it sprinkled over'.

'The next thing that they heard the same Night', Sherring continued, 'was a terrible noise as if it had been a slat of Thunder'. Worse was to follow. Gast's granddaughters, sharing a bed, were terrified by a 'great scratching about the Bedsted, and after that a great knocking with a Hammer against the Beds-Head'. On hearing their cries for help the men rushed upstairs and, in their room, found a hammer, previously 'lockt up fast in the Cupboard', on the bed , 'and on the Beds-head there were near a thousand prints of the Hammer which the violent strokes had made'. The girls told them they had been scratched and pinched in bed 'with a hand [...] which had exceeding long Nails'. This is horrific – someone or something in the dead of night sneaking into a room

---

224 *cf.* Andrew Pickering, 'The Devil's Cloyster: putting Selwood Forest on England's seventeenth-century witchcraft map' in Richard Nate and Julia Klüsener (eds), *Remembered Places: Perspectives from Scholarship and the Arts* (Königshausen & Neumann, 2019), pp. 35-54.

occupied by two sleeping girls who are awakened by the battering of the headboard above them and then feel a hand clawing at them under the bedcovers. Apparently, that night 'many other things of the like nature' occurred.

The second night Sherring stayed in the haunted house he was accompanied by one Thomas Hillary. Further apports occurred: a pair of tongs Sherring had used to hold a coal to light his pipe, found their way to a room upstairs and a pair of Gast's shoes upstairs swapped places with a pair of one of the girls' shoes left beside the fire downstairs. More ominously, 'The same Night there was a Knife carried up into the Chamber, and it did scratch and scrape the Beds-head all the Night, but when they went up into the Chamber, the Knife was thrown into the Loft'. Things from the room below were thrown at them as they went upstairs, and when they went downstairs 'the Old Man's breeches were thrown after them'. In addition, 'there was continual knocking and pinching the Maids, which was usually done every Night'.

On the third night of his visit, Sherring was joined again by Hillary. Odd things continued to happen beginning with some commotion upstairs when, as soon as the family went to bed, clothes were thrown about, extinguishing the candle lighting their room. Next, feathers were plucked out of a bolster filling the room, and peoples' mouths so that 'they were almost choaked'. A little later 'a very hideous knocking at the heads as they lay on the Bed' was heard and Sherring and Hillary went upstairs, with a lighted candle, to investigate. On this occasion 'they saw a Hand with an Arm-wrist hold the Hammer which kept on knocking against the Bedstead'. When Sherring approached 'the Hand and Hammer fell down behind the Bolster and could not be found' even though they pulled back the bedclothes searching for it. However, just as they left and made their way back downstairs, 'the Hammer was thrown out into the middle of the Chamber'.

Sherring recalled other phenomena including the hopping about of a 'very troublesome' saddle, a cloak hanging on the door in the hall which flew into the fire which proved surprisingly hard to recover and yet was unburned, a hat which was struck off Gast's head when he was eating his dinner, and a pole, 'about 14 or 15 foot in length, which', mysteriously and, seemingly, miraculously, 'was brought into the House, and carried up into the Chamber, and thrown onto the Bed'. It was too big to get rid of without removing a pane of glass and shoving it out of the window. Summing up the evidence, 'There were many other things', Glanvill declared, 'which are too long and tedious to write, and it would take great deal of time'. Sherring and Hillary remained in the house for a further four nights but, other than more 'knocking and scratching', nothing else untoward occurred.

Another witness to the haunting, 'Jone Winsor of long Burton', provided an account on 3 July 1677 in which she spoke of her own disturbing experiences in the house at night including 'a great Stone thrown after her' which, fortunately, missed.[225] Another disconcerting episode involved something lifting the bolster beneath her and her bedfellow's heads 'and did endeavour to throw them out'. Jone stayed at the house for three nights 'and the trouble was much after the same Manner'.

16
THE STORY OF THE STIRS, LEASINGHAM, LINCOLNSHIRE, 1679-80

THIS IS THE fifth of the six Relations appended by Henry More to the second edition (1687) of Joseph Glanvill's posthumous *Saducismus Triumphatus* (1681) which was published the year after his own death.[226] Four of these are either wholly or in part 'poltergeist' cases.

The 'stirs', as the disturbances are described, began at Sir William York's house in Leasingham,[227] south-west of Lincoln, when he was away from home in May 1679. For a couple of hours around ten and eleven

---

225 'A wold vergen' (an old virgin), Jone Winsor ('Wenzor'), was buried at Long Burton on 14 December 1691.
226 Henry More, 'A Continuation of the Collection, or, An Addition of some few More Remarkable and True Stories of Apparitions and Witchcraft' in Glanvill, *Saducismus Triumphatus*, (2nd ed., 1688), pp. 509-20.
227 Thought to be the existing Leasingham Manor (*c.* seventeenth century) or its medieval predecessor.

one night someone or something created a great din by continuously lifting the latch of an outside door up and down. Lady York, at home with a few servants, presumed it to be the work of thieves trying to break in but none were found even after a horn was sounded in alarm which 'raised the Town' but did have the effect of causing the noise to cease.

It was heard no more until the following May when, while Sir William was away in London, the same rattling latch sound was heard for two or three nights. At this point it began to be recognized as being something done 'by some extraordinary means'. Some twenty or so members of the household heard the noise but, looking out of the windows overlooking the door, could not see anything or anyone causing it. The night was bright and visibility good but no-one was discovered and the fact that the door in question opened onto a yard surrounded by a ten-foot tall wall made a hasty escape by a villain of the piece most unlikely.

About a month, having returned from London, Sir William had gone to bed, and Lady York was about to do the same, when he heard similar knocking noises. This time they went on for about quarter of an hour and continued to be heard, periodically, through the night. In the later stages it sounded like someone 'thrusting with a Knee, only more violent'.

In the middle of July, when their servants were in the kitchen adjoining the hall of the house awaiting the return of Sir William and his wife from a trip away from home, they heard a noise in the hall 'like the clapping of the door at the feet of the Stairs'. On entering they found the chairs had been moved into the middle of the hall. They restored them to their usual positions and returned to the kitchen. Soon after they heard more noises and found the chairs had now arrived in the passage between the hall and kitchen.

In August, at around nine or ten o'clock one evening, Sir William heard a couple of bursts of violent knocking, as if made with a stout stick, on a door under the stairs. About a fortnight later, again at around ten, he heard further knocking in the same place but, on unlocking and opening the door into the enclosed space under the stairs, nothing untoward was found. This time he resolved to sit quietly in the hall with ten or so members of the household, listening out for further activity. After half an hour, there having been no further disturbance, he retired to bed, taking the precaution of placing the key to the under-stairs door in his pocket. Immediately the noise started up again and did so on four of five further occasions. Each time he rushed downstairs to investigate, the noise stopped and nothing seemed to be amiss.

The noises continued to be heard, most evenings, between about eight and eleven in the evening. By September the knocking sounds were joined by what was taken to be the footsteps of a man walking or running, and sounding at times like he was using stilts, in chambers above the listeners. As time passed the noises 'began to be more dreadful', causing Sir William's elderly father, his wife and children such consternation they began to think they might have to leave the house. By now, three or four times a week, knocking and banging sounds were heard all around the property, inside and out. The disturbance seems to have been most acute when Sir William's brother-in-law, Mr Brown, visited. In accord with the events at John Mompesson's home back in the early 1660s, 'a very great Drumming at a pair of Wainscot Doors, between the Hall and the great Parlour, imitating Drummers in their several ways of beating', but with hands rather than sticks, was heard.

Three or four nights later, at the beginning of October, 'Sir William lighted a Candle, and set it in a high Candlestick in the middle of the Hall' and went upstairs with his whole family to pray in a chamber above. The drumming noise returned and when he went downstairs he 'found the Chairs removed, and the Candle put out, the Snuff hanging bent down, and the Candlestick removed into the Passage between the Kitchin and the Hall'. On at least one occasion he gathered the whole household together in a single room to ensure that no-one among them was the cause of the disturbances.

Sir William was required to attend parliamentary sessions starting on 16 October. As various relations gathered on the eve of his departure, further knocking at the door under the stairs was heard during the night 'but very little to what usually'. Before he left, he gave instructions for his wife and children to be sent to London to join him in the event of there being more paranormal trouble. However, it seems to have abated soon after and 'by God's Blessing from that time to this it was never heard any more'.

17
A HOUSE INFECTED WITH DEMONS: NEWBURYPORT, NEW ENGLAND, 1679

In 1705 John Beaumont (c. 1650-1731) published *An Historical Physiological and Theological Treatise of Spirits, Apparitions, Witchcrafts, and Other Magical Practises*, a 400-page exploration of the theory that a mostly invisible 'spirit' world coexists with the visible 'natural' world:

> I intimate these things only to caution men not to be over hasty in rejecting things that may seem strange, and do not presently fall within their comprehension; and that in opposing adversaries they use due circumspection in attending to the vast extent of the power of nature, and the various manifestations of God in men, many things being evident to some persons, which to others seem wholly incredible.[228]

Beaumont was a Somerset man from a Roman Catholic family based in Ston Easton, a few miles north-east of Wells. His growing reputation, founded on his work in natural philosophy and geology, led to his election to the Royal Society in 1685 where he would count among his colleagues such eminent intellectuals as Sir Hans Sloane, Robert Hooke and John Aubrey. His 1705 treatise contains several cases of supernatural phenomena including the records of Matthew Hopkins' and John Stearne's witch-finding activities in 1645, Cotton Mather's studies in New England, and the remarkable episodes of witchcraft at Salem in 1691. He also recounted his own disturbing experience of encounters with spirits, which we can presume he probably had at his Ston Easton home, and a couple of local episodes he knew of, one concerning apparitions at Bristol, the other concerning poltergeist activity in the village of Butleigh near Glastonbury [Relation 25]. In 1705 Beaumont echoed Glanvill's by now unfashionable argument that

---

228 John Beaumont, *Treatise*, pp. 132-33.

the reality of witches and demons proved the presence of God as the ultimate authority above all things:

> Now, if there are any witches, enchanters, etc., it necessarily follows that there are demons, by whose help and power, they cause these prodigious effects to come to pass, which men wonder at, and look upon with horror and amazement, it being impossible that those things should be done by any human power. The histories therefore and writings of all nations, and even of the heathens themselves, are full of examples of the Devil's apparitions and of their strange effects. Now, [...] if there were any demons (as it cannot be denied) it follows that there is a deity above them, which so restrains them, that they shall not overthrow all things by their might, for they have strength and malice enough to do it.[229]

Beaumont's was just one of at least thirteen books on the subject of witchcraft published between 1680 and 1718.

An enticing, enigmatic case, seemingly of the classic poltergeist mould, appears in his *Treatise of Spirits*, 'not unlike', the author proclaimed, 'the *Demon of Tedworth*' [Relation 11].[230] Beaumont's story, derived from Mather's recently published *The Wonders of the Invisible World* (1693), is set in the house, 'infested with demons', of one Mr William Morse of Newbury, in the year 1679. Here some remarkable things were happening:

> Bricks, Sticks, Stones, Pieces of Wood, etc. were often thrown at the House, a long Staff danc'd up and down the Chimey, and afterward was hung on a Line, and swung to and fro; an Iron Corrk was violently hurried about by an invisible hand; and a Chair flew about the Room till at last it light on the Table, where Meat stood ready to be Eaten, and was like to have spoil'd all.

A chest, also 'by an invisible Hand' moved from one place to another, doors could not be opened, keys went missing from the bunch

---

229 Beaumont, *Treatise,* p. 264.
230 Beaumont, *Treatise,* pp. 132-33.

among which they were tied, 'and the rest flying about with aloud [sic] Noise of their Knocking against one another'. Beaumont declared these were just some among 'many other unaccountable things things of this kind [...] too long here for me to set down'.

This is another case in which a poltergeist's focus might be detected - this time in the shape of 'a little Boy belonging to the Family'. As the 'Principal Sufferer in these Molestations, he was flung about at such a rate that they fear'd his his Brains would've have been beaten out'. He could not be made still, 'his Bed Clothes were pull'd off from his Bed' which was shaken. When a man tried to hold him down in a chair, 'the Chair fell a dancing, and both were very near being thrown into the Fire'. Even worse, various sharp objects were found 'stuck in his Back', including an iron spindle, pins, and, most astonishingly, 'all the Knives in the House [which] the Spectators pull'd out'. The afflicted child 'Sometimes bark'd like a Dog, then clock'd like an Hen'. The boy claimed to see his tormentor who he described as 'a Man call'd P———l'. The entity molested some of the bystanders too by the

The Newbury home of the Morse family 'still standing at the corner of Market street, opposite to saint Paul's church'.
Joshua Coffin, *A Sketch of the History of Newbury, Newburyport, and West Newbury* (Boston, 1845), p. 134.

sound of things: 'They often thought they felt the Hand that scratch'd them, while they saw it not', although 'Once the Fist beating the Man was discernable [sic], but they could not catch hold of it'. On another occasion 'an Apparition of a Blackamoor Child shew'd it self plainly to them', and, 'another time a Drumming on the Board was heard, which was followed with a Voice that sang, *Revenge, Revenge, Sweet is Revenge*'. This last terrifying episode caused the people to pray to God for their deliverance, 'whereupon there follow'd a Mournful Voice uttering these expressions, 'Alas! Alas! We knock no more, we knock no more', and there was an end to it all'.

Thus, we are left by Beaumont with what seems to be an unequivocal poltergeist episode. The case that inspired Beaumont is recalled elsewhere as 'the only recorded case of witchcraft, in Newbury, that was ever subjected to a legal investigation'.[231] Beaumont neglected to mention the Newbury in question was not the town in England but the settlement by that name in *New* England. In 1634 a group of a hundred people had sailed from Wiltshire, first to establish, in that year, the settlement that came to be called Ipswich, and subsequently, in 1635, Newbury. Among this community of Puritan pioneers were William Morse, a shoemaker, and his wife, Elizabeth (*c.*1616-90). She would be sentenced to death by hanging for 'having had familiarity with the devil' on 20 May 1680, forty-five years after she had arrived.[232] The phenomena described by Beaumont were inspired by supposedly paranormal happenings in the Morse family home on Market Street in Newbury (subsequently Newburyport). When Joshua Coffin published a history of the area in 1845, the house was still standing. Its supposed location is now marked by a plaque commemorating the unfortunate Elizabeth Morse.

According to the testimonies of William and his brother, Anthony, the disturbances began towards the end of November 1679.[233] When William and Elizabeth were in bed one night, they 'heard a great noies against the ruf [roof] with stekes and stones throwing against the hous with great vialanse'. William got out of bed to see what was going on but found

---

231 Joshua Coffin, *A Sketch of the History of Newbury, Newburyport, and West Newbury* (Boston, 1845), p. 122.
232 Massachusetts Archives, vol. cxxxv., 18, in Coffin, *Newbury*, p. 126.
233 Coffin, *Newbury*, pp. 123-24.

nothing and no-one. When he got back into bed the commotion started up again. Later that night they were further disturbed by the noise of 'a grete hoge in the hus', which, despite the door being shut, had somehow got inside. William opened the door and let the distressed pig out. The family was also troubled by the bizarre and recurring phenomenon of objects, including 'a pece of a brick', a basket, nails, and a hammer, disappearing from within the house, and reappearing again having been dropped down the chimney. Other objects Anthony believed had come down the chimney included 'a pece of wood, about a fute loung', and 'a fiar brand, the fiar being out'. When William placed an awl in a cupboard after it too had mysteriously been dropped down the chimney, it repeatedly found its way out and back down the chimney '3 or 4 times'. Cattle tied up in William's barn were found untied the following morning. A spinning wheel was turned upside down, 'and many things set upon it as a Stale [stool?] and a Spade Lick [like] the form of a ship'. A hand iron danced up and down 'many times and into a pot and out againe up atop of a tabal [table], the pot turning over and Speling [spilling] all in it'. Among other similar phenomena, William reported (in his own hand):

> My wife went to make the bed the Clothes Ded fly of many times of themselves, and a Chest open and Shut and Dores fli together. My wife going into the Seler [cellar] thinges tumbling done and the dore fling together vialintly.

While he was at prayer at his bedside, 'A Chaire', he complained, 'did often times bow to me then Strike me on the side'. Meanwhile, 'My wife Com out of the other rome A wege of Iron being thrown at her, and A spade but [did] not rech her, and A stone which hurt her much'. William, his wife, and a couple of neighbours saw a stone fly across the room and, several times, strike a lamp as they all sat beside the fire, and, also a shoe, seen indoors in the same room earlier, drop down the chimney. A door slamming shut hit William on the head 'which did much hurte'.

The court case that followed these disturbances is a sorry tale of accusation, a hunt for one or more individuals engaged in foul play or, worse still, diabolism. The pointing finger of the accusers finally rested on Elizabeth. She was found guilty of witchcraft and condemned to death. Although she received a reprieve, she suffered the lasting humiliation of being confined to her home until her death, of natural causes, in around 1690.

18
THE FOUL-FIEND OF ORMISTON: EAST LOTHIAN, SCOTLAND, 1680

GEORGE SINCLAIR'S ELEVENTH Relation in *Satan's Invisible World Discovered* (1685) is a conventional 'poltergeist' case combined with a ghost story concerning the sighting by one Isabel Murray of the apparition of a servant named Isabel Heriot who died 'about the beginning of Winter 1680' and had once worked for, and been sacked by, the minister of the parish of Ormiston. The subsequent haunting of his home, commencing a few days after the apparition was seen by Murray in its vicinity, is loosely attributed to the vengeance of the disaffected servant. However, there is a distance between the poltergeist, defined throughout as 'the Devil', and the ghost of the woman which in the adjoining account of its manifestation is described as a 'foul-fiend in her likeness'. So, setting aside the claims of a woman who thought she saw a ghost, and also the rambling discussion of this spectre and allegations of witchcraft in the parish which are the preoccupation of the second part of the relation, we end up with a self-contained tale of unadulterated poltergeist activity.

This starts as another case of lithobolia with 'a throwing of stones over the Ministers house, and some thrown at the Hall-door and Windows'. Since, the narrator continues, 'The stones were found in the Close the next morning', the inference is that this happened during the night. Another night, as the minister entered the house through the back door, a great stone was thrown at him as he closed it, leaving a dent in the wood. Isabel Murray was hit smartly in back 'coming out of the Minister's house one night, or going into it'. A young man 'that helped the Horses', the account continues, 'after he been at his Devotion, and was going into his bed in the Stable, was by somewhat [something] gripped by the heel to his great amazement'. The stable-lad's cry of alarm roused the minister's wife and other members of the household who found him 'under a great affrightment'. That night clods of earth and more stones were thrown about but no one was hurt. Likewise, the servant evaded injury when a 'an old Horse-comb which had been a wanting for several years, was thrown at the Lads Bedstead with great violence'. The horses in his charge were spooked too and were found the following morning 'standing and lying disorderly, and sometimes all in a great sweat'. When he was working in the garden the stable-boy had 'several Stones thrown at him, but was never touched, save by one, which hit him very favourably'.

In addition to the throwing around of stones and the like, odd sounds, 'some small Noise and Din', were heard. Rather more ominous was the throwing of a burning coal under a bed. One morning a member of the family found his night-cap, 'taken off his Head in the Bed', in the chimney hearth, 'full of Sinders and Ashes'. Such night-time occurrences continued, intermittently, for eight or nine weeks. The 'frequent and fervent Prayers' of the occupants of the haunted house, however, seem to have paid off, for thereafter 'there was no more trouble about the Family'.

As for Isabel Murray's ghost story, this seems to have been an irritation to the minister and his family as they said their prayers to 'drive away the Devil':

> There was much talking of this Ghost, and things spoken rashly, and some out of malice did invent lies and untruths.

The narrator (Sinclair?) himself sounds equally dismissive or, at least, equivocal in commencing the discussion of the apparition episode in warning his reader, 'For what follows', unlike the account of the poltergeist activity in and around the house, 'we have only the simple word of the foresaid Isabel Murray'.

19
STRANGE AND WONDERFUL NEWS: EWELL, SURREY, 1681

Strange and Wonderful News from Yowell in Surrey (1681) is an eight-page pamphlet which starts with the common device of assuring its reader that 'divers ocular and auricular witnesses can and will upon occasion, testifie the truth of what shall be hereafter asserted'.[234] The focus of the poltergeist seems to have been Elizabeth Burgiss, a serving girl in the home of 'Mr. Tuers, a Gentleman' of Ewell, about twelve miles south of the City of London. In equally archetypal fashion her troubles began a couple of weeks after, on Thursday 5 October 1681, she had words with an elderly woman, Joan Butts, who had long had a reputation for being a witch. It is a classic example of the 'charity refused' model for witchcraft accusation – in this instance the girl refused to give the 'witch' a pair of old gloves, adding insult to injury by curtly telling her that, not only 'she had no Gloves for her' but 'if she had she could not spare time to look [for] them'.[235] Fourteen days later, to the amazement of all onlookers, including her master and his wife, she seemed to be the target of a bout of unexplained stone-throwing: 'stones flew about the Yard at such a strange rate, as if it had rained down showers of them, and many of them were as big as a mans fist'. More stones started flying about the house even though the doors leading outside were shut. Although 'they flew so thick about, they hit no body but the Maid'.

The girl fell ill and suffered various strange afflictions. A day or two later, when she was on her way to go milking, she saw Joan Butts again, this time in Nonsuch Park. Here she spotted her 'sitting amongst the Thorns and Bushes, bedaggled [sic] up to the knees in Dew, and

---

234 *Strange and Wonderful News from Yowell in Surrey* (Printed for F. Clarke at the Bible and Harp in West-smithfield, 1681).
235 The 'charity refused' model developed by Keith Thomas and Alan Macfarlane in the 1970s, remains a useful starting place for considering the dynamics of accusation in witchcraft cases.

Strange and wonderful News
FROM
YOWEL in Surry;
Giving a True and Just Account of One
ELIZABETH BURGISS,
Who was most strangely Bewitch-
ed and Tortured at a sad rate, having several great lumps of Clay pulled forth from her Back, full of Pins and Thorns, which pricked so extreamly, that she cry'd and roar'd in a vehement and out-ragious manner, to the great amazement of all the Beholders.

AS ALSO,

How great Stones as big as a Mans
Fist, were thrown at her in the Dwelling House of Mr. *Tuers*, which came flying into the House in a most strange and amazing manner, the Doors being shut and Windows, so that it could not be imagined how they should be conveyed into the House, and that none of the Family was any ways hurt, but this Maid; Also how the Bellows was thrown at her. Mr. *Tuers* her Master, finding his House thus troubled, after some time, sent her home to her Mothers House at *Afteed*, about three Miles off from *Yowel*, where by the way She was most strangely assaulted with Stones as before; and after She came to her Fathers House, the throwing of the Pewter-Dishes, Candlesticks, and other clattering of Houshold-Goods at her, besides the displacing of a Musical Instrument, hanging up her Grand-Fathers Breeches on the top of the Seal-ling.

With many more strange and miraculous things, filling the Spectators with Wonder and amazement.

Printed for *J. Clarke*, Seignior; at the Bible and Harp, in *West-smithfield*, 1 6 8 1.

---

looking like one that lately had converse with some Infernal Fiend'. That evening she fancied she saw the woman again, this time in her master's house, and the next bout of poltergeist activity began. Elizabeth had gone into the room in which she slept to fetch a trunk which was to be sent to London. From here Mr Tuers heard her call out 'Master, master here is the old Woman'! He ran 'hastily to see whether it were or were not so', and, although he could not see Joan Butts, he saw hand irons being thrown after the maid 'and all her own Linnen thrown about at such a rate, as is hard to believe'. Odder still was the sight of the wooden bar used to secure the front door which 'was strangely removed and conveyed up stairs, and came tumbling down after the maid in the sight of her master'.

Three days after all this commotion, a pair of bellows was flung around 'and Candlesticks and other things [were] thrown after the Girl as she passed to and from in her master's house'. When she set off to her parental home in Ashtead, three or four miles away, 'such numberless numbers of stones were thrown at her that she found it hazardous to Travel'. The poltergeist seems to have followed her all the way for, on Sunday 9 October, 'her Grandfathers Britches were strangely found to be on top of the house as near as can be imagined over his Bed, and besides great quantities of Nuts and Acorns flew about, that the Spectators never beheld the like before'. The pewter ware in the house also 'danced about the house in a strange manner' and, equally surprising, was the discovery of an unknown fiddle in a chest. Having been hung up in the room in which it was found, it somehow made its way onto the tester overhanging the bed, and thereafter was not seen again.

On Thursday 18 October, the mother 'of this afflicted maid' met Joan Butts at Ewell Fair. Convinced by now that her daughter had been bewitched she determined to sort the matter out and, in the course of doing so drew the old woman's 'Hellish Blood', and thus, according to tradition, countering her curse, but with what consequences the narrator says, 'I must get time to acquaint you with'.

20
THE STONE-THROWING DEVIL: NEW HAMPSHIRE, 1682

One of the most detailed accounts of poltergeist activity in the seventeenth century is found in a twenty-page pamphlet printed in London in 1698 with the title *Lithobolia: or, The Stone-Throwing Devil*. The British Museum copy of the tract identifies, in what appears to be contemporary handwriting, its author 'R. C.' as Richard Chamberlain ('Chamberline' in the text). It is the record of events in New England in the home of the Waltons of Great Island in New Hampshire. In neighbouring Massachusetts, six years before, the infamous Salem witchcraft trials had begun. According to *The Stone-Throwing Devil*, the case 'is upon record in his Majesties Council-Court held for that [New England] province', of which Chamberlain declares himself a member. This, presumably, is the same Richard Chamberlain who had been secretary of that council in the early 1680s.[236] His preamble, a dedication in effect to 'The much Honoured Mart[in] Lumley, Esq.', presumes that to such 'a Sober, Judicious, and well Principled Person' the story will prove a fascinating one since 'plain Truths are much more agreeable than the most charming and surprising Romance or Novel, with all [its] strange turns and events'. In common with plenty more such literature in the second half of the seventeenth century, it is written in defiance of those sceptical 'Sadduceans' who would maintain 'it's all a Sham'.

His is an account of 'Preternatural [events] not assignable to, or the effect of, Natural Causes' yet not necessarily beyond other, unknown, or unrecognized, laws of physics. Thus, Chamberlain appears to come from the same stable as those natural philosophers exploring demons scientifically and sharing their quest for empirical evidence. Chamberlain, from the start, sounds like someone in complete accord with the views of Joseph Glanvill, Henry More, Cotton Mather, *et al.* His story has much in common with that of the case in North Aston, Oxfordshire, a hundred years or so before [Relation 1], in as much as it is highly detailed and dominated by the lithobolia phenomenon – the throwing of stones by invisible forces. And, for that matter, a great many stones. Also, in common with that of another highly detailed account, that of the Tidworth demon [Relation 11], it went on for a long time: not less than a year and a half, and, it too is an eye-witness ('Ocular Witness') account.

---

236 'America and West Indies: January 1684', in *Calendar of State Papers Colonial, America and West Indies: Volume 11, 1681-1685*, ed. J W Fortescue (London, 1898), British History Online https://www.british-history.ac.uk/cal-state-papers/colonial/america-west-indies/vol11/pp573-581 [accessed 26 April 2025].

It sounds like Chamberlain was back in England when he had his story printed, having, 'Some time ago being in America (in His then Majesty's Service).' The Majesty in question was James II. This 1698 publication in fact concerns events that occurred in 1682, sixteen years before they were printed. Chamberlain was provided with lodgings in the home of George Walton, 'a Planter there'. Walton's farm / plantation was next door to the property of John Amazeen, an Italian, with whom, one 'bright Moon-light Night' on a Sunday at around ten o'clock, he had cause to meet on the boundary between them to try to figure out the unexplained damage done to a fence-gate that had been 'wrung off the Hinges, and cast upon the Ground'. As he and several other visitors to the Waltons that evening made their way back towards the house 'they were all assaulted with a peal of Stones' flung 'by unseen Hands or Agents' although the Waltons' two granddaughters, claimed that 'as they were standing in the Porch-Chamber Window they saw, as it were, a Person putting out a Hand out of the Hall Window' and 'throwing Stones toward the Porch or Entry'. However, Chamberlain was certain that at the time there was no-one in the hall 'except my self and another'. Meanwhile, Chamberlain, who had gone to bed, and others in the house, had been disturbed by the racket of stones hurled 'against the top and all sides of the House'. They looked about the place but withdrew back indoors when the entrance porch was bombarded with stones, 'some as big as my Fist'. Luckily no-one was seriously hurt although a couple of youths were struck, 'one on the Leg, the other on the Thigh'. Chamberlain was certain it was the work of 'the infernal Agent', that 'constant Enemy to Mankind' who 'intended no less than Death or Maim'. They searched the hall and the cellar but found no one and nothing untoward except for the falling, as if from the ceiling, of two small stones, a sure sign that 'it must necessarily be done by means extraordinary and preternatural'. The worst of the damage, in fact, was sustained by Walton's windows which were smashed and battered, not from the outside, but mostly from the *inside*, 'forcing the Bars, Lead, and hasps of the Casements outwards'. Objects of pewter and brass, such as a pair of candlesticks and 'a large Pewter Pot', flew about or fell to the ground. Some of the stones were very hot to the touch when picked up, as if they had just been taken out of a fire. Chamberlain found by chance, and then by experiment, that if he placed fallen stones

LITHOBOLIA:

OR, THE

Stone - Throwing Devil.

BEING

An Exact and True Account (by way of Journal) of the various Actions of Infernal Spirits, or (*Devils Incarnate*) Witches, or both; and the great Disturbance and Amazement they gave to *George Waltons* Family, at a place call'd *Great Island* in the Province of *New-Hantshire* in *New-England*; chiefly in Throwing about (by an Invisible hand) *Stones*, *Bricks*, and *Brick-bats* of all Sizes, with several other things, as *Hammers*, *Mauls*, *Iron-Crows*, *Spits*, and other Domestick Utensils, as came into their Hellish Minds, and this for the space of a Quarter of a Year.

By R. C. Esq; who was a Sojourner in the same Family the whole Time, and an Ocular Witness of these Diabolick Inventions.

The Contents hereof being manifestly known to the Inhabitants of that Province, and Persons of other Provinces, and is upon Record in his Majesties Council - Court held for that Province.

LONDON,

Printed, and are to be Sold by *B. Whitlook* near Stationers-Hall, 1698.

on a table and turned his back on them for just a few moments one or two would go missing.

After over four hours of havoc, Chamberlain, tired out, had had enough and decided to go back to bed. However, as soon as he had fallen asleep he was awoken again, this time with a violent crash on the other side of a thin partition wall in his bedroom. 'I could not imagin it less', he wrote, 'than the fracture and downfall of a great part of the Chamber, or at least of the Shelves, Books, Pictures, and other things, placed on that side, and on the Partition-Wall between the Anti-Chamber and the Door of mine'. Members of the rest of the company in the house that night rushed upstairs to see what was going on and assured Chamberlain that the wall of the room next door looked fine. However, they did present him with a single great stone weighing some eight and a half pounds which seemed to have been hurled with such force at his bedroom door that it had flung open, before, judging by the dent in the floorboards he found the next morning, ricocheting back into the room.

Having asked everyone to leave, Chamberlain shut his bedroom door and went back to bed. However, he was soon disturbed by the crash of another missile, which turned out to be a brick, hurled against the door in the neighbouring room. Nevertheless, he managed to get back to sleep and lay undisturbed for the rest of the night.

The next day, Monday, he was 'inform'd by several of the Domesticks of more of the same kind of Trouble'. This included the disappearance of the roasting spit which had been standing in a corner of the chimney. All of a sudden it came down the same chimney and lodged itself, spike first, in a log in the hearth. Despite being placed by a member of the family on the other side of the chimney, it next appeared outside a window in the room that opened onto the back of the house. Meanwhile a heavy 'pressing-iron' was found on a ledge in the chimney and that too ended up mysteriously 'convey'd invisibly into the Yard'.

Having decided it would be sensible to keep 'as a Proof and Evidence' the very large stone that had been thrown at his door the night before, Chamberlain, took it up to his room, laid it on a table, and returned downstairs, locking the door after him. Having returned to the house after attending to business elsewhere, Chamberlain was informed by his landlady that soon after his departure those downstairs heard a great noise above and discovered the stone had been thrown into the antechamber. Chamberlain recovered the stone and kept it for a long time 'to show, for the Satisfaction of the Curious'.

Many more stones were hurled around the place that morning, both in the house and in the fields 'where the Master of the House was, and the Men at Work'. In the afternoon Chamberlain and a local minister, Mr Woodbridge, saw a stone 'lighting near, and jumping and tumbling on the Grass'. 'So did one Mrs. Clark', Chamberlain continued, 'and her Son, and several others; and some of them felt them too'. When someone there insisted some boys working in the vicinity must be the culprits, Mrs Clark's little boy was struck in the back by a flying stone 'which caused him to fall a crying'. Mother and child made a hasty departure.

In the evening, having 'sup'd in the outer Room before mine', Chamberlain began to play 'a little Musical-Instrument'. It was warm and he had the door 'set open for Air' when 'a good big Stone came rumbling in, as it were to lead the Dance'. The noise of it on the floorboards 'brought up the Deputy-President's Wife, and many others of the Neighbourhood that were below' who were then treated to the sight of many more stones, as well as a pewter spoon, falling into the room for them to gather as souvenirs of these bizarre developments. While all this was happening a black cat was spotted by a couple of youths in the orchard and adjoining fields, which managed to avoid being hit by more stones before fleeing out of sight.

That night, 'about the Hour it first began there, were more Stones thrown in the Kitchin, and down the Chimney', and also, as Chamberlain was going upstairs to bed, 'in an upper Chamber, and down those Stairs'. These were witnessed by 'one Captain Barefoot, of the Council for that Province', among others.

The following night, on Tuesday, five or six more stones were thrown, this time, smashing windows in the 'Maid's Chamber near the Kitchin', one of them hitting her 'as she lay'. At the same time, two young men in the house heard 'an odd, dismal sort of Whistling'. Thinking it must be that of the stone-thrower, these 'youths' dashed outside to catch the perpetrator, but all they encountered was another curious sound that they likened to that of 'the trampling of a young Colt', 'stepping a little way ahead of them', before it faded away. The next curious discovery was made by Chamberlain four days later when he found two stones on the stairs. More were mysteriously 'convey'd into the Room next [to] the Kitchin' on the Sunday night.

The following week things took an unusual turn in seventeenth-century poltergeist cases: the phenomena moved well beyond the confines of the haunted house. Mr Walton had left with a team of men, by water, on the Monday to work in the woods, 'where his son was placed', 'in a place called Great Bay'. After staying at the son's house overnight, the men set to work felling trees and carrying the lumber to the boat. On two occasions they were showered with stones. Each time they were gathered up and saved in a hat, which they nearly filled. The first time this happened the hat was found empty a while after it had been filled; the second time, the hat was found some distance away from where it had been left. When they returned to Walton's son's place there was a further episode of stone-throwing and young Walton must have been especially alarmed by the discovery of 'half a brick thrown into a Cradle, out of which his Child was newly taken up'.

Chamberlain also learned that on another occasion, when George Walton and his men were returning home up-river from the Great Bay with a cargo of hay, his boat began to take in water. They discovered 'a Plug or Stopple in the bottom of the Boat', designed to release rainwater on dry land, had been pulled out. This act of sabotage, which threatened to sink the vessel and drown its crew, was attributed by Chamberlain to witchcraft: 'a Contrivance and Combination of the old Serpent and the old Woman, or some other Witch or Wizard'.

On the Wednesday the team had further bizarre experiences in the woods. While they were at work 'on a sudden they heard something gingle like Glass, or Metal, among the Trees' as an object fell among them. It turned out to be a stirrup Walton happened to have placed carefully in the boat under some timber. He returned it to its place in the boat only to have it thrown back at him shortly afterwards. This time he secured it to the 'Girdle or Belt he wore about his Waist'. However, due to the heat of the day, he later had cause to remove the belt. Although it was carefully buckled, the stirrup attached to it had vanished by the time he came to recover his belt, never to be seen again. Once again, they were troubled by odd and potentially hazardous occurrences on their journey: 'the Graper, or little Anchor of the Boat, [was] cast overboard, which caus'd the Boat to wind up; so staying and obstructing their Passage'. Likewise, 'the setting-Pole was divers times cast into the River [...] which put them to the trouble of Paddling, that is, rowing about for it as often to retrieve it'.

When he returned home 'Mr. Walton was charg'd again with a fresh Assault in the out Houses; but we heard of none within doors until Friday after'. This time a handful of stones was thrown about in the kitchen, one which was hot to handle, seemingly taken out from the fireplace. Chamberlain was present when Walton was subjected to more stone-throwing on his return from his 'middle Field, (as he call's it)' where his men were at work mowing. Six or seven stones, 'his old troublesome Companions', were thrown, two of which hit Chamberlain, one on the thigh causing him 'to smart a little'. That evening, as Chamberlain and a party of visiting 'Persons of Note' were walking along a lane by the Middle Field, they heard the 'rustling Noise' of a substantial stone which then fell out of the dry stone alongside them. That night some of them were witnesses to further episodes of 'Stonery', including stones that 'flew into the Hall a little before Supper'. Engaged as he was, not in mere story-telling but finding proof of the preternatural, Chamberlain declared he 'made a Memorandum, by way of Record' to their testimonies and added their names and brief profiles to his own account. These were listed under the following heading:

> These Persons under-written do hereby Attest to the Truth of their being Eye-Witnesses of at least half a score Stones that Evening thrown invisibly into the Field, and the Entry of the House, Hall, and one of the Chambers of George Walton's.

The names that followed included the Governor of West Jersey, Samuel Jennings, the Deputy-Governor of Rhode Island, Walter Clark, John Hussey and his wife, Arthur Cook, Matthew Borden of Rhode Island, a merchant from Barbados by the name of Oliver Hopton, another merchant identified as Mr T. Maul, and Captain Walter Barefoot. The presence of such dignatories at the Waltons' home is reminiscent of the interest, at the highest levels, aroused by several cases investigated back in England.

~~~

CHAMBERLAIN FOLLOWED HIS summary of these odd occurrences at George Walton's estate of which he was made aware around the time of his arrival, with a more detailed account of developments between Saturday 24 June and Wednesday 9 July 1682,[237] some of which he had already alluded to. It begins, 'On Saturday, 24 [June]. One of the Family, at the usual hour of the Night, observ'd some few (not above half a dozen) of these natural (or rather unnatural) Weapons to fly into the Kitchin, as formerly'.

Chamberlain clarified his view on the matter when he wrote about the further antics of 'the malicious Demon' on the Sunday and Monday nights. The commotion began, 'more furiously than formerly', with the hurling of a large stone in the kitchen followed by the clatter of pewter dishes and the like, falling down of their own accord. Around midnight two substantial stones, each weighing over thirty pounds (13.6 kilograms), which were kept in the fireplace, perhaps for heating pots of water, 'were in the former, wonted, rebounding manner, let fly against my Door and Wall in the ante-Chamber, but with some little distance of time'. Chamberlain, of course, was woken up and the crashes also brought up 'the Men from below'. They discovered pictures in Chamberlain's room had fallen off the wall and an 'abundance of things' had been displaced.

Unable to sleep, Chamberlain got out of bed while the commotion continued. Stones and 'great pieces of Bricks' flew about smashing windows, some seemingly thrown from outside and some from within. He grabbed a candlestick, but the candle was 'struck out' before he could light it. He made his way to join others in the house when 'a wooden Mortar [bowl]' landed on the floor besides him having somehow been moved from its former position at 'the other end of the Kitchin'. All of this was accompanied by a strange whistling sound heard several times by those in the house.

The following Monday night, 26 June, the disturbances were even worse. They began with more stone-throwing in the kitchen and then, while Chamberlain was in his ante-chamber eating his supper,

---

237 The date given in the text, 'Saturday, July 24', is clearly an error according to the dates thereafter.

'the Window near which I sate at Table was broke in 2 or 3 parts of it inwards'. As the window panes shattered he was showered with, but not hurt by, small fragments of glass. Preferring not to be alone, he went to join members of the family and a neighbour in the kitchen. Here, once again, they were troubled by missiles – stones and 'an old hosing Iron,[238] from a Room hard by, where such Utensils lay'. This time he seemed to be the principal target: 'most of the stones that came (the smaller I mean) hit me, (sometimes pretty hard) to the number of above 20, near 30, as I remember, and whether I remov'd, sit, or walk'd, I had them'. Some larger stones fell softly into his lap as he sat and others bounced harmlessly off the wall next to him. Meanwhile more stones were being hurled around in rooms upstairs, much to the consternation of the children trying to sleep in their bedrooms. 'And for Variety', Chamberlain continued, 'three great, distinct Knocks, sometimes five', as if made with 'a great Maul [mallet]' were heard several times. In describing these rooms as being 'infested' by an entity he anticipated the application of the same term in the study of poltergeists by Harry Price in the mid-twentieth century.[239]

Things got back to normal the next day only to be followed by more stones being thrown about the place on the Wednesday (28 June). The following morning Chamberlain found several objects hanging on nails in his ante-chamber had been knocked off the walls, including 'a Spherical Sun-Dial'. That day though George Walton had the worst of it: while out in his fields he was pelted with stones and hit about forty times. On this occasion, in a highly unusual development in early modern poltergeist stories, he was severely hurt. Chamberlain dolefully remarked he reckoned he would be troubled by his injuries 'even to his dying day; and I observ'd he did so, he being departed this Life since'. Meanwhile his crop of 'Indian Corn' was vandalised: 'struck up by the Roots almost, just as if they had been cut with some edged Instrument'. Men working in the fields, and Chamberlain too, once more heard weird noises, 'like that of Snorting and Whistling', and, Ashe was leaving, he 'receiv'd a pretty hard Blow with a Stone on the Calf of my Leg'. The whistling was likened by Walton and one of his labourers to the sound 'of a Bullet discharg'd from a Gun'.

---

238 Iron for hosiery (stockings).
239 Price, *Poltergeist*, p. 1.

The following Saturday (July 1), Chamberlain made a visit to a neighbour, one Captain Barefoot. Just as he arrived, he and Barefoot's man at the door saw '3 or 4 Stones fall just by us in the Field, or Close, where the House stands, and not any other Person near us'. Back at the Waltons', just as he was going to bed 'a great Stone fell in the Kitchin' and the pewter utensils fell to floor. More stones flew about and candles, again were gutted while the sound of 'Snorting' was heard. A maid was 'hit on the Head in the Entry between the Kitchin and Hall with a Porringer [basin] from the Kitchin'. A heavy 'pressing-Iron clattered against the Partition Wall between the Hall and the Chamber beyond it 'which Chamberlain seems to have been sharing with 'Mr. Randolph, His Majesty's Officer for the Customs'.

A few more stones were flung around on the Sunday morning after which things settled down. On the Monday morning (3 July), however, Walton 'and 5 or 6 with him in the Field' were targeted by more flying stones and, once more, heard the now familiar sound of 'Snorting and Whistling'. That afternoon Walton received further painful blows from flying stones 'as he was in his Boat that lay at a Cove [be]side his house'.

One night soon after, 'the Devil', as Chamberlain now described the unseen perpetrator of all this mischief, played another 'very odd prank' – a further act of petty, wanton vandalism. This involved messing about with the freshly made 'Cocks [heaps] of Hay' in the orchard which were undone, thrown into the trees, and scattered across the orchard and even through the house. Various objects inside were moved around – a great log was placed on the outside of Walton's door, preventing him from opening it, a 'Form'[240] was moved from the porch and placed beside a fireplace, with a napkin, two pewter pots and a candlestick set upon it, and a cheese-press had 'a Spit thrust into one of the holes of it, at one end; and at the other end of the Spit hung an Iron Kettle; and a Cheese was taken out, and broke to pieces'.

On another occasion, one Sunday night, Chamberlain's window 'was all broke with a violent shock of Stones and Brick-bats', just missing him and smashing a great hole in a cabinet containing books and another ripping through the canvass of a picture on the wall. 'After this', Chamberlain remembered, 'we were pretty quiet, saving now and

---

240 This, probably, denotes a wooden bench.

then a few Stones march'd about for Exercise, and to keep (as it were) the Diabolical hand in use, till July 28, being Friday, when about 40 Stones flew about, abroad, and in the House and Orchard, and among the Trees therein, and a Window broke before, was broke again, and one Room where they never used before'.

What follows this in Chamberlain's report is a fascinating, graphic account of 'witch-bottle' counter-magic in a forlorn attempt to bring it all to an end. After another bout of stone-throwing and smashing of a window on Wednesday 1 August, 'they tried this Experiment; they did set on the Fire a Pot with Urin and crooked Pins in it , with design to have it boil, and by that means to give Punishment to the Witch, or Wizard, (that might be the wicked Procurer or Contriver of this Stone Affliction) and take off their own; as they had been advised'. 'As the Liquor begun to grow hot', Chamberlain continued, 'a Stone came and broke the top or mouth of it, and threw it down, and spilt what was in it; which was made good again, another Stone, as the Pot grew hot again, broke the handle off, and being recruited and fall's the third time, was then with a third Stone quite broke to pieces and spilt; and so the Operation became frustrate and fruitless'.

The following day, Thursday 2 August; more stones were thrown and windows smashed. That night Chamberlain and 'many more' in the kitchen witnessed 'one great Stone that lay on a Spinning-Wheel to keep it steady [...] thrown to the other side of the Room'. The next day the gate between Walton's land and that of his neighbour, John Amazeen, was taken down and thrown into Amazeen's field where it landed with a crash that sounded like the firing of 'a great Gun'.

At this late stage in his account, Chamberlain revealed the chief suspect was a woman from another neighbouring property who had often threatened Walton 'he should never enjoy his House and Land'. On Friday 4 August a fence between the Waltons and these unnamed neighbours was 'maliciously pull'd down to let in their Cattel into his Ground'. When Walton and his men set about repairing it they were pelted with dozens of stones. Meanwhile labourers working for the Waltons elsewhere were also subjected to further lithobolic assaults, and 'A Woman helping to Real (among the rest) was hit 9 or 10 times, and hurt to that degree, that her left Arm, Hip, Thigh, and Leg, were made black and blue there with'. Two men visiting Chamberlain – a clergyman called Woodbridge and a merchant by the name of Jefferys – were also hit with stones. Chamberlain doubtless showed them the devastated kitchen in which one of the battered windows 'was now quite broke out, and unwindow'd, no Glass or Lead at all being left and 'a Glass Bottle broke to pieces, and the Pewter Dishes (about 9 of them) thrown down, and bent'. The Waltons' 'invisible Adversaries' continued to trouble those working in the fields and impeding the harvest by damaging the sickles they relied upon, hitting them with such force that they cracked.

Things settled down between Sunday 6 July and the following Tuesday, but on Wednesday 9 July 'above 100 Stones (as they verily thought) repeated the Reapers Disquiet in the Corn-Field', some, 'as big as a Man's Head'. Mrs Walton received a nasty blow on the shoulder, and more sickles were violently knocked out of the hands that held them and rendered unusable. And then it all seemed to be over with no further disturbances throughout the rest of July and the whole of August. However, George Walton's demon had one last game to play: as he set out in his canoe from his Great Island home to present himself before the Council at Portsmouth concerning these matters, 'he was sadly hit with three pebble Stones as big as ones Fist; one of which broke his Head'. Chamberlain was present when Walton showed this injury to the President of the Council.

Thus, Chamberlain's tale was concluded. His closing remarks clarified his reasons for sharing this news of extraordinary events from a distant colony all those years before, ending with an urgent plea for acceptance of seemingly empirical proofs for belief in a world of spirits:

> Who, that peruses these preternatural Occurrences, can possibly be so much an Enemy to his own Soul, and irrefutable Reason, as obstinately to oppose himself so, or confusedly fluctuate in, the Opinion and Doctrine of Demons, or Spirits, and Witches? Certainly he that do's [does] so, must do two things more: He must temerariously unhinge, or undermine the Fundamentals of the best Religion in the World; and he must disingenuously quit and abandon that of the Three Theologick Virtues or Graces, to which the great Doctor of the Gentil[e]s gave the Precedence, Charity, through his Unchristian and Uncharitable Incredulity.

21
THE SHE-DEMON OF SPREYTON: DEVON, 1682

A *NARRATIVE OF* the *Demon of Spraiton*, a nine-page pamphlet, combines accounts of apparitions and poltergeist activity. It was printed in London in 1683 and, a year later, appeared as the fourth Relation in Richard Bovet's *Pandaemonium*.[241] A further account, 'Transportation by an Invisible Powere', was recorded by John Aubrey in his *Miscellanies* (1696). Bovet implied he was responsible for the original pamphlet, having transcribed the account from a letter sent to 'a Gentleman in London' by one 'J. G. Esquire' who apparently lived close to the village of Spreyton in Devon at the time of the phenomena that began in November 1682. J. G.'s letter was dated 11 May 1683. Bovet's 1684 version is close to the original but not quite the exact transcription he declared it to be.

Bovet knew of a further version 'related by the Reverend Minister of Barnstable [sic]' thirty miles north of the village of Spreyton. A few days before J. G. sent his, this unnamed minister[242] had sent the account to Andrew Paschall, the Somerset clergyman who also provided Henry More with one of the poltergeist stories he added to Joseph Glanvill's *Saducismus Triumphatus* (1681) [see Relation 10 in this collection]. Paschall was the Rector of Chedzoy in Somerset and it is his summary of the case in a letter he wrote to Aubrey in May 1683 which provided the entry in *Miscellanies*. Although the language and syntax in the later Aubrey version is less archaic, the story and the structure of its telling, sentence by sentence, is much the same. Thus, a single source accounts for the three contemporary versions. Its anonymous author (J. G. perhaps) is described throughout as the 'Narrator' or the 'Relator'.

The pamphlet begins with a Glanvill-esque rant against 'your Hobbs [sic], your Scots, your Websters, with their Blasp[h]emous denyals of

---

241 Bovet (ed. Summers), *Pandaemonium*, pp. 107-13.
242 Paschall described him as 'a Learned Friend [who] was of my time in Queens College in Cambridge'.

the Existence of Spirits'[243] and a commendation of the works of Henry More and Glanvill in this ongoing philosophical war of words in which Bovet had picked up the baton, the *Triumphatus Saducismus* providing the model for Bovet's slighter *Pandaemonium*. Bovet, or whoever else it was who produced the pamphlet, clarified his purpose in his closing sentence:

> If it conduce to the Conviction of any one of the adverse Party, or move in others (more Sober) Resolutions to Walk seriously, and with an Awful Frame before the Omnipotent Creator of all things; and to take heed of Satanical Delusions, I have my Aim; and let God have the Glory.

The tale begins as a ghost story. First, a twenty-year-old servant of one Philip Furze, by the name of Francis Fry (Fey in Bovet), encounters the ghost of Furze's father who gives Fry certain directions regarding certain incomplete financial affairs. All goes well until the ghost of old Furze's second wife – 'That Wicked Woman' - appears. Up to this point the action has taken place outside but now this second apparition is seen inside as well as out, 'sometimes in her own shape', but dressed in her daughter-in-law's clothes, 'sometimes in shapes more horrid, as of a Dog belching Fire, and of an Horse' and Fry is attacked, leaving him 'bruised and bloody', by an invisible foe, a demon, in his master's house. While the 'Woman Spectre' concept is sustained throughout the story, in this curious hybrid of two allied folkloric traditions, the conventional ghost story gives way to a demonic poltergeist infestation.

In addition to severe physical provocation, including near strangulation as unseen hands pulled tight the neckerchief Fry wore around his neck, the shape-shifting 'Female Demon' moved certain objects around and destroyed others. The wig on Fry's head 'was torn all to pieces' and the box containing his finest peruke was forced open and 'the Wig torn all to slitters'. The buckles fell off Mr Furze's garments, and the laces freed themselves from his shoes and 'crisp'd and curl'd' in his serving maid's hand 'like a living Eel'. Fry's clothes and those of one Anne Langdon (the maid?) 'were torn to pieces on their backs'.

---

243 Influential early modern English philosophers considered by the author as sceptics regarding the existence of sprits: Reginald Scot, Thomas Hobbes, and John Webster.

Meanwhile 'a great Barrel full of Salt [marched] out of one Room into another', and on top of a pan of milk warming over the fire a hand iron was found overlaid by two glitches of bacon.

The servant, Francis Fry, continued to be the focus of attention and, 'Divers times the feet and leggs of the young man afforementioned have been so entangled about his neck, that he hath loosed with great Difficulty. Sometimes they have been so twisted about the frames of chairs and stools that they have hardly been set at Liberty.'

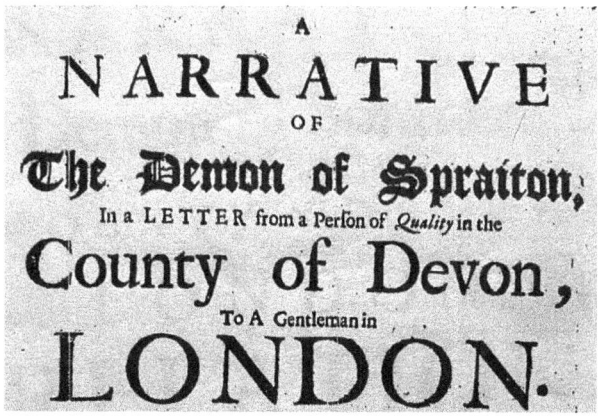

On Easter Eve Fry went missing until 'he was heard Singing and whistling in a Bogg or Quagmire, where they found him in a kind of Trance, or Extatick Fit'. This, apparently, was not the first time he had been found in this condition but the narrator, who happened to be there on this occasion, did not know if these fits predated the arrival of the 'She-Demon', as Bovet described it. On this occasion, when he recovered 'about an hour after' he insisted 'he was taken up by the skirt of his doublet, by this Female Demon' which 'carried him so high, that his Masters House seemed to him to be but a hey-cock' [heap of hay]. He prayed to God 'not to suffer the Devil to destroy him, and [...] he was suddenly set down in that quagmire'. His bizarre story was reinforced by the finding of his shoes which seemed to have fallen to the ground, one 'on one side of his Masters house, and the other on the other side'. More compelling was the discovery the following morning of his peruke wig 'hanging on the top of a tree'. Not long after, he fitted again and somehow sustained a blow that resulted in a great bruise on his forehead. He claimed a bird had 'flown in at the Window, with a stone in its beak, which had dashed directly against his forehead'. The offending stone was searched for where he suggested it might be found but instead of a stone 'a weight of Brass or Copper, which it seems the Demon had made use of on that occasion' turned up.[244] More surprising still to the incredulous reader is the narrator's closing remark: 'The persons present were at trouble to break it in pieces, every one taking a part, and preserving it in memory of so strange an Accident'.

Paschal's account in Aubrey's *Miscellanies* provides further interesting details. It transpires 'the poor afflicted People' in the haunted house 'called to their assistance none but Nonconforming Ministers'. Paschal knew he would not be welcome there, despite being 'so near' and having 'passed by the very Door' since he had 'given Mr. Furze a great deal of trouble the last Year about a Conventicle[245] in his House, where one of his Parish was the Preacher'. He also mentioned that he had received a visit from Francis Fry's distressed mother who had told him 'that the Day before he had five Pins thrust into his Side'. His advice was 'that she should remove him thence by all means', but he doubted she would. In addition, he reported one Anne Langdon, who seems to have been a maid servant in the house, was also 'grievously troubled', as much as Fry, by the demon. Although she was not levitated, 'her Fits and Obsessions seem to be greater, for she Scrieches in a most hellish tone.' Meanwhile, he remarked, one 'Thomasin Gidley (though removed) is in trouble, as I hear'.

22
A THIEF DISCOVERED BY A DEMON: BRIGHTLING, SUSSEX, c.1690

ONE MR COLINS, a 'Pious Credible Person' and 'Eye-witness of much of it', related his account to Richard Baxter of recent poltergeist

---

244 In Aubrey's *Miscellanies*, his informer, Andrew Paschal, had heard it was neither brass nor copper but was some kind of 'a strange Mineral'.
245 An assembly, in this instance, of religious non-conformists.

activity in Brightling, Sussex. His narrative subsequently appeared in Baxter's *Certainty of the Worlds of Spirits* (1691).[246] The disturbances were preceded by the arrival of an old woman who, at around noon one Monday, appeared at the home of Joseph Cruttenden of Brightling and his wife, and advised a servant girl there of 'sad Calamities [...] coming upon her Master and Dame'. Their home, she declared, 'should be Fired, and many other troubles befal them'. Before her departure she warned the girl, 'That if she spake of what she had told her, the Devil would tear her to pieces'.

That night, when Cruttenden and his wife were in bed, 'Dirt and Dust, etc. was thrown at them, but they could not tell whence it came'. They rose and started praying and the disturbances ceased but they started up again as soon as they went back to bed. 'Dust, Dirt, and several things' were thrown at them again at noon the following day. And then the direst part of the old woman's prophecy took shape:

> Before Night, a part of one end of their House Fired; they rake it down, it flashes somewhat like Gunpowder; as they stop'd it there, it began in another place, and thence to another, till the whole House was burnt down.

Another feature of this supposedly unnatural fire was that, although the property was 'burnt down to the Ground it flamed not'. The owner of the property, Colonel Busbridge, 'bid them go into another of his Houses in the Parish'. They moved in with the goods they had salvaged but their troubles were far from over for 'such like Disturbances were there also; the House Fireth, endeavours are made by many to quench it, but vain, till the Goods are thrown out, when it ceased with little or no help'. This seeming rejection by haunted houses of their Cruttenden incumbents caused their neighbours to refuse taking them in and, homeless, they found shelter in a hut. Even here, the story continues, their goods, including pewter dishes and knives, were 'thrown upside down', and brickbats were hurled about although, curiously, when they struck them they 'hurt them not'. When two ministers, Mr Bennet and Mr Bradshaw, intervened to pray with the family, Bennet was hit,

---

246 Baxter, *Worlds of Spirits*, pp. 41-3.

harmlessly, by a knife which glanced off his chest, and had 'a Bowl or Dish thrown at his Back'. With so many gathering there they conducted their prayers outside and 'a Wooden Tut [?stool] came flying out of the Air' and struck Joseph Cruttenden. A horseshoe 'was observ'd of its own accord to rise' and also 'fly to the Man, and strook him in the midst of a hundred People'. At this point Cruttenden felt compelled to make a public confession 'that he had been a Thief'.

Despite this positive outcome, once the servant girl's story of her visit by the old woman got out, a suspect, with a reputation for witchcraft, was rounded up, exposed to a search for any physical signs of diabolism, such as an additional teat for feeding her familiar, closely watched for twenty-four hours and probably deprived of sleep, while a look-out was kept for anything unusual such as the appearance of her familiar. The girl declared the woman resembled the one she had met but would not swear to it.

23
THE VIOLENT INFESTATION OF A HOUSE IN RERRICK: DUMFRIES AND GALLOWAY, SCOTLAND, 1695

THIS SUBSTANTIAL ACCOUNT of poltergeist activity is set in a house occupied by Andrew Mackie and his family in southern Scotland between February and May in 1695. It was attested by multiple witnesses, and written down by Alexander Telfair, minister of Rerrick parish in Galloway, and published as a pamphlet in both Edinburgh and London in 1696.[247] The witnesses, all visitors to the house, included

---

247 Alexander Telfair, *A True Relation of an Apparition, Expressions and Actings, of a Spirit, which Infested the House of Andrew Mackie* (Edinburgh: 1696); Alexander Telfair, *A New Confutation of a Saducismus, being a true Narrative of the wonderful Expressions and Actions of a Spirit, which infested the House of Andrew Mackie* (London: 1696). The quotations that follow are mostly derived from the original Scottish version but, where appropriate, for the sake of greater clarity, also from the revised copy printed in

five clergymen and two lairds [lords/landowners]. Once again this is proclaimed as a case concerning a spirit which 'infested' a house - the term used centuries later by Harry Price to describe the behaviour of poltergeists.[248] Early modern poltergeists were perceived to haunt houses as much as the families occupying them. This house was built, we are told, about twenty-eight years before the poltergeist outbreak (c.1667). The account indicates it was built of stone, with a chimney breast and loft, and a timber and thatch roof, while retaining the traditional long-house design with a barn at one end. Telfair's purpose in telling the story is unequivocal. In his preface, dated 22 December 1695, he denounced the 'conviction and Confutation of that prevailing Spirit of Atheism, and Infidelity in our time, denying both in Opinion and Practice the Existence of Spirits, either of God or Devils; and consequently a Heaven or Hell'. His narrative provided further evidence for the reality of spirits as well as being a dire warning to those God might choose to punish by letting Satan loose in their homes as a punishment for their irreligious ways. This is providential, polemical literature, springing from the same well of righteous concern as most English language 'poltergeist' narratives in the period. Without this imperative an argument for the rise of the poltergeist in this period would be unsustainable.

Telfair's conviction that hauntings, ultimately, were divinely permitted, if not ordained, must have made the case, for him at least, all the more puzzling since the family occupying the haunted house 'in Ringcroft of Stocking'[249] in his parish seem to have been decent, godly folk. Mackie, a mason, Telfair declared, 'is outwardly Moral, there is nothing known to his Life and Conversation, but honest, civil and harmless'. Seemingly devout, plagued by a demon, he 'did pray to the great satisfaction of many'. Telfair was unconvinced by gossips who spoke of Mackie's dealings with the Devil through supposed participation in the mysterious masonic rites with which the trade was already associated. 'As for his Wife and Children', Telfair continued,

---

London.
248 Price, *Poltergeist*, p. 1.
249 This has been identified as a farmstead close to Auchencairn, on its north-west side. The 1849 Ordnance Survey map marks a site 'The Ring (now in ruins)' beneath the crest of 'Stocking Hill'.

'none have imputed any thing to them as the rise of it, nor is there any ground, for ought I know, for any to do so'.

In the February of 1695 the Mackies' troubles began. First, odd things happened to their livestock which broke loose of their bindings during the night on at least two occasions. Worse than that, one night the family was awakened by the smell of smoke to find 'a great Quantity of Peat', cut and stored for fuel, smouldering 'in midst of the house floor'. Fortunately, the fire was extinguished before any further damage was done, 'and though they made a narrow search' they 'could neither hear nor see any Agent'.

On Wednesday 7 March 'there were stones thrown in the House, in all the places of it, but it could not be discovered from whence they came, what, or who threw them'. This continued during the day and, especially, at night. The stone-throwing proved to be especially frequent on the Sabbath (i.e. Sundays), particularly when anyone was at prayer. It was noted that when people were hit by these stones they seemed to be struck more lightly than might be supposed, as if the stone was half its natural weight.

On the Saturday (10 March) the children, had a fright when they thought they saw somebody wrapped in a cloak sitting at the fireside. The youngest child who was nine or ten years old, recognized the blanket as his own and ran over to it pulling it off what 'they found to be a four footed Stool set upon the end, and the blanket cast over it'.

The following day 'the Pot-hooks and Hanger' disappeared from their place in the chimney. They searched high and low for them over the next four days before they 'were found at last in a Cockloft, where they had searched for them several times before'. This was attested by the owner of the property, Charles Maclellan, Laird of Collin, and one John Cairns of Hardhills.[250] That same day the narrator of the tale, Telfair, after delivering his sermon, heard all about these events from Mackie. He visited the house the following Tuesday (13 March), stayed a while, and prayed with the family during which time there were no disturbances. Then, as he was about to leave and was 'speaking to some men at the barn end', he saw 'two little stones drop down on the

---

250 Collin is close to the village of Auchencairn, today one of the two principal settlements in the parish of Rerrick, the other being Dundrennan; Hardhills is directly to the south-east of Auchencairn.

Croft[251] at a little distance from me'. At the same moment people came rushing out of the house telling him 'it was as ill as ever within'. Telfair re-entered and returned to his prayers during which 'it threw several stones at me, but they did no hurt, being very small'.

After this episode 'there was no more trouble' until the following Sunday (18 March) when it began to throw more stones, larger than before, which struck with greater force. This continued until the following Wednesday (21 March). Telfair returned to the house and stayed there for much of the night during which 'stones, and several other things were thrown at me'. He was not alone, and others there heard the thud of the unseen great staff as it struck him 'several times on the sides, and shoulders'. 'That same Night', he continued, 'it pull'd off the side of a Bed[252] [and] knock'd upon the Chests and Boards, as People do at a Door'. This was attested by his companions, Maclellan and John Tait of Torr.[253] At one point Telfair felt his arm being raised and, looking up, he fancied he saw for a moment, before it vanished, a disembodied 'little white Hand and an Arm, from the Elbow down'.[254] Other supposed apparitions in the course of the haunting included the sighting by one of Mackie's friends of 'a young Man, red faced, with yellow hair, looking in at the Window', and several sightings of a 'a young Boy about the age of 14 years with gray Cloths [*sic*], and a bonnet on his head'. The London version leaves out these sightings of unidentified visitors to the property. The next day (or, most likely, night) 'it grew more troublesome', beating family members and visiting neighbours, including Laird Maclellan and Andrew Tait of Torr, 'with Stones and Staves, and compelled some of them to leave the House'. By now, visitors to the property had stones hurled at them both as they arrived and departed. Mackie had his hair pulled by the increasingly violent poltergeist, he was wounded on the forehead, 'thrust several times at his shoulder', and 'felt something like the Nails of one's Fingers scratch the Skin of his Head'. Several people were dragged 'about the House by their Clothes'. A miller from Auchencairn, John Keige, had

---

251 'Field' in the London version.
252 One of the four wooden panels forming the shape of a seventeenth-century bed.
253 Torr and Torr point are one the north-east side of Auchencairn.
254 This strange manfestation of a hand and the lower part of an arm occurs in other accounts of this kind (see, for example, Relation 15).

A TRUE RELATION OF AN Apparition, Expressions and Actings, OF A SPIRIT,

Which Infested the House of *Andrew Mackie* in *Ring-Croft* of *Stocking*, in the Paroch of *Kerrick*, in the Stewartry of *Kirkcudbright*, in *Scotland*.

By Mr. *Alexander Telfair*, Minister of that Paroch: and Attested by many other Persons, who were also Eye and Ear-Witnesses.

Eph. 6. 11. *Put on the whole Armour of God, that ye may be able to stand against the wiles of the Devil.*
Verf. 12. *For we wrestle not against flesh and blood, but against Principalities, and Powers,* &c.
James 4. 7. —— *Resist the Devil and he will flee from you.*

EDINBURGH,
Printed by GEORGE MOSMAN, *And are to be sold at his Shop in the Parliament-Closs*, 1696.

the horrible experience of something so powerful tugging him on one side that he feared he would be torn apart. 'That same Night', Telfair reported, the children asleep in bed were struck on the hips, 'the Noise whereof was distinctly heard by the People in the House, as if it had been done by a Man's Hand'. John Telfair of Auchenleck,[255] among others, swore he had seen the 'bar of the Door, and other things [...] move about the House as if one had been carrying them in their Hand, yet nothing could be seen doing it'.

The supposed entity continued throwing stones, rattling beds and chests, and beating people, and then, from Tuesday 3 April 1695 it began to whistle and articulating what sounded like the words, 'Hush, Hush, at the close of every Sentence in Prayer'.[256] The following day Maclellan and Mackie went to a place identified as Buittle, seventeen miles north of Auchencairn, to meet a group of ministers who proceeded to engage in public prayers on behalf of the Mackie family. Two of these, Andrew Ewart and John Murdo, ministers of the neighbouring parishes of Kelton and Crossmichael respectively,[257] now visited the house where they passed a night in fasting and prayer. Here 'it was very cruel against them, especially by throwing great Stones some of them about half a stone weight'. Ewart was wounded 'twice in the Head', causing him to bleed effusively, and his wig was pulled off. Murdo was also hit several times. Indeed, 'There were none in the House that Night escaped from some of its fury and cruelty' – a burning piece of peat was thrown into their midst at one point and 'the Stones poured down on all who were in the House to their hurt'. The two ministers, together with Maclellan and Tait, attested to this.

On Thursday 5 April straw for thatching was set on fire in the yard, and that night, despite being full of family and neighbours, stones were hurled about the house. Mrs Mackie had noticed 'a broad stone near the door' wobble when she stepped on it and, the following morning, when she lifted it, she found, wrapped in old, soiled paper, seven small bones and an amount of flesh and blood. Alarmed, she ran to Collin, quarter of a mile away, to see her landlord, Maclellan. Meanwhile, things had really got out of hand at Ringcroft with many more stones being flung around as well as 'fireballs' both in and out of the house. A 'Hot-stone'

---

255 Auchenleck is a short distance to the east of Auchencairn.
256 'Hush, Hush' is the English version of 'Wisht, Wisht' in the original printed in Edinburgh.
257 'Kel and Carsmichel' in the Edinburgh version and 'Kells and Corsmichael' in the London.

somehow ended up in a bed between the children lying there and burnt a hole through the bedclothes. It was removed by the Mackie's eldest son but, when Maclellan turned up and held it, an hour and a half later, it was still too hot to handle. A staff (whether visible or not is unclear) was thrust through a wall of the house above the children's bed, a groan was heard and, only after prayers and more stone throwing, did the commotion cease when Maclellan removed the collection of small bones under the slab by the door. Maclellan then summoned Telfair who arrived at the house to pray. He was hit by more stones that night but evaded injury, and, eventually, things quietened down.

On 7 April a local blacksmith, William Mackmin, according to his own testimony, was wounded on the head by stones hurled at him, and he was also made the target of a flying ploughshare. A trough weighing three stone (6.35 kg.) fell on his back but he was not injured. That night the house (its thatched roof perhaps) was set alight twice but both times it was saved by the Mackie's attentive neighbours. The same day the Mackies' son, John, on coming to the house, was suddenly bathed in light just before he stepped inside.

No doubt Mackie must have been shocked when, the following morning, he found a letter in the yard, written and sealed in blood, and containing an abstract, poorly written, but seemingly dire warning commanding repentance for some unspecified crime or conduct. Still, it was enough to cause the local civil magistrate, to whom the mysterious bones were sent, to convene meetings with all those who had lived in the house since it was built. At these meetings Maclellan, Telfair and others investigated evidence of foul play at the property. However, nothing untoward was discovered. Nevertheless, Telfair and five more local ministers gathered at the house 'to spend so much time in Fasting and Praying as we were able'.

Telfair was back at the house on 10 April when stones were thrown at him the moment he opened his mouth to commence his prayers. By now 'It came often with such force upon the house that it made all the house Shake'. A hole was broken through the timber and thatch roof and through it 'poured in great Stones'. One of these, 'more than a Quarter weight', hit James Monteith, Minister of Borgue, on the back, but, surprisingly, he was not injured. Likewise, when a rock bigger than a man's fist hit him with great force on the chest he was unhurt. The strategy of policing the hole in the roof from outside, with ministers taking turns to stand guard, seems to have prevented more stones falling into the house through the roof but, instead, 'it forced open the Barn-door, broke down the Partition-wall, and threw Stones into the House that way, but without doing much hurt to the People'. What followed was equally alarming as some of those attendant, including Laird William Lennox of Millhouse and Telfair himself, felt an invisible hand grab them by the ankles. Thus the commotion continued until ten o'clock that night.

Things got even worse over the next three days – 'worse than it ever was before'. Everyone who visited the house suffered a blow of some sort. On one of these nights three men visiting with Andrew Tait were all clouted with a dead seabird - a fulmar - which Tait's dog had caught on the way to the house and had been left outside when he entered. One of Tait's colleagues, Samuel Thomson, was especially alarmed when he felt something grip him 'hard by the Side and Back, and thrust an Hand, as he conceived beneath his Clothes and into his Pocket'. In fact, he was so frightened it made him ill.

On the Sunday (14 April) things took another serious turn when straw in the yard beside the barn was set alight and more stones were thrown about until ten o'clock that night. Meanwhile, a spade for digging ditches, 'with the Mouth toward him', was hurled at Mackie, and a grain sieve was thrown around the house which he managed to catch but found difficult to hang onto. Somehow the mesh of the sieve separated from the rim and, bundled up, was thrown at Thomas Robertson of Aires who subsequently attested to the truth of the matter.

The following evening Maclellan made another visit, this time in the company of a drover, William Anderson, and Anderson's son-in-law, James Paterson. Later that night Mackie's sons accompanied Maclellan home and on their return 'they were Cruelly stoned, and the stones Rolled amongst their Legs like to break them'. Shortly after they got back inside, Anderson was hit on the head and there was a 'great Effusion of his Blood'. When prayers were said the company heard something whistle, groan and cry, 'Hush, Hush'. The next day, 16 April, more whistling and groaning was heard, more stones were thrown during prayers, and men were shaken 'back and foreword' and hoisted up 'as if it would lift them off their knees' as the supplicants prayed. Further words were heard, this time sounding something like, 'Bo, Bo, Kick, Cuck'. The Mackie family fled from the house leaving 'five Honest neighbours' to watch over it for the rest of the night. Nothing untoward happened to them or to any of the departed Mackie family. The only oddity was the unexplained untying of cattle in their stall. After the family had returned the following day, similar things happened to their livestock in the 'sheep-house' in the night but the family indoors was not disturbed. The following day, Thursday 19 April, straw in the barn for threshing was set alight which Mackie quickly put out. Meanwhile staves of some sort were pushed through the partition wall 'at him' but he came to no harm. There was more stone-throwing, whistling and 'hushing' the next day. When someone got hit John Tait swore it said, 'Take you that'. He also heard it say, more than once, 'Take you that till you get more' after which its unfortunate target was bound to get hit again. Its antics continued over the next three days with more stone-throwing and beating with unseen staves, and it also threw lumps of peaty mud in the faces of everyone in the house.

By now, and probably well before, the troubles endured by the Mackies were the concern of the whole parish. A 'day of Humiliation' was declared for observance on Tuesday 24 April, of which the entity seems to have taken a dim view:

> all that day from Morning to Night, it continued in a most fearfull maner [sic] without intermission, throwing Stones with such cruelty and force that all in the House feared lest they should be killed.

It threw stones all night on the twenty-fifth and, again, the following evening. This time however it also knocked on a chest and began to speak, calling those present 'Witches and Rooks' and saying, 'it would take them to Hell'. This was followed by a substantial dialogue in which it declared it was acting on God's commission 'to warn the land to repent' and, seeming to reveal its diabolical intent, commanding those present to 'Praise me, and I will whistle to you, Worship me, and I will trouble you no more'. The conversation closed with the dire threat it would burn the house down. Sure enough, the following day the house was set on fire seven times – 'as it was quenched in one part, instantly it was fired in an other'. Failing to burn the house to the ground, the demon proceeded to cause the collapse of one end of the house, pulling down 'all the stone-work thereof', and obliging the family to shelter and make their fire in the stable. Things took an especially horrific turn the following night when, according to two witnesses, William Mackminn and John Corsby, 'it pulled one of the Children out of the bed, gripping him as he thought by the craig [neck] and shoulders, and took up the block of tree [wood], as great as a ploughing-head, and held it above the Children, saying, if I had a Commission [from God?] I would brain them'! Whatever it was, 'it continued Setting fire to the house' the following day, even after Mackie had 'poured water upon the Hearth' and 'there was no Fire within an quarter of an Mile of the house'. While he was threshing in the barn he heard his name whispered twice – 'Andrew, Andrew'. When he refused to respond, he heard in an angry voice command, 'Answer' and 'Speak'. It then told him he would be troubled no longer, apart from the throwing of a few more stones, if he agreed to take away the straw form his threshing barn. Whether he did so or not is not stated by Telfair. That night however Telfair himself was back at the house where he stayed until around four in the morning. During the time he was there it attempted to set fire to the house once more, and a couple of small stones dropped down by the fireplace just as he came in.

When Maclellan and several neighbours were at prayer in the barn on the night of Tuesday 30 April, he saw a 'black thing' in a corner, 'and it did increase, as if it would fill the whole house'. It was formless, cloud-like, to its alarmed onlookers. It then proceeded to throw barley-chaff and mud in their faces, and gripped some 'by the Middle, Arms, and other Parts, so hard, that for five days after they felt those Gripes'. All this spanned a period of an hour or two after which things returned to normal. Macclelan and four others attested to the truth of this.

The next day, 1 May, 'a little Sheep-house' was burnt down, but the sheep were saved. The demon in the house, of course, was blamed. This was, it seems, it's final act. Telfair concluded his narrative with the admonition: 'Be sober, be vigilant, because your adversary the Devil, as a roaring lyon walketh about seeking whom he may devour; whom resist steadfast in the Faith'.

24
THE DEVIL OF DEPTFORD: DEPTFORD, 1699

T*HE DEVIL OF Deptford* tells the tale of 'the strange Disturbances, Ludicrous Feats, and Malicious Pranks of an Evil Spirit in the House of Mr. G. living in Back Lane at Deptford near London, in April and May, 1699'. It claims 'a great number of Inhabitants of that Town' could attest to its veracity. As a demonological text it can be counted among the many pieces written between the Restoration (1660) and the end of the century, and through the heated debate concerning the reality of demons and other supernatural possibilities that was conducted by theologians and philosophers. It takes the form a two-sided broad-sheet and amounts to around 1500 words. Its unnamed author declares it has been published (by Nathaniel Crouch in Poultney in 1699) 'to prevent false reports'. From the start it is clear in its purpose to assert the reality of spirits, evil ones in this instance, in retaliation to a supposed tide of atheism.

Unlike so many ghost stories before and since, this one is set in broad daylight, not in the dark nor at midnight. It begins around noon on Saturday, 25 April 1699, when a stone smashed the glass of a window facing onto the street in Mr G.'s parlour. While some boys in the street were being accused of doing it - which they denied - another stone was thrown through a second windowpane. Thereafter, for several days, many more stones were thrown at windows at the back of the house and on the side-wall, seemingly being hurled from adjacent fields. Glass was smashed and window lead was pock-marked causing the residents to close the shutters to prevent further damage. Stones continued to be hurled at the house with even more 'fury'. One great stone shattered the shutters of a window. Consequently, strong pine boards were nailed up on the outside of the broken windows after which the disturbances ceased on the outside of the house but now moved inside. On one occasion all the china cups and glasses were removed from the mantle-piece in the parlour and placed

> **The Devil of Deptford.**
>
> Being a true Relation of the ſtrange Diſturbances, Ludicrous Feats, and Malicious Pranks of an Evil Spirit in the Houſe of Mr. G. living in *Back-Lane* at *Deptford* near *London*, in *April* and *May*, 1695.
>
> *The Truth whereof is known, and can be atteſted by a great number of the Inhabitants of that Town.*
>
> Publiſhed to prevent falſe Reports.

on the floor. On another occasion several earthenware plates and dishes were smashed. After all the pieces had been gathered up by the lady of the house they were thrown about with great force before they were gathered up again and taken off the premises. Several pewter plates were seen leaving the kitchen and going into the parlour of their own accord, and an iron heating device (? a warming pan) somehow made its way upstairs into the lady's bedroom where it was thrown at her head, striking her under the ear with such violence that it made her bleed. Reeling from the first blow she sustained a second after the heater rose from the floor and hit her on the other side of her head. A maid was instructed to take it into the garden but about an hour later Mr G. saw it come in at the parlour door to strike his wife a third time, this time on the collarbone, causing her a good deal of pain. A small barrel, large enough to contain about four gallons, got to the top of the cellar stairs before another gentleman kicked it back down again. Soon after, a maid going down the same stairs met it coming up again with the head uppermost. Mr G. also saw the barrel on the move and another one too which followed it soon after. A noise on the first floor revealed that a candle and candlestick, hitherto in the dining-room which was locked at the time, had been thrown upstairs. In addition to all this, part of a loaf of bread went missing and, after a long search, it was found under a kettle in the cellar. Some butter in a pan was thrown onto the earth floor and the pan itself was smashed.

In one very odd episode a small book was seen to leave a drawer in which it had been placed and to hover across the room, a couple of feet off the ground, as if it was being blown, before it fell at Mrs G's feet. As soon as she put it back in the drawer it came out again and moved towards her. This was repeated five times until it disappeared entirely before it was found, some time later, in the corner of a closet. Likewise, a hat and hat-case moved around a room without human aid, and a small stool rose from the ground and fell upon a chest of drawers, jumping off again sometime later and landing neatly on its feet. Candles, tobacco-pipes and a wig stand ('head-block') were also seen to move about of their own accord. For security a maid took strings ('links') of sausages upstairs but no sooner had she done so than they began to make their way back down again. 'Stop the links!', she cried out, but the sausages 'were too nimble for her' and disappeared from view. When, eventually, they were found, they were in a grubby corner in the cellar. Nevertheless, after they had been washed and fried, Mr G. and his wife enjoyed them for supper although they agreed thereafter they should have avoided doing so, not knowing through what infernal hands they had passed. Once, when she opened the trunk in which she kept her clothes she saw them heaving up as though a cat was lying beneath them. The same thing happened in her maid's trunk but in both instances no animal was found to explain the phenomenon. The linen in a chest of drawers was found crumpled despite having been laid flat, and a chest of drawers was turned upside down. Beds made in the morning were found disordered with the bedclothes thrown off two or three times a day, and the pillows found at the foot of the stairs.

One day, when Mr G. was walking in his garden, a stone was somehow conveyed into his hands which he was holding behind his back. His wife saw one coming towards her but it flew sufficiently slowly for her to be able to catch it in one hand without injury. Indeed, they were often hit by stones but never with great force. It was reckoned about a thousand stones were thrown around the place within a month. Although watchers were placed around the house in the streets, fields, and gardens, the culprit was not discovered even while stones continued to be flung about.

At length Mr G. decided to sit up all night with some friends, praying and reading. However, they soon realized that the disturbances only took place between eight in the morning and eleven o'clock at night, the 'spirit' thus enabling everyone to get a decent night's sleep.

They also discovered that the more company they had at the house the less likely they were to be troubled. Nevertheless, certain ministers who were made aware of their troubles were certain they defied rational explanation and thus must be caused by 'an Invisible and Supernatural power'. However, it was also apparent that the phenomena started about ten days after 'one Person came into the Family' who stayed with them for about five weeks. The moment this individual left the disturbances came to an end. One wonders, who was this person? Was he or she the cause, conduit, or target of these bizarre events? The damage sustained by the windows and the window fittings was considered tangible evidence of supernatural forces and, according to our source, 'the whole town of Deptford, almost, will be Vouchers for the reality thereof'.

25
A HOUSE INFECTED WITH DEMONS: BUTLEIGH, SOMERSET, c.1704

IN 1705 JOHN Beaumont published an account of a recent case of demonic lithobolia at Butleigh, close to the author's Somerset home.[258] Of this and other similar cases, Owen Davis has noted that 'Through rumour and gossip, the act of stone-throwing, if continued for long enough without detection, could accrue supernatural associations that were not present in the first place'.[259] The tale is short enough to warrant including here in its entirety:

> There are many Relations of Houses infested with demons by Magical Practices, causing Noises in them, throwing stones, etc. [...] There was an instance of this kind last year in Somersetshire, at Butley near Glastenbury [sic]. Here lives one Mr. Pope, whose Son, being about 13 or 14 Years of Age, fell often into Fits, and in his Fits said, his

---

258 Beaumont, *Treatise*, pp. 305-06.
259 Davies, *The Haunted*, p. 31.

AN
Historical, Physiological and Theological
TREATISE
OF
SPIRITS,
Apparitions, Witchcrafts,
and other Magical Practices.

CONTAINING

An Account of the *Genii* or *Familiar Spirits*, both Good and Bad, that are said to attend Men in this Life; and what sensible Perceptions some Persons have had of them: (particularly the Author's own Experience for many Years.)

Also of Appearances of Spirits after Death; Divine Dreams, Divinations, Second Sighted Persons, &c.

Likewise the Power of Witches, and the reality of other Magical Operations, clearly asserted. With a Refutation of Dr. *Bekker's World bewitch'd*; and other Authors that have opposed the Belief of them.

By JOHN BEAUMONT, Gent.

Præstat aliqua probabiliter nosse de rebus superioribus & Cœlestibus, quàm de rebus inferioribus multa demonstrare.
Arist. Moral. 9.

London: Printed for D. Browne, at the Black Swan without Temple-Bar; J. Taylor, at the Ship in St. Paul's Church-Yard; R. Smith, at the Angel without Temple-Bar; F. Coggan, in the Inner-Temple Lane; and T. Browne without Temple-Bar, 1705.

Father's House would be Burnt by Spirits, whom he sometimes saw; and the House was Burnt down accordingly, and a Stall with three Oxen in it, and some Wheat Mows in his backside; and Stones were seen to come in at the Windows in the Day time, no man perceiving from what Hand they came; as a Person of Glastenbury told my self, the last summer at Wells, in the said County; he, upon his being in the House, having seen many stones to come in at the Windows. This vexation continued for a long time, though now I hear it's ceas'd, and the House is rebuilding. There are many more particulars to be brought concerning this Fact, and, if any Man can make out, that all these things were done by Trick, and Contrivance (as some say they were) they may do well to satisfie the World of it.

26
'OLD JEFFRIES' AND THE WESLEYS: EPWORTH RECTORY, LINCOLNSHIRE, 1716-17

DESCRIBED BY HARRY Price as 'a classic – perhaps *the* classic of the early cases', the tale of the haunting of Epworth Rectory, the Wesley family home from 1695 to 1735, is contained in the family papers.[260] It boasts the fullest record of both events and context. There are multiple family and other accounts of what happened when the Wesley family home was infested by a demon, and a wealth of material revealing the family's history.

The Reverend Samuel, Rector of St Andrew's, Epworth, and his wife, Susanna, set up home in the parish in 1695. Samuel, a staunch royalist, and a Tory who demanded the strict observances of his parishioners, seems to have made enemies in the locality; his crops were burnt, his animals maimed, and the destruction of his timber-framed and thatched rectory by fire in 1709 could have been the result of arson.

---

260 Price, *Poltergeist*, p. 81.

Epworth Old Rectory *c.*1890

Little survived beyond the chimney survived the fire and a new, grander rectory was built around it in place of the original structure. Price's further observation that the record has probably only survived because the family happened to produce two very famous sons, John and Charles Wesley (1703-81, 1707-88), founders of Methodism, is equally valid. Letters written by their mother and other family members to their older brother, Samuel (1690-1739), when he was a teacher at Westminster School, tell the story as it unfurled. These and related papers were published by Joseph Priestly in 1791 in *Original Letters by the Rev. John Wesley.*[261] They include a full account written by John a decade later,

---

261 Priestly, *Letters*, pp. 118-66.

based on one by his father. This material, around two dozen separate documents, was collated and annotated by Price in a dedicated chapter in *Poltergeist Over England* (1945).[262] That it had a significant and lasting impression on John Wesley, even though he was living away from home in a boarding school at the time, is indicative in the fact that he chose to publish his episodic version of the events, towards the end of his life, in the *Arminian Magazine* (October-December 1784).[263] If there is some kind of truth in the notion that the poltergeist is the product of anxiety, underpinned by a strong belief in the reality of malevolent spirits, this tale supports it.

The story begins with 'several dismal groans, like a person in extremes, at the point of death' heard in the entrance hall by Nanny Marshall, the family's maid, on 1 December 1716.[264] Molly Wesley and two or three of her sisters were in the dining-room when Nanny, with a bowl of butter in her hand, burst in and told them about it. Although the girl was terrified and it 'caused the up starting of her hair, and made her ears prick fourth at an unusual rate',[265] no-one was much concerned when told, and, instead, 'endeavoured to laugh her out of her fears'.[266] It was suggested she might have heard the mournful complaint of one Mr Turpin, 'who had the stone' (kidney stones), as he passed by the house.[267]

According to John's later narrative, the following day his father's manservant and one of his sisters, were in the dining room at around ten o'clock one evening when they heard knocking at the door which opened into the garden. Brown opened the door but there was no-one there. Soon further knocking was heard, together with a groan, and, once again, nobody could be seen.

---

262 Price, *Poltergeist*, Chapter VII 'The Wesley Poltergeist', pp. 81-110.
263 John Wesley, 'An Account of the Disturbances in My Father's House', *Arminian Magazine*, Volume VII, 1784, October, pp. 548-50, November, pp. 606-8, December, pp. 654-56.
264 Nanny Marshall had started her employment at the rectory on 11 November 1716. To Samuel Wesley from his mother, 12 January 1716/17; Priestly, *Letters*, p. 120.
265 To Samuel Wesley from his sister, Susannah, 24 January 1716/17; Priestly, *Letters*, p. 128.
266 To Samuel Wesley from his mother, 12 January 1716/17; Priestly, *Letters*, p. 120.
267 From Molly Wesley to her brother John ('Jack'), August 27 1726; Priestly, *Letters*, p. 157.

About ten days later Emily, one of the Wesley sisters, told her mother that there was a general alarm among the servants and younger children who had been reporting more groans, and also unaccountable knocking about the house, usually three or four knocks at a time. These began to be heard two or three nights after Nanny heard the groans in the hall.

Another of the Wesley daughters, Sukey, who was in her early twenties, sat up in 'the best chamber' upstairs one night 'on purpose to hear it'.[268] '[E]arnestly desiring to hear it', she was not disappointed when she began to hear knocking which seemed to emanate from the room below which she knew was locked and, presumably, unoccupied. Several years later she told her brother John ('Jack') 'I was frightened, and leapt into bed with all my cloaths on'. Thereafter, 'at all hours of the day and night' she heard knocking and, on one occasion, the crash of what sounded like a falling chain.

Not long after the haunting had begun, Sukey and her sixteen-year-old sister Nancy, were sitting in the dining room when 'We heard something rush on the outside of the doors that opened into the garden, then three loud knocks, immediately after [an]other three, and in half a minute the same number over our heads'.[269] The next day, Sukey and another sister, twenty-year-old Molly, who were still up after most of the family had gone to bed, 'heard three bouncing thumps under our feet, which soon made us throw away our work, and tumble into bed'.[270] They continued to be disturbed, this time by 'the tingling of the latch and warming pan'[271] before the supposed entity departed. Molly later declared, '[the] windows jarred, and the house shook from top to bottom'.[272] Not long after, but maybe on another night, they 'heard a noise as if a great piece of metal was thrown down on the outside of our

---

268   Susannah 'Sukey' Wesley (1695-1764).
269   Anne 'Nancy' Wesley (born 17 March 1701).
270   Mary 'Molly' Wesley (1696-1734), Molly was reading at the dining room table; To Samuel Wesley from his sister Susannah, 24 January 1716/17; Priestly, *Letters*, p. 129.
271   To Samuel Wesley from his sister, Susannah Wesley, 24 January 1716/17; Priestly, *Letters*, p. 129.
272   Account given to John Wesley by his sister Molly, August 27 1726; Priestly, *Letters*, p. 158.

Epworth Old Rectory in 2024 [Photo: author]

chamber'.[273] A few days later, between five and six in the evening, Molly was by herself in the dining room when 'The door seemed to open, though it was still shut, and somebody walked in a night gown trailing on the ground (nothing appearing) and seemed to go leisurely round me'.[274] She promptly fled upstairs to tell her mother and older sister, Emily, all about it.

The eldest daughter in the family, Emily, who turned twenty-five at the time of the haunting, was, initially, sceptical of her sisters' claims until, 'one night, about a week after the clock had struck ten, I went down

---

273   To Samuel Wesley from his sister, Susannah Wesley, 24 January 1717; Priestly, *Letters,* p. 129.
274   Account given to John Wesley by his sister Molly, August 27 1726; Priestly, *Letters,* p. 158.

RELATIONS   211

stairs to lock the doors, which I always do'.²⁷⁵ She had hardly got to the top of the main staircase, 'when I heard a noise, like a person throwing a vast coal in the middle of the fire kitchen, and all the splinters seemed to fly about from it'. She and Sukey went downstairs together to check all the rooms downstairs, 'but there was nothing out of order'.²⁷⁶ The dog was fast asleep and the family's one cat was at the other end of the house. However, she had just gone back upstairs, and was undressing for bed in the nursery, when she heard a great crash as if a large stone had been thrown into the midst of the empty bottles that were stored under the main staircase.²⁷⁷ Somewhat alarmed, she got into bed as quickly as she could. Her sister Hetty, who was around nineteen-years-old, was still up, ready 'to wait on my father going to bed' as was her custom. She was sitting on the bottom step of 'the garret stairs' with the door at the foot of the stairs closed, when she heard coming 'down the stairs behind her, something like a man, in a loose night gown trailing after him, which made her fly rather than run to me in the nursery'.²⁷⁸

From that night on, Emily recalled in 1726, 'I heard it every night, for two or three weeks.' She came up with a nickname for the entity bothering the family. She called it 'Jeffrey'.²⁷⁹ He was named after a man who had died in the house some time ago.²⁸⁰

At first, Mrs Wesley was of the opinion the cause must be rats or, possibly, weasels, declaring that the best way to deal with them was by the continuous blowing of a horn to scare them away. Molly was 'much displeased' by this suggestion for, 'if it be anything supernatural, it certainly would be very angry, and more troublesome', but her mother went ahead and a 'horn was blown in the garrets'. Perhaps Molly's warning was well-founded since, 'before the noises were always at night,

275   Emilia 'Emily' Wesley (31 December 1692-1771).
276   To Samuel Wesley from his sister Emily, *c.* February 1716/17; Priestly, *Letters*, p. 136.
277   As the eldest daughter Emily had responsibilities for the care of her younger siblings, the youngest of whom, in December 1716, was seven-year-old Kezia ('Kezzy').
278   To Samuel Wesley from his sister Emily, *c.* February 1716/17; Priestly, *Letters*, p. 136.
279   To Samuel Wesley from his sister Emily, *c.* February 1716/17; Priestly, *Letters*, p. 137.
280   Wesley, 'An Account of the Disturbances in My Father's House', pp. 548-50, 606-8, 654-56.

from this time they were heard at all hours, day and night'.[281] These were heard in the garret but most often in the nursery, or green chamber (it is unclear if these were two separate rooms or one and the same). What sounded like the footsteps of a man going up and down stairs, were heard through the night, together with great rumblings downstairs, and in the attics. 'The noises', Mrs Wesley told her son, Samuel, 'were more loud, and distinct, both day and night, than before [...] beyond the power of any human creature'.[282]

At about seven o'clock on what Mr Wesley later calculated was probably the morning of 23 Sunday December, Emily persuaded her mother 'to go into the nursery, where I should be convinced they were not startled at nothing'. Sure enough, she heard knocking noises at her feet and at the head of the bed. Doubtless aware of the concept of the sentient poltergeist, she addressed it directly, 'I desired, if it was a spirit, it would answer me, and knocking several times with my foot on the ground, with several pauses, it repeated under the sole of my feet, exactly the same number of strokes, with the same intervals'. Emily's seven-year-old sister, Kezzy, joined in by stamping on the floor and 'the same sounds were returned that she made many times, successively'. When Susanna Wesley looked under the bed she appears to have found the culprit for, 'something ran out pretty much like a badger, and seemed to run directly under Emily's petticoats, who sat opposite to me on the other side'.[283]

Everyone in the household, with the exception of Samuel, seems to have heard these odd noises in the first couple of weeks of December. For a time, his wife choose not to mention the matter to him since he might be quick to think it was knocking for him or foretelling some imminent misfortune within the family. When she finally did tell him he proposed somebody was playing games but, the following night, on Friday 21 December, 'as he was in bed, it knocked loudly nine times,

---

281 Account given to John Wesley by his mother in August 1726; Priestly, *Letters*, pp. 152-5.
282 To Samuel Wesley from his mother, 25 or 27 January 1716/17; Priestly, *Letters*, p. 125.
283 Account given to John Wesley by his mother in August 1726; Priestly, *Letters*, p. 153.

just by his bedside'.²⁸⁴ It sounded as if it was coming from the room next door but when he looked for a perpetrator he found none. Nevertheless, he presumed there must be an intruder and, he later declared, 'having got a stout mastiff, hoped he would soon rid me of it'.²⁸⁵ Thereafter he was disturbed by the noise as much as the rest of the household.

'One night', Susanna wrote to their eldest son, Samuel, 'it made such a noise in the room over our heads, as if several people were walking', ran up and down the stairs, 'and was so outrageous that we thought the children would be frighted, so your father and I rose, and went down in the dark to light a candle'.²⁸⁶ It was about one o'clock in the morning. Holding onto each other in the dark, just as they reached the foot of the staircase they heard a great noise as if a bag of coins was being emptied at their feet, together with what sounded like all the bottles stored under the stairs were being 'dashed to a thousand pieces'. The mastiff came with them but, after a bout of barking, quietened down and 'seemed more afraid than any of the children'. They passed through the hall into the kitchen to fetch a candle and returned upstairs to check on the children. They were all fast asleep. They still heard it 'rattle and thunder in every room above or behind us, locked as well as open'. At around two in the morning they got back to bed 'and were pretty quiet for the rest of the night'.²⁸⁷ This all happened on the night of Thursday 27 December.

The following day Wesley invited Joseph Hoole, the rector of nearby Haxey (1712-37), 'an eminently pious and sensible man', to stay the night.²⁸⁸ He agreed to do so, and they stayed up until one or two in the morning. They all heard the usual knocks, usually three at a time, and other odd sounds. That night Sukey bravely chose to sleep in the nursery 'where it was very violent'.²⁸⁹ In addition to vigorous

284 To Samuel Wesley from his mother, 12 January 1716/17; Priestly, *Letters*, p. 120.
285 Wesley, 'An Account of Noises and Disturbances in my House'; Priestly, *Letters*, p. 143.
286 To Samuel Wesley from his mother, 12 January 1716/17; Priestly, *Letters*, p. 120.
287 Wesley, 'An Account of Noises and Disturbances in my House'; Priestly, *Letters*, p. 144.
288 Wesley, 'An Account of the Disturbances in My Father's House', pp. 548-50, 606-8, 654-56.
289 To Samuel Wesley from his sister Susannah 24 January 1716/17; Priestly, *Letters*, p. 129.

knocking which made the bed the younger children were sleeping in shake, she 'heard something walk by my bedside, like a man in a long night gown'.[290] In the account she sent her brother John some years later she provided further details of the events that night:

> One night hearing it was most violent in the nursery, I resolved to lie there. Late at night several strong knocks were given on the two lowest steps of the garret stairs which were close to the nursery door. The latch of the door then jarred, and seemed to be swiftly moved to and fro, and presently began knocking about a yard within the room on the floor. It then came gradually to sister Hetty's bed, who trembled strongly in her sleep. It beat very loud, three strokes at a time, on the bed's head.[291]

Mr Hoole, 'with fear', according to his own account, and Sukey's father, 'with a great deal of hope', heard the commotion and came to investigate.[292] Mr Wesley went into the nursery and 'adjured it to speak' but the knocking continued around the room before seeming to move into the garret room above. Sukey had had enough and left the nursery to join her mother and sister Emily in their mother's room. She suggested they play a game of cards but they had only just begun when a knocking began under their feet. Although this soon stopped, they could hear it knocking in the nursery until early in the morning.

Molly recalled how her father was infuriated when the entity did not respond when, on more than one occasion, he attempted to communicate with it in the nursery, and he 'spoke sharply, called it *deaf and dumb devil*, and repeated his adjuration' to explain why it was troubling his family. She remembered her sisters were 'terribly afraid it would speak'. According to John Wesley's retelling of Hoole's recollections, 'Mr. Wesley observing, that they were much affected though asleep, sweating and trembling exceedingly, was very angry, and pulling out a pistol,

---

290 To Samuel Wesley from his sister Susannah 24 January 1716/17; Priestly, *Letters*, p. 129.
291 Account given to John Wesley by his sister, Susannah, in c. September 1726. Priestly, *Letters*, p. 160.
292 Account given to John Wesley by Reverend Hoole, September 16 1726. Priestly, *Letters*, p. 163.

was going to fire at the place from whence the sound came'. Hoole persuaded him that, since this was 'something preternatural' he had no power to hurt it, and that such a reaction might only empower it.[293] In a parting gesture it knocked on the bed's head 'so exceedingly violently, as if it would break it to shivers, and from that time we heard nothing till a month after'.[294] The earliest known correspondence regarding the case, Susanna Wesley's letter to her son, written on 12 January 1717, suggests the house had been quiet since 28 December.[295] On 24 January Sukey assured her brother, 'It is now pretty quiet', its knocking more or less reserved for family prayers, at the point when Mr Wesley prayed for the king.[296] On 11 February his father wrote, 'As for the noises, etc. in our family, I thank God we are now all quiet'.[297] Nevertheless the strange phenomena lingered a while longer. On 17 March 1717, Sukey informed him that 'last Sunday, to my father's no small amazement, his trencher danced upon the table a pretty while, without any body's stirring the table'.[298] On 1 April, Emily declared 'the spright was with us last night, and heard by many of the family, especially by our maid and myself'. This maid, Nanny Marshall presumably, saw the dining room door open of its own accord and, a while later, close itself, 'then it began to knock as usual'.[299]

When, at the end of January 1717, Samuel asked his mother if the two recently hired servants in the house, Marshall and Brown, might be playing tricks on the family, she assured him this was not the case since they were both terrified by the disturbances, and 'we have often the noises when they were in the room by us', particularly she added 'at family prayers'. Nanny 'was in such a panic, that she was almost

---

293 Wesley, 'An Account of the Disturbances in My Father's House', pp. 548-50, 606-8, 654-56.
294 Account given to John Wesley by his sister Molly, August 27 1726. Priestly, *Letters*, p. 159.
295 To Samuel Wesley from his mother, 12 January 1717. Priestly, *Letters*, pp. 121-22.
296 To Samuel Wesley from his sister Susannah, 24 January 1716/17; Priestly, *Letters*, p. 130.
297 To Samuel Wesley from his father, 11 February 1716/17. Priestly, *Letters*, p. 134.
298 To Susannah Wesley from her brother, Samuel, 27 March 1716/17; Priestly, *Letters*, p. 139.
299 To Mr. N. Berry from Emilia Wesley, 1 April 1717; Priestly, *Letters*, p. 140.

The principal staircase of Epworth Old Rectory and focus of poltergeist activity, 1716-17. [Photo: author]

incapable of all business, nor durst ever go from one room to another, or stay by herself a minute after it began to be dark'. As for Robert, he 'was most visited by it lying in the garret, and has been often frighted down bare foot, and almost naked, not daring to stay alone to put on his cloaths'.[300] Although one or more of the Wesley daughters could be considered a focus of the poltergeist's attentions, Robert Brown also claimed to have been bothered as he lay in his garret sleeping quarters. This is John Wesley's summary of the vivid (and entertaining) recollection of Robert's haunting which he shared with him in 1726:

> The first time Robert Brown, my father's man, heard it, was when he was fetching down some corn from the garrets. Somewhat knocked on a door just by him, which made him run away down stairs. From that time it used frequently to visit him in bed, walking up the garret

---

300 To Samuel Wesley from his mother, 25 or 27 January 1717. Priestly, *Letters*, p. 126.

stairs, and in the garrets, like a man in jack boots, with a night gown trailing after him, then lifting up his latch and making it jar, and making presently a noise in his room like the gobling [sic] of a turkey cock, then stumbling over his shoes or boots by the bed side. He was resolved once to be too hard for it, and so took a large mastiff we had just got to bed with him and left his shoes and boots below stairs; but he might as well have spared his labour, for it was exactly the same thing, whether any were there or no. The same sound was heard as if there had been forty pairs. The dog indeed was a great comfort to him, for as soon as the latch began to jar, he crept into bed, made such an howling and barking together, in spite of all the man could do, that he alarmed most of the family.

Soon after, being grinding corn in the garrets, and happening to stop a little, the handle of the mill was turn round with great swiftness. He said nothing vexed him, but that the mill was empty. If corn had been in it old Jeffrey might have ground his heart out for him; he would never have disturbed him.[301]

The whole family was baffled by their bizarre, shared experience. Emily wrote to Samuel shortly afterwards: 'A whole month was sufficient to convince any body of the reality of the thing, and to try all ways of discovering any trick, had it been possible for any such to have been used'. Of course, this was a deeply religious family and, at the same time, like every ghost-hunter since, Emily *wanted* reason to believe in a supernatural cause: 'I heartily rejoice at having such an opportunity of convincing myself past simple doubt or scruple, of the existence of some beings besides those we see'. 'But', she continued, 'whatever it was, I perceived it could be made angry [...] It was more loud and fierce if any one said it was rats, or any thing natural'. It tended to be active from ten or eleven at night, announcing its arrival with something that sounded to Emily like ' the quick winding up of a jack, at the corner of the room by my bed's head, just the running of the wheels and the creaking of the iron work'.[302]

301 Account given to John Wesley by Robert Brown in August 1726; Priestly, *Letters*, pp. 164-65.
302 To Samuel Wesley from his sister Emily, *c.* February 1716/17; Priestly, *Letters*, pp. 135-37.

As in so many poltergeist cases the most remarkable aspects of the Epworth tale are the abundance and duration of odd phenomena, the fact that it was witnessed by so many, and that, despite appropriate investigation, no obvious explanation was discovered. 'I went out of doors', wrote Mr Wesley, 'some times alone, at others with company, and walked round the house, but could see or hear nothing'. One day, soon after the troubles began, Emily, according to her brother John's account, 'heard knocking at the back-kitchen door. She ran to it, unlocked it softly, and when the knocking was repeated, suddenly opened it: but nothing was to be seen'. She shut it and more knocks followed. She opened it again but no-one was there and 'when she went to shut the door, it was violently thrust against her: she let it fly open but nothing appeared'. The second time she tried to shut it, it 'thrust against her: but she set her knee and her shoulder to the door, forced it to, and turned the key'. The knocking started up again but this time she ignored it and went to bed, however, 'from that time she was thoroughly convinced, that there was no imposter in the affair'.[303]

~ ~ ~

P. G. Maxwell-Stuart has written of the case, 'Samuel Wesley senior clearly assumed, on the strength of groaning repeated more than once, he was dealing with a ghost'. Although the term 'ghost' is, of course, open to interpretation, this claim, if we use the conventional definition, is questionable. While the entity was given a jocular nickname of 'Jeffrey' or 'Old Jeffries', after a previous incumbent, the poltergeist as the ghost of the human-departed explanation does not tally with what we know of their beliefs from the Wesley correspondence. As we have already seen Emily considered it a work of witchcraft, and the Reverend Hoole, according to John Wesley, stated that Mr Wesley, on refusing to leave his haunted home, declared, 'I will never flee from the devil'. The implication here, and elsewhere, is clear: the entity was, by his reckoning, a demon, and Wesley thus falls in line with the demonic traditions of the previous century as opposed to the future obsession with

---

303 Wesley, 'An Account of the Disturbances in My Father's House', pp. 548-50, 606-8, 654-56.

ghosts. There are of course 'ghostly' elements in the accounts, notably the occasions when members of the household thought they heard the sound of trailing apparel and heavy footsteps prompting speculation regarding a masculine entity dressed in a long nightshirt.

Roger Clarke, in his *Natural History of Ghosts* (2912), also, as befits his title, calls the Epworth poltergeist a ghost,[304] whereas, in the correspondence of its witnesses, it was beyond human (and, for that matter, gender) - a 'thing' consistently identified simply as 'it'. To the Wesleys, in jest, it was dead old Mr Jeffrey, but when they dared take the matter seriously, they had to conclude that, even if it sounded like a person or, on one occasion, it *looked* like a person, they were dealing with something much more dangerous. If it was not a living mischief-maker or rats, it had to be a demon. Maxwell-Stuart has noted that, according to Hoole, he was invited by Wesley to Epworth 'to conjure' this demon. Hoole himself was unclear as to Wesley's meaning and purpose beyond sitting up with him to listen out for Jeffrey, but Maxwell-Stuart's hypothesis is that it was an allusion to the principle, if not Wesley's intended practice, of exorcism.[305]

Some years after the drama of December 1716, John Wesley noted in a memorandum, 'The first time my mother ever heard any unusual noise at Epworth was long before the disturbance of old Jeffrey'. Following a squabble between Sukey and a brother who had 'lately come from London' – Samuel, presumably – 'the door and windows rung and jarred very loud' in the room above where their mother was sitting. This was accompanied by three distinct knocks. 'From that night', John concluded, 'it never failed to give notice in much the same manner, against any signal misfortune, or illness of any belonging to the family'.[306] And Susanna Wesley was no stranger to misfortune; just ten of her nineteen children survived their early childhood. Among other things she heard in the winter of 1716/7 was the sound of a cradle being rocked vigorously in the nursery. By now her youngest child, Kezzy, was nearly eight years old and 'no cradle had been there for some years'.[307]

304 'The ghost was called by the family Old Jeffrey'; Clarke, *Ghosts*, p. 98.
305 Maxwell-Stuart, *Poltergeists*, p. 162.
306 Memorandum of John Wesley; Priestly, p. 150.
307 Wesley, 'An Account of the Disturbances in My Father's House', pp. 548-50, 606-8, 654-6.

Despite the earnest advice of 'Several Gentlemen and Clergymen [...] to quit the house' Samuel Wesley and his family stayed put. The worst of it was over by the end of January 1717.

~ ~ ~

ONE OF THE many pieces of evidence for the Epworth Rectory case, a letter written by Samuel Wesley in London to his mother in the haunted house, is worth transcribing in full since it exemplifies the cultural shift in attitudes to the supernatural that had occurred in the second half of the seventeenth century. By 1717, at the start of which year Samuel wrote his letter, belief in the supernatural, and, more particularly, the reality of spirits, was no longer universal. Instead, sceptics in such matters, then as now, were disposed to seek 'rational' explanations for strange occurrences rather than resort to that of divine Providence. Samuel and, for that matter, his famous brother John, were men moulded in the tradition of theologians like Richard Baxter. In the dying embers of what has been dubbed the Glanvill-Webster debate[308] it is evident in this letter and other writings where their sympathies lay.

> Those who are so wise as not to believe any supernatural occurrences, though ever so well attested, could find a hundred questions to ask about those strange noises, you wrote me an account of; but for my part, I know not what question to put, which if answered, would confirm me more in the belief of what you tell me. Two or three I have heard from others. Was there never a new maid, or man, in the house, that might play tricks? Was there no body above in the garrets, when the walking was there? Did all the family hear it together when they were in one room, or at one time? Did it seem to all to be in the same place, at the same time? Could not cats, or rats, or dogs be the sprights? Was the whole family asleep, when my father and you went down stairs? Such doubts as these being replied to, though they could not, as God himself assures us, convince them who believe not Moses and the prophets, yet would strengthen such as do believe. As to my

---

308 The dispute between Joseph Glanvill and John Webster and their supporters regarding the reality of witches and demons.

particular opinion, concerning the events forboded by these noises, I cannot, I must confess, form any - I think since it was not permitted to speak, all guesses must be vain. The end of spirits actions is yet more hidden than that of men, and even this latter puzzles the most subtle politicians. That we may be struck so as to prepare seriously for any ill, may, it is possible, be one design of providence. It is surely our duty and wisdom to do so.[309]

27
'ALL NIPPED TO PIECES': KINROSS, SCOTLAND, 1718

THE FOLLOWING ACCOUNT, apparently, was recorded first in 'a curious printed sheet'[310] printed in June 1718. It had the equally curious title *Endorism, or a strange Relation of Dreamers or Spirits that trouble the Minister's House of Kinross*. The elusive original 'broadside'[311] appears as a transcription in nineteenth-century sources including an 1834 cultural history of Scotland by James Maidment,[312] an 1871 reprint, with additions, of George Sinclair's *Satan's Invisible World Discovered* (1685),[313] and a history of witchcraft in Scotland by Charles Kirkpatrick Sharpe published in 1884.[314] The editor of the Sinclair reprint, Thomas

---

309 Samuel Wesley to his mother, January 17 1716/17; Priestly, *Letters*, pp. 123-24.
310 Sharpe, *Instruments*, p. 177.
311 If it was published as a single-sheet broadside in 1718, as has been claimed, I am not aware of an extant copy; it does not appear in the massive digital archive of such texts, *Early English Books Online*.
312 James Maidment, *Analecta Scotica: Collections Illustrative of the Civil, Ecclesiastical, and Literary History of Scotland* (Edinburgh, 1834), pp. 195-97.
313 George Sinclair, *Satan's Invisible World Discovered* (Edinburgh, 1871, supplement V), pp. xci-xciv.
314 Charles Kirkpatrick Sharpe, *A Historical Account of the Belief in Witchcraft in Scotland* (London,1884, 177-80).

George Stevenson, an Edinburgh publisher and bookseller, declared he had found it 'in a folio volume of Miscellaneous Papers consisting of Dying Speeches, Elegies [etc.]'.[315]

Despite its title, invoking the biblical 'Witch of Endor',[316] and the old assumption that witchcraft was the foundation of poltergeist infestation, the narrator was somewhat ambivalent: 'what is the essence of spirits, or what way the devil makes use of these deluded creatures [...] it's hard to determine'. Equally, he/she seems to have had little doubt the minister of Kinross's troubles were the work – 'the supernatural molestation'[317] - of one or more spirits. The minister in question was Robert McGill who served in this capacity from 1698 until 1726. Contrary to belief that sinfulness invited the unwonted attention of demons, this narrator declared, in justifying the revelation of their activity in the minister's home, 'the godly are the only objects of the devil's fury, for such as the devil is sure of, he does not heed them, until he has them'.

The first odd occurrence in the McGill household was the disappearance of some silver spoons and knives 'which were found in the barn among the straw some time afterwards, stuck up in the floor, with a big dish all nipped to pieces'. After this pins kept turning up in their food, including, on one occasion, the large pin that Mr McGill used to fasten his gown. A pair of their sheets, put out to dry on the green alongside their neighbours' washing, was also 'all nipped to pieces' while everyone else's linen was left alone. By now the house had attracted attention and, one night 'several went to watch the house' for further disturbances. While one of these was praying 'down falls the press, wherein was abundance of lime vessels, all broke to pieces'. As in certain other cases clothing locked up in a coffer and, even while being worn, was cut, torn, destroyed and 'clipt away'. A 'certain girl' ate some food, in the house presumably, and fell sick before throwing up five pins, and a stone which came down the chimney, 'wambled' across the floor, 'and then took flight out at the window'. Among other odd occurrences, the

---

315 George Sinclair (ed. T. G. Stevenson), *Satan's Invisible World Discovered* (Edinburgh, 1871) supplement V, xci; his description of his source, incidentally, does not match the content of Maidment's 1834 volume in which it had previously been retold.
316 Biblical witch consulted by Saul to raise the spirit of the prophet Samuel.
317 Sharpe, *Instruments*, p. 177.

minister's Bible was thrown into the fire but, amazingly, did not burn, while a plate and two silver spoons which also somehow ended up in the fire 'melted immediately'. The narrator ended the account of these troubles with the lament:

> Now, is it not very sad, that such a good and godly family should be so molested, that employ their time no other way but by praying, reading, and serious meditation, while others who are wicked livers all their lifetime, and in a manner avowedly serve that wicked one, are never troubled.

Still, no-one was hurt, nor could they have been in the narrator's opinion, for 'these bad spirits [had] no power over their bodies', but they certainly had the power to give them a fright.

AFTERWORD

WHILE WHAT IS now regarded as the poltergeist may have been a British folkloric commonplace through the medieval period, there is a dearth of documentary and archaeological evidence to prove this. Conversely there are many accounts of poltergeist activity in the period between $c.1590$ and $c.1720$. These coincided with England's so-called witch craze and, it is commonly presumed, were an aspect or consequence of it. The flourishing of poltergeist literature after $c.1650$ coincides with what has been dubbed 'England's Last Witch Craze'.[318] The archaeology of counter-magic house protection in the form of witch-bottles, concealed shoes, engraved *Ave Marias*, daisy wheels, scorch marks, and the like, paint a similar picture. While the decay of material over time, including the demolition of old houses, must be taken into consideration, the comparative abundance of such things dated to the era of the 'great rebuilding' is striking. There is good reason to suppose that the scale of concern in seventeenth-century England regarding the threat of demonic invasion of people's homes was unprecedented.

The general character of English homes of the period can be discovered at multiple places including the reconstructions at open-air museums of architecture, notably the Weald and Downland Living Museum near Chichester, and *in situ* restorations such as the exquisite cottage of the Hathaway family in Stratford-on-Avon. Sadly, few of the haunted houses mentioned in this book still stand. The exact location of the majority is unknown and most of the others have gone including the Mompessons' fine house in Tidworth and the old royal castle at Woodstock. However, you can visit Epworth Rectory, now a Wesley family museum and international shrine to Methodism. In this extraordinary, evocative place the past resonates in the present but 'Old Jeffries' in his cockloft lair left a long, long time ago. Early modern

---

318 McAleavy, *The Last Witch Craze*.

poltergeist cases were relatively short-term affairs, normally lasting for just a few weeks or months.

Occasionally people living in such houses had genuine experiences akin to those put down to poltergeists in the twenty-first. The evidence invites a range of interpretations: supernatural intervention, paranormal science, psychology and the imagination, misinterpretation and fraud. Observers and commentators in the early modern period were as tuned-in to these possibilities as the sceptics and believers of present times.

It is hard, probably impossible, to prove there was an increased experience of supposed poltergeist activity in the seventeenth century. However, the proliferation of cases in conjunction with theological shifts, changing political and social structures, and economic anxieties, which have been cited as factors in the contemporary witch craze, are equally valid in consideration of what looks like the take-off of a 'poltergeist craze' in the second half of that century. In particular, it found expression in demonological texts in the period which themselves were in large part manifestations of acute existential fears in the wake of the challenge of fledgling atheism. The natural philosophers of the Royal Society, notably, Robert Boyle, Henry More, John Aubrey, Joseph Glanvill, Justinian Isham, Robert Plot, and John Beaumont. and their correspondents, played the leading role in the second half of the seventeenth century in the development of interest in poltergeists in intellectual circles. When the case studies they accumulated were derived from seemingly reliable sources, and multiple witnesses, they presented them as empirical evidence for the reality of spirits.

The rise of English poltergeist cases in the historical record coincided exactly with the resurgence of interest in the middle of the seventeenth century in witchcraft cases and other strange phenomena, including demonic possession. Poltergeist cases were another version of the latter in which homes, as opposed to individuals, were infested by unclean spirits. Occasionally the two phenomena elided but, nevertheless, they should be regarded as distinct paranormal genres in the period.

Just as these cases were the product of the age in which they emerged, they were also, in part, the product of the places in which they occurred. The rebuilds and new-builds of the seventeenth century provided an abundance of domestic structures that provided perfect playgrounds for

AFTERWORD

mischievous poltergeists or their human imitators, much better suited than the simpler single-storey open halls of yesteryear.

The sprites haunting these houses in early modern England, and in the imaginations of the people living there, had yet to find an identity. As commentators struggled to make sense of a wave of novel accounts, a new type of supernatural / paranormal entity was evolving. It might have had its origins in other folk traditions – be it fairy-legend or pulpit-demonology – but this phenomenon was distinct and unique. It would be another two hundred years before the rise of the English poltergeist around the middle of the seventeenth century would find its name.

APPENDIX

Poltergeist cases mentioned in the text and their principal sources for the period c.1590 to c.1720.

Date	Location	Principal Source(s)
1591-92	George Lee's farmhouse, North Aston, Oxfordshire	*A True Discourse* (1592)
1630s	Home of Peter Pain, shoemaker, Mary Peol Street, Bristol	Bovet, *Pandaemonium* (1684)
c. 1635	Home of a Puritan minister, Edinburgh	Baxter, *Certainty* (1691)
1645	Home of Paul Fox, silk-weaver, West-Ham, near London	*Strange and fearfull newes* (1645) Glanvill, *Saducismus* (1681)
1647	Kirkby Malory, Leicestershire	Baxter, *Certainty* (1691)
1649	Woodstock Manor (royal palace), Oxfordshire	*The Woodstock Scuffle* (1649-50) Widows, *The Just Devil* (1660) Glanvill, *Saducismus* (2nd edition, 1682) Aubrey, *Miscellanies* (1696)
1650	Home of the Merryday family, Greenwich, near London	Magomastix, *The Strange Witch* (1650)
1654	Home of Gilbert Campbell, weaver, Glenluce, Wigtownshire, Scotland	Sinclair, *Hydrostaticks* (1672) Glanvill, *Saducismus* (2nd edition, 1682)
1658	Home of the Cowley family, Welton, Northamptonshire	Glanvill, *Saducismus* (1681)
c. 1659	Home of Walter Meyrick, Bleddfa, Powys, Wales	Glanvill, *Saducismus* (1681)

APPENDIX

1661	Home of the Paschall family, Soper Lane, London	Glanvill, *Saducismus* (1681)
1662-63	Home of John Mompesson, Justice of the Peace, North Tidworth, Wiltshire	Miles, *A Wonder of Wonders* (1663) Glanvill, *A Blow* (1668) Glanvill, *Saducismus* (1681) State papers in Hunter, 'New Light' (2005), pp. 338-53
1670	Home of Elizabeth Bridges, Weobley, Herefordshire	*The Demon of Burton* (1671)
1674	Home of a 'gentlewoman', London Wall, London	*Strange and Wonderful News* (1674)
1675	Home of the Pitts family, Puddle Dock, London	*News from Puddle-Dock* (1674-75)
1677	'Old Gast's House', Little Burton, Dorset	Glanvill, *Saducismus* (1681)
1679-80	Home of Sir William York, Leasingham, Lincolnshire	Glanvill, *Saducismus* (2nd ed., 1682)
1679	Home of the Morse family, Market Street, Newburyport, Massachusetts	Mather, *The Wonders* (1693) Beaumont, *An Historical . . . Treatise* (1705)
1680	Home of a minister, Ormiston, East Lothian, Scotland	Sinclair, *Invisible World* (1685)
1681	Home of 'Mr Tuers, a Gentleman', Ewell, Surrey	*Strange and Wonderful News from Yowell* (1681)
1682	The Walton family estate, Great Island, New Hampshire	Chamberlain, *Lithobolia* (1698)
1682	Home of the Furze family, Spreyton, Devon	*Narrative of the Demon of Spraiton* (1683) Bovet, *Pandaemonium* (1684) Aubrey, *Miscellanies* (1696)
c. 1690	Home of the Cruttenden family, Brightling, Sussex	Baxter, *The Certainty* (1691)
1695	Home of Andrew Mackie, mason, Rerrick, Dumfries & Galloway, Scotland	Telfair, *A True Relation* (1696)

1699	Home of 'Mr G.', Back Lane, Deptford, London	*Devil of Deptford* (1699)
1704	Home of the Pope family, Butleigh, Somerset	Beaumont, *An Historical . . . Treatise* (1705)
1716-17	Home of the Wesley family, Epworth Rectory, Lincolnshire	Wesley, 'An Account' (1784) Priestly, *Original Letters* (1791)
1718	Home of Robert McGill, minister, Kinross, Perth & Kinross, Scotland	*Endorism* (1718) Maidment, *Analectia Scotica* (1834)

BIBLIOGRAPHY

Early Modern sources

Anon., *A True Discourse of such strange and woonderfull accidents, as happened in the house of M. George Lee of North-Acton, in the countie of Oxford, being in truth and and matter of such special weight and consequence, as sildome hath the like bene heard of before* (London, 1592)

—., *The Woodstock Scuffle, or, Most Dreadful Apparitions that were lately seene in the Mannor-Hose of Woodstock neere Oxford, to the great Terror and wonderfull Amazement of all there, that did Behold them* (1649)

—., *The Devil of Deptford, Being a true Relation of the strange Disturbances, Ludicrous Feats, and Malicious Pranks of an Evil Spirit in the House of Mr. G. living in Back Lane at Deptford near London, in April and May, 1699* (London, 1669)

—., *The Demon of Burton, or A true Relation of Strange Witchcraft or Incantations lately practiced at Burton in the Parish of Weobley in Herefordshire* (London, 1671)

—., *Strange and Wonderful News from London-Wall, being A Full and True Relation of a House miserably disturb'd ever since Friday the Third of the Instant April, where Bedding, Linnen, Apparel, and Household-stuff of great*

Value, have at several Times, both in the Day and Night, been Cut to Pieces by Invisible Means; Knives Removed out of a Drawer in the Kitchin, and scattered in the Chambers and Garret, and things fast lock't upon Trunks and a chests, Cut and Spoiled in an unheard of Manner (London, 1674)
—., *News from Puddle-Dock in London* (London, 1674/5)
—., *Strange and Wonderful News from Yowell in Surrey* (London, 1681)
Aubrey, John, *The Natural History of Wiltshire* (London, 1691)
—., *Miscellanies* (London, 1696)
Baxter, Richard, *The Certainty of the Worlds of Spirits.* (London, 1691)
Beaumont, John, *An Historical Physiological and Theological Treatise of Spirits, Apparitions, Witchcrafts, and Other Magical Practises* (London, 1705)
Bernard, Richard, *Guide to Grand-Jury Men* (London, 1627)
Bovet, Richard, *Pandaemonium, or, The Devil's Cloyster being a further blow to modern sadduceism, proving the existence of witches and spirits, in a discourse deduced from the fall of the angels, the propagation of Satans kingdom before the flood, the idolatry of the ages after greatly advancing diabolical confederacies, with an account of the lives and transactions of several notorious witches: also, a collection of several authentick relations of strange apparitions of dæmons and spectres, and fascinations of witches, never before printed.* (London, 1684)
Chamberlain, Richard, *Lithobolia: or, The Stone-Throwing Devil* (London, 1698)
Freke, William, *A full enquiry into the power of faith* (London, 1693)
Glanvill, Joseph, *Some Philosophical Considerations Touching Witches and Witchcraft.* (London, 1666)
—. *A Blow at Modern Sadducism in some philosophical Considerations about Witchcraft.* (London, 1668)
—. *Saducismus Triumphatus, or, full and plain Evidence concerning Witches and Apparitions.* (London, 1681, 1688)
Hutchinson, Francis, *Historical Essay Concerning Witchcraft* (London, 1718)
Lavater, Lewis, *Of Ghostes and Spirites Walking by Nyght, and of Strange Noyses, Crackes, and Sundry Forewarnynge* (London, 1572)
Magomastix, Hieronymous, *The Strange Witch at Greenwich, (Ghost, Spirit, or Hobgoblin) haunting a Wench, late servant to a Miser, suspected a Murtherer of his late Wife* (London, 1650)
Miles, Abraham, *A Wonder of Wonders; Being A true Relation of the strange and invisible Beating of a Drum, at the House of John Mompesson, Esquire, at Tidcomb in the County of Wilt-shire* (London, 1663)
More, Henry, *An Antidote against Atheisme, or, an Appeal to the natural Faculties of Minds of Man, whether there be not a God* (London, 1653)
Moulin, Peter du, *The Devill of Mascon: A true Relation of the chiefe things*

which an uncleane Spirt did, and said at Mascon in Burgundy, in the house of Mr Francis Perraud Minister of the Reformed Church in the same Towne (Oxford, 1658)

Plot, Robert, *The Natural History of Oxford-shire* (Oxford and London, 1677)

Priestly, Joseph, *Original Letters by the Rev. John Wesley, and His Friends, Illustrative of his Early History, with Other Curious Papers* (Birmingham, 1791)

Scot, Reginald, *Discoverie of Witchcraft* (London, 1584)

Sinclair, George, *The hydrostaticks, or, The weight, force, and pressure of fluid bodies, made evident by physical, and sensible experiments together with some miscellany observations, the last whereof is a short history of coal, and of all the common, and proper accidents thereof, a subject never treated of before* (Edinburgh, 1672)

—. *Satan's Invisible World Discovered* (Edinburgh, 1685)

Telfair, Alexander, *A True Relation of an Apparition, Expressions and Actings, of a Spirit, which Infested the House of Andrew Mackie* (Edinburgh, 1696)

—. *A New Confutation of a Saducismus, being a true Narrative of the wonderful Expressions and Actions of a Spirit, which infested the House of Andrew Mackie* (London, 1696)

Wesley, John, 'An Account of the Disturbances in My Father's House', *Arminian Magazine*, Volume VII, October 1784, pp. 548-50, November, pp. 606-8, December, pp. 654-56

Wesley, Samuel, 'An Account of Noises and Disturbances in my House, at Epworth, Lincolnshire, in December and January, 1716' (transcribed by his son, John Wesley, in 1726 and further transcribed, from this version, by John's brother, Samuel, in 1730) in Priestly, Joseph, *Original Letters by the Rev. John Wesley, and His Friends, Illustrative of his Early History, with Other Curious Papers* (Birmingham, 1791), pp. 141-49

Widows, Thomas, *The Just Devil of Woodstock, Or, A True Narrative of the Several Apparitions, the Frights and Punishments, inflicted upon the Rumpish Commisioners Sent thither, to Survey the Mannors and Houses belonging to His Majestie.* (London, 1660)

Modern sources

Ashton, John, *The Devil in Britain and America* (Ward and Downey, 1896)

Banks, S. E., and Binns, J. W., *Gervaise of Tilbury: Otia Imperlialia* (Oxford University Press, 2002)

Bath, Jo, and Newton, John, '"Sensible Proof of Spirits": Ghost Belief during the Later Seventeenth Century', *Folklore* 117, no. 1 (2006), pp. 1-14

Bennet, Gillian, 'Ghost and Witch in the Sixteenth and Seventeenth Centuries', *Folklore* 97, no. 1 (1986), pp. 3-14

—. *'Alas, Poor Ghost!' Traditions of Belief in Story and Discourse* (Colorado, 1999)

Briggs, Katharine, *The Fairies in Tradition and Literature* (Routledge and Kegan Paul, 1967)

Brunskill, R. W., *Vernacular Architecture: An Illustrated Handbook* (4th ed., Faber & Faber, 2000)

Bryson, Bill, *At Home: A Short History of Private Life* (Doubleday, 2010)

Carrington, Hereward, and Fodor, Nandor, *The Story of the Poltergeist Down the Centuries* (Rider and Co., 1953)

Chesters, Timothy, *Ghost Stories in Late Renaissance France: Walking by Night* (Oxford University Press, 2011)

Clarke, Roger, *A Natural History of Ghosts* (Penguin, 2012)

Coffin, Joshua, *A Sketch of the History of Newbury, Newburyport, and West Newbury* (Boston, 1845)

Collins, Pat, 'Things that Go Bump in the Night', *The Furrow* 56, no. 2 (2005), pp. 94-98

Davidson, Jane P., and Duffin, Christopher John, 'Stones and Spirits', *Folklore* 123, no. 1 (2012), pp. 99-109

Davies, Owen, *The Haunted: a Social History of Ghosts* (Palgrave Macmillan, 2007)

Davies, Owen, and Houlbrook, Ceri, *Building Magic: Ritual and Re-Enchantment in Post-Medieval Structures* (Palgrave Macmillan, 2021)

Dingwell, E. J., and Langdon-Davies, John, *The Unknown: Is It Nearer?* (Cassell, 1956)

Eire, Carlos, *They Flew: A History of the Impossible* (Yale University Press, 2023)

Elmer, Peter, *Witchcraft, Witch-Hunting, and Politics in Early Modern England* (Oxford University Press, 2016)

Ewen, C. L'Estrange, *Witchcraft and Demonianism* (Heath Cranton, 1933)

Finucane, Ronald C., 'Historical introduction: the example of Early Modern and Nineteenth-Century England' in James Houran and Rense Lange (eds), *Hauntings and Poltergeists: Multidisciplinary Perspectives* (McFarland, 2001)

Gibson, Marion, *Reading Witchcraft: Stories of Early English Witches* (Routledge, 1999)

Gaskell, Malcolm, 'The Pursuit of Reality: Recent Research into the History of Witchcraft', *Historical Journal* 51, no. 4 (2008), pp. 1069-88

Harte, Jeremy, *Fairy Encounters in Medieval England: Landscape, Folklore and the Supernatural* (University of Exeter Press, 2024)

Harvey-Lee, John, and Potts, Marcus, *North Aston: A Millennium* (Information

Press, 2007)

Hoggard, Brian, *Magical House Protection: The Archaeology of Counter-Witchcraft* (Berghahn, 2019)

Holder, Geoff, *Poltergeist over Scotland* (The History Press, 2013)

Hole, Christina, *Haunted England: A Survey of English Ghost-Lore* (Batsford, 1940)

Hoskins, W. G., 'The Rebuilding of Rural England', *Past and Present*, no. 4 (1953), pp. 44-59

—. 'The Great Rebuilding', *History Today* 5, no. 2, (1955), pp. 104-11

—. *The Making of the English Landscape* (Hodder and Stoughton, 1955)

Houran, James, and Lange, Rense, (eds), *Hauntings and Poltergeists: Multidisciplinary Perspectives* (McFarland, 2001)

Hunter, Michael, and Schaffer, Simon, (eds), *Robert Hooke: New Studies* (Boydell Press, 1989)

Hunter, Michael, 'New light on the 'Drummer of Tedworth': conflicting narratives of witchcraft in Restoration England', *Historical Research* 78, no. 201 (2005), pp. 311-53

—. *Boyle: Between God and Science* (Yale University Press, 2009)

—. *The Decline of Magic: Britain in the Enlightenment* (Yale University Press, 2020)

Iman, Sheeha, '"Mistress, Look out at the Window": Women, Servants and Liminal Domestic Spaces on the Early Modern Stage', *English Literary Studies*, supply. Special Issue 29: Door-Bolts, Thresholds, snd Peep-Holes: Liminality and Domestic Spaces in Early Modern England (2020), pp. 1-18

Johnson, Matthew, 'Rethinking the Great Rebuilding', *Oxford Journal of Archaeology* 12, no. 1 (1993), pp. 117-25

—. 'Houses, Power and Everyday Life in Early Modern England' in *Constructing Power: Architecture, Ideology and Social Practice*, ed. by Joseph Maran, Carsten Juwig, Hermann Schwengel, and Ulrich Thaler (Lit Verlag, 2006)

Krylova, Olga, Earn, David J. D., 'Patterns of smallpox mortality in London, England, over three centuries', *PLOS Biology* doi: 10.1371/journal.pbio.3000506, 27, accessed 11/03/2024

Lang, Andrew, *Cock Lane and Common-sense* (Longmans, Green, and Co., 1896)

Laurence, Anne, *Women in England, 1500-1760: A Social History* (Phoenix Press, 1994)

Lipman, Caron, *Co-habiting with Ghosts: Knowledge, Experience, Belief and the Domestic Uncanny* (Routledge, 2016)

MacCarthy, Fiona, William Morris (Faber & Faber, 1994)

Machin, R., 'The Great Rebuilding: A Reassessment', *Past and Present* 77, no.

1 (1977), pp. 33-56

Marshall, Peter, *Invisible Worlds: Death, Religion and the Supernatural in England, 1500-1700* (SPCK, 2017)

Maxwell-Stuart, P. G., *Poltergeists: A History of Violent Ghostly Phenomena* (Amberley, 2011)

McAleavy, Tony, *The Last Witch Craze: John Aubrey, the Royal Society and the Witches* (Amberley, 2022)

Notestein, Wallace, *A History of Witchcraft in England from 1558 to 1718* (The American Historical Society, 1911)

Nuttall, Geoffrey K., and Keeble, N. H., (eds), *Calendar of Correspondence of Richard Baxter, Vol 2: 1660–1696* (Clarendon Press, 1991)

O'Connor, Sean, *The Haunting of Borley Rectory: The Story of a Ghost Story* (Simon & Schuster, 2022)

Oldridge, Darren, *The Devil in Tudor and Stuart England* (The History Press, 2010)

Owen, A. R. G., *Can We Explain Poltergeists?* (Garrett Publications, 1964)

—. *Joseph Glanvill and the Demon Drummer* (New Horizons Research Foundation, 1984)

Owens, Susan, *The Ghost: A Cultural History* (Tate Publishing, 2019)

Parsons, Coleman O., 'Ghost-stories before Defoe', *Notes and Queries* 3, no. 7 (1956), pp. 293-98

Pearson, Jacqueline, '"Then she asked it, what were its Sister's names?" Reading between the lines in seventeenth-century pamphlets of the supernatural', *The Seventeenth Century* 28, no. 1 (2013), pp. 63-78

Pickering, Andrew, *The Devil's Cloister: Wessex Witchcraft Narratives* (HHA Press, 2017).

—. 'Great News from the West of England: Witchcraft and Strange Vomiting in a Somerset Village', *Magic, Witchcraft and Ritual* 13, no 1 (2018), pp.71-97

—. 'The Devil's Cloyster: putting Selwood Forest on England's seventeenth-century witchcraft map' in Richard Nate and Julia Klüsener (eds), *Remembered Places: Perspectives from Scholarship and the Arts* (Königshausen & Neumann, 2019), pp. 35-54

—. *The Witches of Selwood: Witchcraft Belief and Accusation in Seventeenth-Century Somerset* (The Hobnob Press, 2023)

—. 'The Rise of the English Poltergeist, *c.*1590-*c.*1720', *Folkore* 136, no. 2 (2025), pp. 314–55.

Pickering, David, *Dictionary of Superstitions* (Cassell, 1995)

Playfair, Guy, *This House is Haunted* (White Crow Books, 2011)

Price, Harry, *Poltergeist Over England: Three Centuries of Mischievous Ghosts*

(Country Life, 1945)
Robins, Danny, *Into the Uncanny: A Real-Life Investigation into the Paranormal* (BBC Books, 2023)
Rojoewicz, Peter M., 'The 'Men in Black' Experience and Tradition: Analogues with the Traditional Devil Hypothesis', *The Journal of American Folklore* 100, no. 396 (1987), pp. 148-60
Schmitt, Jean-Claude, *Ghosts in the Middle Ages: The Living and the Dead in Medieval Society* (Chicago University Press, 1998)
Scott, Walter, *Letters on Demonology and Witchcraft* (Routledge, 1885)
Sitwell, Sacheverell, *Poltergeists: An Introduction and Examination Followed by Chosen Instances* (Faber and Faber, 1940)
Stratton, J. M., *Agricultural Records, A.D. 220-1977* (John Baker, 1978)
Sugg, Richard, *A Century of Supernatural Stories* (Createspace, 2015)
Summers, Montague, *Pandaemonium by Richard Bovet, 1684* (EP Publishing, 1951)
Thomas, Keith, *Religion and the Decline of Magic: Studies in Popular Beliefs in Sixteenth- and Seventeenth-Century England* (Weidenfeld & Nicholson, 1971)
Thorpe, Lewis, (trans.), *Gerald of Wales: The Journey through Wales* and *The Description of Wales* (Penguin Books, 1978)
Tucker, S. D., *The Hidden Folk: Are Poltergeists and Fairies Just the Same Thing?* (CFZ Press, 2016)
—. *Blithe Spirits: An Imaginative History of the Poltergeist* (Amberley, 2020)
Vernon, Alice, *Ghosted: A History of Ghost Hunting, and Why We Keep Looking* (Bloomsbury, 2025 pending)
Walsh, Brendan C., '"He Could Raise and Lay Ghosts at His Will": Victorian Folklorists and the Creation of Early Modern Clerical Ghost-Laying', *Folklore* 134, no. 3 (2023), pp. 281-303
Wilson, Colin, *Poltergeist: A Study in Destructive Haunting* (New English Library, 1981)

Databases

British History Online
Clergy of the Church of England Database
Early English Books Online
FreeREG
Heritage Gateway
The Oxford Dictionary of National Biography (ODNB)
Victoria County History (VCH)

INDEX

Addison, Joseph, 68, 71, 141
Aubrey, John, 70, 105–6, 163, 185, 188, 226

Baxter, Richard, 26–7, 53, 65, 87–8, 143, 188–9, 220
Beaumont, John, 26, 59, 69, 163–6, 226
Bleddfa, Powys, 120-2
Bovet, Richard, 9, 26, 56, 84, 86–7, 185–7
Boyle, Robert, 18–20, 22–4, 26, 105, 111, 226
Brightling, Sussex, 188-91
Bristol, 84-7
Butleigh, Som, 204-6

Chamberlain, Richard, 26, 173–84
Charles II, king, 17, 20, 22, 95, 126, 136
Civil War, the English, 17, 34, 88, 107
Clerke, Gilbert, 117–20
Cock Lane poltergeist case, 10, 20, 27, 68
Coggeshall, Ralph of 13
Conway, Anne, 23
Counter-magic, 40–2, 44, 93, 183, 225
Creed, William, 134–6, 138, 140, 143

Deptford, London, 201-4
du Moulin, Peter, 18, 31

East Lothian, Scotland, 168-70
Edinburgh 87-8
Enfield poltergeist case, 5, 50–1, 110

English Civil War, the, 17, 34, 88, 107
Epworth, Lincs, 206-21
Ewell, Surrey, 170-2

Fairy traditions, 10, 13–14, 16, 136, 227

Gerald of Wales, 13
Glanvill, Joseph, 9, 20–7, 49, 51, 64–71, 92, 111, 117, 120, 122, 124, 126–7, 131–2, 143–6, 160, 163, 173, 185–6, 226
Glanvill-Webster debate, 220
Glenluce, Scotland, 110-17
Great Rebuilding, the, 35–6, 38, 40–1, 43–5, 225
Greenwich, 107-10

Harrison, William, 38
Hobbes, Thomas, 66, 185–6
Hutchinson, Francis, 26–7

Isham, Justinian, 117, 226

Kelmscott Manor, 37
Kinross, Scotland, 221-3

Lang, Andrew, 10, 20, 23, 122
Lavater, Lewis, 14–16, 140
Leasingham, Lincs, 160-3
Lithobolia, *see* Stone throwing
Little Burton, Dorset, 157-60
Little Ice Age, 32
London, Puddle Duck, 153-7
London, Soper Lane. 122-6

London Wall, 151-3
Lutterworth poltergeist case, 53

Mâcon, Devil of, 18, 20, 31, 105
Mather, Cotton, 163–4, 173
Mechanical philosophy, 8, 21–2, 69, 111
Mompesson family, 10, 22, 33, 50, 56, 60, 63
74, 126–46, 225
More, Henry, 9, 20–7, 49, 64–5, 69, 90, 92, 105, 111, 113, 117, 120–2, 125, 157, 159–60, 173, 185–6, 227
Moulin, Peter du, 18, 31

Neoplatonism, 34
New Hampshire, 172-85
Newburyport, New England, 163-8
Nicholas, Edward, 135
North Aston, Oxon, 74-84
Notestein, Wallace, 27
Paschall, Andrew, 50, 122–5, 185, 188
Philosophy, Mechanical, 8, 21–2, 69, 111
Pierce, Thomas, 135, 137
Plaistow, London 88-94
Plot, Robert, 105, 227
Poltergeist activity, characteristics of, 48
Poltergeist activity, stages of, 54
Price, Harry, 7, 9–11, 15, 24, 39, 48, 50–1, 181, 192, 206–8
Purgatory, 8, 44, 65, 125

Ragley Hall 23
Ralph of Coggeshall 13
Rebuilding, the Great, 35–6, 38, 40–1, 43–5, 225
Reformation, the, 44, 59
Rerrick, Scotland, 191-201
Restoration, the, 20–1, 33, 69, 96, 108, 135
Royal Society, the London, 18–19, 23–6, 69–70, 92, 105, 111, 117, 122, 126, 163, 227

Scot, Reginald, 13, 16
Scott, Walter, 33, 107
Sinclair, George, 26, 73, 106, 110–16, 168–9, 221–2
Spreyton, Devon, 185-8
Stone throwing (lithobolia), 14, 20, 26, 48, 52–5, 57, 75, 77–8, 80–4, 90–2, 97, 102–4, 106, 108–9, 113, 116, 120–1, 160, 164, 166–84, 188, 193–201, 203–4, 206, 211, 222

Telfair, Alexander, 191–200
Tidworth (Tedworth), Wilts, 126-46
Trickster tradition, 8, 10

Wales, Gerald of, 13
Webster, John, 220
Weobley, Herefs, 146-51
Wesley family, 1, 9–11, 27, 31–2, 37–9, 41, 43, 50–1, 53, 56, 61, 65–6, 70, 206–21, 225
Witch-bottles, 40–2, 185, 225
Woodstock, Oxon, 94-107
Wren, Christopher, 70

York, William, 56, 160–1

'I Know [w]hat I Heard and Saw'

Joseph Glanvill concerning his 'poltergeist' experience
at Tidworth in 1663

www.ingramcontent.com/pod-product-compliance
Lightning Source LLC
Chambersburg PA
CBHW061246230426
43662CB00021B/2444